Performance Measurement, Evaluation, and Incentives

Harvard Business School
Series in Accounting and Control
Series Editor, Robert S. Kaplan

Board of Advisers
   Germain B. Boer   Vanderbilt University
   Thomas R. Dyckman   Cornell University
   Robert K. Elliott   KPMG Peat Marwick
   George Foster   Stanford University
   Hein Schreuder   University of Limburg

Rewarding Results
   Motivating Profit Center Managers
   by Kenneth A. Merchant

Measures for Manufacturing Excellence
   Edited by Robert S. Kaplan

The Information Mosaic
   by Sharon M. McKinnon and
   William J. Bruns, Jr.

Performance Measurement, Evaluation, and Incentives
   Edited by William J. Bruns, Jr.

Performance Measurement, Evaluation, and Incentives

Edited by
William J. Bruns, Jr.

Harvard Business School Press
Boston, Massachusetts

The paper used in this publication meets the requirements of the American National
Standard for Permanence of Paper for Printed Library Materials Z39.49–1984.

LIBRARY OF CONGRESS CATALOGING-IN-PUBLICATION DATA
Performance measurement, evaluation, and incentives / edited by
William J. Bruns, Jr.
    p.   cm.—(Harvard Business School series on accounting and
control)
    Includes bibliographical references and index.
    ISBN 0-87584-350-6
    1. Employees—Rating of—Congresses.   2. Employee motivation—
Congresses.   3. Incentives in industry—Congresses.   I. Bruns,
William J.   II. Series.
HF5549.5.R3P477   1992
658.3'125—dc20   91-44880
                                                     CIP

Contents

v

Performance Measurement, Evaluation, and Incentives

Introduction

William J. Bruns, Jr.

O N June 25–26, 1990, a colloquium held at the Harvard Business School discussed problems and issues in the measurement and evaluation of performance and the management of incentive compensation systems.[1] Ten papers by sixteen professors from universities in the United States and Europe were presented to and discussed by an audience of sixty-six executives, consultants, and academics. The call for the colloquium was stimulated by the unsatisfactory state of knowledge about how organizations measure performance of managers and business units and how incentive compensation systems are developed and used in organizations. Although economists, accountants, organization theorists, and personnel specialists have written much about how organizations might or should use these related systems, the literature about solving problems in managing such systems was scanty. Early in 1989, a group of academic researchers who were conducting field studies on performance measurement systems and incentives in organizations was invited to report on its research at the colloquium.

Specifications for research included in the call for participation were quite general. Studies were to focus on one or more issues covered by the proposed colloquium title, "Performance Measurement and Incentive Compensation." The only other constraint was that reports were to be based on data collected in the field from organiza-

1

tions with interests in problems or solutions to problems implied by the working title.

Some researchers chose to focus on one organization and one or more systems used in evaluating and measuring performance, or compensation. Others took a cross-sectional approach, examining the same issue in several organizations. In more than one instance work was initiated but later abandoned because of difficulties in the research or the deadline imposed by the schedule for the colloquium. The criteria that are evolving for successful use of research methods in field study—important questions, investigated at carefully selected sites, richly described, triangulated observations, and cautiously presented results—mean that extensive time and effort are required to produce results such as those reported here.

Ten of the research projects were completed, resulting in the reports that were the basis for the colloquium. Each paper was subsequently revised to incorporate comments by discussants and commentators, and the revised reports appear in this volume.

Problems in measuring performance are necessarily entwined with need and desire to evaluate the contribution that individuals and units in an organization make to the organization's success. That is why six of these ten studies are about systems for evaluating performance. Such systems are the link between measurements made by systems or by individuals and the kinds of incentives that organizations design and employ. Sometimes measurement is the sole basis for evaluation. In other instances, evaluation goes beyond comparing performance measures to expectations and incorporates matters of style and effectiveness. In most organizations, incentives are intended to motivate performance. Except in very small organizations, incentives and incentive systems include recognition, pay, or promotion to positions of greater responsibility and authority. To keep rewards from appearing capricious, organizations find ways of measuring and evaluating performance that do not produce dysfunctional consequences.

By doing field studies, contributors could go beyond merely describing the systems employed by the organizations they studied. Most writers of these reports attempt to examine how systems were intended to work and how they have evolved as managers and organizations try to improve them. None of these organizations, once they had a system, was content to use it without continual modification. The obvious ingenuity in the design of adopted systems requires continuous rethinking and tinkering as the organization tries to make measurement, evaluation, and incentives more effective motivators. Several contributors have captured the state of a system at that time, but their descriptions reveal that future changes are inevitable.

You will notice one difficulty that both human beings and organizations have: they often find it hard to link incentives, particularly monetary rewards, to performance and evaluation. Increasing incentives or paying more for performance does not necessarily lead to higher performance in the future. Similarly, denying incentive compensation can stimulate future performance but may also have the opposite effect, causing withdrawal from future participation. The reports presented at the colloquium make it clear that organizations and their managers struggling with these issues have the same difficulties and experience just as much curiosity as do academics interested in writing prescriptions for better systems.

The ten papers presented at the colloquium are grouped in three categories for this volume: performance evaluation and incentives, performance and organizations, and performance measurement and productivity. Each of the six papers in Part I deals directly with procedures and systems for evaluating performance in organizations. The purposes and cultural complications of evaluation stand out in the first and last papers, and the remaining four are case studies in individual settings of the development, evolution, problems, and effectiveness of attempts to evaluate performance and link them with financial and other incentives.

Papers in Part II deal with issues that arise from the ways in which work is organized for individuals and in organizations. An individual's place in an organization—the job—is more complex than any job title implies. Every incumbent comes from somewhere, seeks reward, and may or may not move on to another role. Recent prescriptions for improving productivity and performance suggest that team assignments may be a more effective way for an organization to achieve its goals amid complex competitive settings. The two papers in this part raise questions often ignored before the organization considers performance measurement evaluation and incentives.

The two papers that comprise Part III raise questions about measuring performance in two kinds of settings. When it is difficult to measure outputs implied in an organization's objectives, control mechanisms other than directly measuring the organizational performance may be necessary. The appropriate measures may be determined as much by sponsorship as by stated objectives. In these as well as in more conventional profit-seeking organizations, some have suggested attempting to measure how much each factor contributes to the organization's performance or productivity. A look at the complications encountered by an organization that uses total-factor productivity measurement concludes the volume.

Performance Evaluation and Incentives

"Evaluation" was not among the words used in describing the topics and issues to be discussed at the colloquium. Nevertheless, the idea was clearly implied. Organizations measure performance to evaluate alternatives for future action and to reward those who have performed. Most modern corporations and many other organizations spend much to develop, maintain, and perfect systems for evaluating or appraising performances. Each of the six research reports in this part contributes to a picture of the state of such systems in modern organizations.

In their field research, Bruns and McKinnon interviewed managers in twelve corporations. In five of these, managers' performance was evaluated at least annually, using procedures that all managers interviewed could describe. In five other companies, managers were evaluated at least annually, but the procedures were either not uniform throughout the organization or were not understood by those evaluated. Two corporations had no regular evaluations of managers' performance. In most corporations, incentive compensation depended on accomplishing individual objectives or on the evaluation plus the level of corporate profitability.

Bruns and McKinnon ask if a system for performance evaluation helps managers understand the tasks and activities expected of them. Their research is based on the belief that managers who explicitly understand the performance expected of them, and whose performance is regularly evaluated, will focus their activity and accomplish their individual objectives. They conclude that schemes for evaluating performance are associated with the managers' way of seeing their tasks, activities, and objectives. These effects are strongest when the nature of the future evaluation is known to managers in advance and performance can be measured more precisely against expectations. In corporations making no evaluations or with managers who were not sure how their performance was evaluated, the descriptions of managerial activities and tasks were less specific and therefore failed to provide a basis for self-direction and control. Evidence on the effect of schemes for incentive compensation is less clear.

Although performance evaluation schemes are established to support multiple objectives, the linkage between performance evaluation and financial incentives greatly interests managers. The allure of a system that provides greatest reward for superior performance is matched only by the difficulty of designing and using an evaluation with no dysfunctional consequences. The remaining five studies in this part attest to both the allure and the difficulty. The first study is a report on a mature system that evolved at Merck & Co., Inc. Two report on the design and influence of new systems in companies that previously had none. One reports on new incentives introduced after a leveraged buyout changed the objectives and control structure at O. M. Scott & Sons, Inc. The final study reports on a failed attempt to use a performance evaluation and incentive compensation plan.

Merck has often been recognized as a well-managed and much-admired company. Kevin Murphy studied how its performance appraisal and salary administration program evolved from 1978 through 1989. At Merck, compensation is determined by characteristics of the job (which determine a base level of salary) and merit (as measured by performance ratings). By March 1985, the 1978 Performance Appraisal Program was not identifying the top and bottom performers in the organization. Furthermore, the differences in rewards for superior performance and penalties for low performance were small. Revision was therefore undertaken in 1985.

The 1986 Performance Appraisal Program mandated that performance evaluation be distributed across five categories. The intent was to spread performance ratings and so broaden distribution of awards to more closely match contributions to the organization. The effect was that relative performance measures were introduced to the organization. Without announcing it, the company also quietly and informally instituted a Discretionary Award Program to further reward superior performers.

After two years, the 1986 program was reviewed and modified, adding gradations of performance within the largest category of mandated distributions. Furthermore, the new plan allowed for differences in employee-rating distributions, depending on how the employee's division performed for the year. Murphy concludes that these changes mitigate problems in using a "forced distribution" and that they will promote collegiality and reduce incentives for sabotage. The new program allows for substantially increased variation and rewards from salary revisions and cash bonuses, so that Merck's financial performance, which has been high relative to that of their closest competitors, seems to support the conclusion that it has created an effective organizational incentive structure.

Merchant and Riccaboni conducted their field study at the Fiat Group in Italy. Most European firms have not used formal performance-based monetary incentives as an important part of their management-control systems. At the time it introduced performance-based incentives, Fiat was reviewing its competitive environment and restructuring. Merchant and Riccaboni investigated why Fiat managers decided to implement a formal incentive system in 1983, the factors that influenced the managers' choices as they refined the system, and the effects of having a formal incentive system.

The findings show that Fiat implemented the system to replace a discretionary bonus plan that had provided small cash awards to only a few senior managers. The incentive system was introduced as an integral part of a major restructuring of the company's management systems. The most significant performance-based system introduced is an MBO program, designed to provide incentives for middle- and senior-level managers. In many characteristics the system is similar in design and effects on behavior to those used in many U.S. firms.

In spite of its success, the Fiat MBO program is still evolving. In 1990 and 1991, efforts were made to give the program a longer-term orientation. Nonfinancial targets were introduced, and multiyear incentives were employed. Attention was also given to using fewer objectives and making sure that managers knew about them early enough so that they could direct attention and activity throughout the management-evaluation period.

Merchant and Riccaboni conclude that cultural differences between incentive practices used by firms in the United States and Italy may not be significant. They attribute part of Fiat's successful introduction to its being started during a time when operating performance was improving. Another positive factor was that the incentive system was compatible with the direction implied by the corporate restructuring. The Fiat system provided limits on managers' bonus potential that were large enough to attract attention but small enough to discourage earnings management or managerial gaming. They also conclude that wanting to create longer-term incentives is a sign of a maturing incentive system in a growing business.

Otley investigated the development and introduction of a

performance-related reward plan in a major British clearing bank with a branch network in England and Wales. Such systems were unusual in the United Kingdom before 1985. Similarly, the bank's competitive environment lacked overt competition and aggressive pursuit of new business opportunities. The performance-related scheme conflicted with the company culture and was a reaction to the changing conditions in which the bank found itself.

The performance-related reward scheme provides monetary bonuses for meeting preset targets. It is part of a more general performance appraisal system that rewards long-term performance, assessed more subjectively, by merit increments and promotions on predefined salary scales.

The field study indicated that performance targets were set in a highly top-down manner. Although most targets were achievable, many managers felt the goals were often set too high for their individual units, causing general dissatisfaction. Although performance targets were achieved, most managers thought the scheme had little influence on their own efforts and performance. Younger managers and those with more education were especially likely to feel that way. Higher grades of management were more dissatisfied with the scheme than the junior managers.

Otley was able to compare high- and low-performing regions, indicating that the style in which targets were used and involvement in target-setting are significant variables. Although the scheme was focused on short-run performance, it has not yet caused dysfunctional side effects. Overall, Otley concludes that the performance-related reward scheme has succeeded because it has given positive direction and motivation. Longer-term aspects of performance also need to be monitored, which is primarily done by subjecting overall performance to a more subjective general appraisal that gives much more significant rewards; that is, promotion, in the long term. As junior managers become more actively involved in setting their own targets as well as achieving them, the plan is expected to break down traditional hierarchic distinctions.

The fifth paper in Part I is a study of organizational changes at O. M. Scott after a leveraged buyout. For fifteen years before the buyout, Scott was a subsidiary of the ITT Corporation. The company's principal controls and incentives were imposed by the corporate parent. After the buyout was complete in 1986, Clayton & Dubilier, a private firm specializing in leveraged buyouts, worked with management to come up with new incentives.

The major changes introduced after the buyout were substantial increases in salary and even greater increases in bonuses that managers could earn by meeting corporate performance targets. More managers participated in the program, and factors that determined bonuses now included corporate performance, divisional performance, and individual goals and performance.

The plan was designed so that the payoff was extremely sensitive to changes in performance. Average bonuses as a percentage of salary for the top ten managers increased from 10% and 17% in the two years before the buyout to 66% and 39% in the two years after, during which period operating income increased by 42%. Personal objectives were set by managers and their superiors, and achievement against those objectives was monitored by superiors.

In addition to changes in the performance evaluation and incentive systems, the board of directors at Scott actively monitors decisions and performance. The close attention by board members affiliated with the buyout firm drastically changed corporate governance at Scott. Baker and Wruck conclude that their results are applicable to organizations that combine high leverage, ownership of equity by management, and active boards of directors. If this assessment is correct, then we may ask why such organizational controls are not observed in other companies with the same characteristics.

Bento and Ferreira studied an organization in which a performance evaluation and incentive compensation plan did not succeed. They were interested in exploring how well the organization's culture matched the incentive contract design that had been adopted. They conclude that because the assumptions about culture implicit in the design appeared false during their post-implementation review, the plan was doomed to failure.

Using five dualities of culture that influence performance evaluation and compensation—equality versus inequality; certainty versus uncertainty; controllability versus uncontrollability; individualism versus collectivism; materialistic versus personalistic—they show how the designers of the evaluation and compensation plan failed to appreciate the cultural characteristics honored and desired by those who would take part in the plan.

They conclude that plan designers who fail to explore culture before trying to tailor performance evaluation and incentive compensation contracts to an organization and its participants will inevitably be disappointed. In their disappointment will be found the seeds for revising the plan and continuously adapting to a more realistic view of the organization's cultural environment.

These six papers leave no doubt that performance evaluation and appraisal and some of their effects are important. Evaluation and appraisal, particularly when coupled with incentive compensation, hold managers' attention and direct their activity. But in the field studies designed to evaluate the effectiveness of such systems, we observe their instability. Systems and processes that were constructed with confidence that they would be effective frequently are modified within a year of their introduction and replaced completely after only a few years. Perhaps change in such systems is another way to keep managers' attention focused on the conditions and key result variables of the moment. Perhaps continuous change reflects the difficulty in developing systems that evaluate and reward human beings amid the always-changing competition that besets an organization.

Performance and Organizations

Lazear considers a vital and provocative question: Is "job" an important concept? Much is at issue in the answer. If a job is just an organizational slot to be filled by a qualified individual for whom another can be substituted, then who fills the slot and how they perform may reflect little more than luck or other factors. On the other hand, if workers invest heavily in productivity-enhancing skills, then the job may be less important for what they earn, how much wealth they accumulate, and how much they contribute to the organization. A growing body of analytic literature emphasizes jobs or slots.

If internal labor markets behave like tournaments, assignments to jobs are based on relative rather than absolute performance. Wages are assigned to the slots and not to individuals. Wages may be paid whether standards are met or not.

Hierarchies assume that jobs create authoritarian positions and relationships in an organization and imply rigid structure. Compensation to workers may differ with working conditions, with differences in compensation determined by the job's pleasantness or undesirability and not by the job holder. These new job-based theories require better understanding of "job."

Using data covering a thirteen-year period in one firm, Lazear concludes that a number of job-related questions can be answered.

Job change is the key to wage growth, and those who change jobs start with higher wages than those who do not change jobs. Turnover in jobs is greatest during the first few years on the job. Low-wage jobs are the ones most likely to produce a promotion. And a job can be classified as a feeder or a dead end. All these ideas have major implications for designing systems for evaluating performance measurement and incentives.

Mohrman, Mohrman, and Lawler differ distinctly with Lazear, focusing on neither job nor individual but assuming that organizations increasingly need to foster teamwork and achieve lateral integration in order to learn and compete effectively in today's environment. For them, analytical organizing principles and hierarchic controls work against successful lateral integration.

Using a diagnostic model and survey data from three large organizations that are trying to redesign performance appraisal and pay-for-performance practices, they seek to isolate relationships among practices for workgroup self-appraisal, special awards, pay-for-performance, workgroup effectiveness, and individual performance.

Their work leads to two questions. First, which attributes and designs for reward and performance management systems encourage continuous improvement in organizational learning? Second, do group-level rewards and other performance management techniques make any difference in performance compared to individual approaches? Their data suggest that when interdependence is high between activities of participants in the organization, the old individual approach offers little performance leverage.

They conclude by identifying several challenges in the performance measurement of a more team-oriented lateral approach that they feel is necessary. These design challenges include identifying and measuring performance units, matching organizational team with individual performance, stimulating team interdependence, coordinating overlapping membership on teams, and solving a number of measurement issues, including economic performance of organizational units and distribution of rewards to groups rather than just to individuals.

These two studies provide a comprehensive, if not an all-inclusive, summary of issues too often overlooked. What is the focus of performance measurement and evaluation? Are we evaluating individuals, or their performance against a job description, or is a larger unit in the organization our aim? The answers are important if systems for measuring and evaluating performance are to be made more effective.

Performance Measurement and Productivity

The two papers that conclude this volume deal with two ways of thinking about difficult problems in measuring performance. Euske chose to do his field study in two environments where technology and output are not easily defined and specified. When the connection between the means that an organization employs and the end it wishes to achieve is not clear, many possibilities for target-setting, performance measurement and appraisal, and incentive compensation are eliminated.

Two child care centers and one fire department that Euske studied maintain a profit orientation. In these environments, although the organizations' stated outputs may not be profit, the ability to measure financial success adds control mechanisms not found in nonprofit organizations.

A second aspect of control Euske examines is the organization's source of funding. When funding is provided by clients, the clients themselves are able to observe performance and success and thus influence performance. In block funding, or funding supplied by those who are not clients that is for the benefit of clients, the organization's performance or success is influenced not only by service provided to clients but also by the appearance of success to the funding groups. To emphasize this distinction, Euske found that nonprofit, client-funded child care centers were more willing to operate below potential rates of enrollment to stress the view that they were serving clients than were the block-funded centers, which were eager to emphasize how well they were serving their client group.

In privately funded versus publicly funded fire protection organizations, budgets were used to create efficiency in the privately funded organization, but to create legitimacy for the public organization. The fire department getting the resources from a municipal government was eager to maintain the status quo in its funding relationship with the city, whereas the private fire department wanted to find ways of promoting the appearance of efficiency.

The study does clarify control mechanisms and performance

measurement problems in organizations with ill-defined technology and output, but it also raises questions. How do subsidies affect the evaluation of efficiency if efficiency is considered in evaluating and rewarding managerial behavior? What resources should be included when efficiency is not the primary criterion by which performance will be evaluated? How is efficiency to be measured?

Kiran Verma closes this volume by examining the status of total-factor productivity measurement at Ethyl Corporation. Interest in measuring productivity was stimulated in 1972 in response to the U.S. Price Commission's requirement that requests for rate changes by regulated firms include productivity measures. Competitive pressures encouraged nonregulated industry to increase its attention to monitoring productivity as well. The American Productivity Center (APC) was founded in 1977 with a principal objective to develop and promote measurement of productivity at the firm level.

Ethyl worked with the APC and later devised a total-factor system for measuring productivity. The new system, intended to go beyond a cost improvement program already at work, was an attempt to relate productivity and price recovery programs to greater profitability. After years of trial, a review showed that managers were not making adequate use of the total-factor productivity measurement system. Managers complained that the measures that the system reported were reported too late, were too difficult to understand, and were strategically misleading. Furthermore, they were resentful that the system had been imposed from the top. A study of the system led to changes.

In 1989, Ethyl introduced the Performance Measurement System, which attempts to determine the effect on profits of productivity, inflation, production volume, other manufacturing costs, product distribution, selling price, and sales volume. Its aim is to develop complementary systems to track productivity, quality, and other performance measures. Frequency of analysis was changed from annual to quarterly or more often. A newly created data base allows analyses for strategic business units defined as a product, a group of products, or a division. Under the revised system as under the old, the productivity measurement system is not tied to compensation.

Verma concludes that total-factor productivity measurement is useful only if it incorporates the detail necessary to relate to day-to-day operations. Furthermore, managers at Ethyl were more comfortable with labels that related their system to variables such as "quality" or "quality of manufacturing" instead of productivity. Finally, Verma reveals the importance of user-friendly performance measures that enable managers to see and understand relations among decisions, actions, performance measures, and improved productivity.

Summary

These ten reports are not a comprehensive summary of performance measurement, evaluation, and incentive compensation as these are practiced in organizations today. Instead, they form a compendium of problems and practices as a few managers grapple with improving their systems to promote organizational performance, effectiveness, and efficiency. The issues are here, as are many of the questions; the answers are not.

Nevertheless, these papers are an important step forward. Unlike academic models or theory based on logical deductions from assumed premises, they reveal the complex culture and environment in which performance measurement and evaluation must function. What should be measured is often not clear. How measurements should be evaluated is often uncertain. We can understand how measurement and evaluation will affect the behavior of managers and others only by getting more data on how such systems actually work in organizations.

Finally, vexing questions arise from any study of incentive compensation. People seek employment and give their effort to corporations and other organizations for many reasons, some of them relating to money. Monetary reward is a motivating factor for many individuals in many circumstances. But in attempting to increase individual productivity and performance, organizations seek an elusive link between additional performance and increased pay. The systems they design are ingenious. The assumptions they make about behavior are often complex, but they are also tenuous. The frequency with which new schemes are developed, modified, and discarded reminds us how difficult the questions are to which we seek answers.

These studies are an attempt to consolidate observations and form a basis for constructing tentative theories that can be tested in further research. If they stimulate further thought by those dealing with issues, or research by those concerned with theory and hypothesis testing, they will have served their purpose. To academics it must be sobering to realize that, with our analytic and large data-base studies, as we struggle to understand the effects of performance measurement and appraisal and the principles for designing more effective systems for performance evaluation and incentive compensation, managers are measuring and evaluating and compensating and designing and changing their systems even as we conduct further research. Practice and theory can and must move forward together.

NOTE

1. The colloquium was the third in a series on field studies in accounting, measurement, and control. Papers from the first colloquium, held in June 1986, were published in William J. Bruns, Jr., and Robert S. Kaplan, eds., *Accounting and Management: Field Study Perspectives* (Boston: Harvard Business School Press, 1987); papers from the second colloquium, held in January 1989, were published in Robert S. Kaplan, ed., *Measures for Manufacturing Excellence* (Boston: Harvard Business School Press, 1990).

PART I

Performance Evaluation and Incentives

CHAPTER 1

Performance Evaluation and Managers' Descriptions of Tasks and Activities

William J. Bruns, Jr., and Sharon M. McKinnon

SYSTEMS for evaluating and appraising performance are important elements in many systems for managing human resources and organizational control. When a performance evaluation scheme is used to communicate expectations about job context and goals of performance, we can assume that objectives will be an explicit part of the expectations against which managerial performance will be measured (Latham and Wexley, 1981; Latham, 1986; Locke and Latham, 1990). In these situations, evaluation may focus managerial activities and attention on assigned tasks.

Levinson (1970) lists these purposes for performance appraisal and review, specifically emphasizing clarification of job requirements and performance expectations:

- To measure and judge performance.
- To relate individual performance to organizational goals.
- To foster the increasing competence and growth of the subordinate.

*Financial support for this research from the Society of Management Accountants of Canada and the Division of Research of the Harvard Business School is gratefully acknowledged, as are helpful comments on an earlier draft by Michael Beer, Susan Harmeling, and Robert S. Kaplan.

- To stimulate the subordinate's motivation.
- To enhance communications between superior and subordinate.
- To serve as a basis for judgments about salary and promotion.
- To serve as a device for organizational control and integration.

In the typical performance evaluation system, superiors and subordinates share responsibility for establishing goals and expectations and measuring individual accomplishment, and the superior is in a position to render final judgment on how well performance has met goals and objectives (Beer, 1981).

These are the principal questions we sought to address in our field research:

1. Does a well-defined and understood performance evaluation scheme enable and assist managers to be more specific in describing their roles, tasks, and activities?

2. Does incentive compensation based upon individual performance evaluation succeed in motivating managers to focus more specifically on tasks and activities comprising their jobs?

A positive answer to either question could justify establishing and maintaining schemes for performance evaluation or for incentive compensation for corporations that wish to focus managers' attention on specific tasks and activities or on specific roles.

Managers' task and activity descriptions must be specific for at least three reasons. First, managers who know what is expected of them and how to perform up to those expectations are more likely to be efficient than managers who are not aware (Meyer, Kay, and French, 1965; Odiorne, 1965 and 1990). Efforts are more likely to be focused, and less unproductive effort is apt to be expended. In working groups or teams too, a clear idea of explicit expectations fosters more efficient organization and operations.

Second, specific job descriptions allow an organization's designers and senior managers to identify redundancies and omissions in job responsibilities. They can thus facilitate realization of economies through modifications such as dividing tasks, changing procedures, or changing the organizational structure.

Third, if each manager understands tasks and activities, management will have more control and can prevent failures of control systems. Planning is facilitated, as is the ability to design effective and meaningful information and performance measurement systems.

When managers know what is expected of them when they are doing the right things, and when they have performed as expected, control failures are likely to be held down.

Some organizations mandate the procedures, processes, and even forms for periodically evaluating an individual manager's performance as part of the corporate system for managing human resources. Others may provide guidelines but give managers greater latitude in evaluating their subordinates' performance. At the other extreme, an organization may require no regular evaluation of subordinates' performance; evaluations may still take place, but their frequency, form, and focus vary depending on the evaluators' interest and skill (Porter, Lawler, and Hackman, 1975).

Managers in twelve corporations were asked to describe how their performance was evaluated and whether incentive compensation was associated with the evaluations. In five companies, managers' descriptions of annual performance evaluations were consistently uniform. In five other companies, performance evaluation procedures showed greater diversity or were not understood by those evaluated. In two companies, evaluation procedures were sporadic at best but essentially nonexistent at upper-management levels. We sought to learn whether an acknowledged, well-understood performance-evaluation system focused managers' attention and had high potential to change their work activities (Flanagan and Burns, 1955; Meyer, Kay, and French, 1965; Kaplan and Atkinson, 1989; Odiorne, 1965 and 1990).

Field Study Procedures

The field study was undertaken to learn more about relationships between managers' tasks and activities and their information needs. We conducted interviews with seventy-one managers in twelve manufacturing corporations in North America. During each interview, managers were asked to describe how their own performance was evaluated. From their descriptions we could determine whether procedures each company used were uniform, and whether incentive compensation was based on evaluations. Managers were also asked to describe in detail their day-to-day tasks and activities.

The corporations taking part in this study were a nonrandom sample of manufacturing companies in the United States and Canada. Companies were selected for location and accessibility, personal contacts, and expected willingness to help with the research. When possible, companies similar to those already selected were contacted in hopes of keeping some control on organizational diversity. All companies surveyed are engaged in manufacturing, marketing, and distribution, and each is in one of three groups: heavy manufacturing of basic materials and products, high-tech manufacturing, and manufacturing of consumer-branded products. All but three corporations are large organizations, and all have a significant presence in their respective industries. Exhibit 1-1 briefly describes and summarizes some characteristics of the companies that took part in this study.

We initially established contact with each company by a personal telephone call to a corporate contact known to the researchers, research sponsors, or a referee who had agreed to participate. We described the purpose of the research and the procedures and elicited a preliminary agreement to participate. A follow-up letter was sent to the person initially contacted, giving more details and requesting that an interview schedule be established, including managers responsible for manufacturing, marketing, sales, and financial management. Visits to interview sites were scheduled around the availability of the managers selected by each company contact. Prior to each interview managers were given a very general description of the research objectives; the effects of performance evaluations were not mentioned.

Interviews were conducted on site, mostly in the office of the interviewee. A structured interview protocol was used as a basis for all interviews, each of which was recorded for later analysis. Although the interviews were structured, we allowed managers to describe in their own words their activities, information used, performance evaluation, and computer use. Most interviews were about one hour long, with the shortest lasting 40 minutes and the longest about 90 minutes. Demographic data on each manager were collected, along with documents relating to the manager's activities when these were available.

The interview was focused on each manager's description of the tasks and activities comprising his or her job and work. Most of these descriptions took up more than half of the interview. Descriptions of the performance evaluation system or scheme were always elicited after tasks and activities had been described in detail. Managers were not asked to link in any way the performance evaluation scheme or incentive compensation to their selection of activities. Questions on performance evaluation were also separated from discussion of activities by questions about other disparate subjects. Exhibit 1-2 summarizes the general features of the performance evaluation and incentive compensation schemes as they were described to us by the interviewees.

Exhibit 1-3 lists by job title the managers interviewed in each group of companies, classified by descriptions of uniformity of performance evaluation scheme provided by managers. The job titles reveal that most managers interviewed had major responsibility for sales and marketing, production and manufacturing, or staff functions. Time in job, in functions, and with company confirmed that they were experienced managers. We made no attempt to determine if they were effective managers, though most had been promoted to present responsibilities after several years of experience in their company.

Analysis of Data

We asked each manager to describe in his own words job tasks or activities in which he regularly engaged. No manager described fewer than two tasks or activities and none more than four. The question that interests us here is whether the descriptions of tasks and activities are more specific in companies with well-developed and mandated performance-evaluation schemes. In other words, does a scheme for regular performance evaluation help managers understand what is expected of them and focus their attention on the activities necessary to meet targets and goals?

Task and activity descriptions were scored by each researcher separately, using a naive scoring system:

1 = very specific description of task, activity, and supporting information

2 = less specific description of activity

3 = vague description of task or activity or general activity with no focus

When researchers disagreed on how specific a manager's description of activity was, the disagreement was resolved by discussion. Disagreement was atypical because interview notes and tapes left little doubt about how specific managers' descriptions were. All tasks were scored before we began analyzing performance evaluation schemes or incentive compensation schemes.

An example will clarify how we scored descriptions of tasks and activities. A vice president of operations (production and manufactur-

Exhibit 1-1 Corporations and Companies Participating in the Research (names are disguised)

Companies (in order of size)	General Descriptions	Comments	Number of Managers Interviewed
Worldwide Computer Co.	Manufactures, sells, and services computer and system hardware and software to diversified industry markets.	Well known for distinctive management style and systems. Currently restructuring major functions.	5[a]
Canadian Oil & Gas, Ltd.	Large producer, refiner, and marketer of petroleum materials and products.	Integrated operations from field to retail sales locations.	6
Belton Foods Company	Manufactures and distributes branded consumer food products throughout the world.	Strong brands and high-volume sales in United States dominate competitors in several product lines.	10
Dell Chemicals, Ltd.	Large producer and distributor of industrial chemicals, coatings, and explosives.	Integrated producer for both external sales and downstream products.	8
Stanga Steel, Ltd.	Large iron and steel manufacturer serving construction and manufacturing industries in both United States and Canada.	Manufacturing and sales of both specialty and commodity steel products.	6

Communications Equipment, Ltd.	International manufacturer and supplier of telephone and communication equipment and systems.	Developing worldwide markets from a strong national base.	5
Plastex, Inc.	Specialty producer of rubber, latex, and polymer products for military, industrial, and consumer markets.	Repositioning after change in strategic focus. Decentralized management of market segments.	5
Cancoil, Ltd.	Manufacturer and distributor of wire and cable products to utilities and industrial markets.	Subsidiary of primary metals producer.	5
Garrison's	Large producer and seller of specialized lines of branded consumer foods.	Centrally managed until recently when international expansion was undertaken.	6
Scitron	Large producer of electronic instruments for sale to worldwide market.	Dominates some market segments where quality and sophistication are needed.	6
Engineering Software, Inc.	World competitor in creation, sales, and support in computer-aided engineering and design (CAE/CAD).	Rapid growth in traditional and new market segments has not changed centralized management style.	4
Puraire, Ltd.	Major supplier of paper filters for air and fluid systems.	One of five competitors in industry where manufacturing and distribution costs will determine who survives.	5

[a]Not included in analysis. Please see text.

Exhibit 1-2 Performance Evaluation Schemes and Incentive Compensation

Companies	Performance Evaluation Scheme	Incentive Compensation Described
Worldwide Computer Co.	All managers described annual written evaluation against personally established goals.	Salary freeze in effect. Incentive compensation only in form of stock options based on corporate performance.
Canadian Oil & Gas, Ltd.	Managers described various procedures for evaluation not universally applied.	Basis for incentive compensation not clear to most managers but based on unit or corporate performance.
Belton Foods Company	All managers described annual written evaluation against multiple personally established goals.	Incentive compensation based in part on personal goal accomplishment and in part on corporate performance.
Dell Chemicals, Ltd.	All managers described annual written evaluation against personal goals, but without common format.	Incentive compensation based on corporate performance only.
Stanga Steel, Ltd.	No performance evaluation.	Incentive compensation based on corporate performance only.

Communications Equipment, Ltd.	Performance evaluation required but managed by superior only.	Incentive compensation based on corporate performance only.
Plastex, Inc.	No formal performance evaluation except for production manager.	Incentive compensation based on corporate performance only.
Cancoil, Ltd.	No formal performance evaluation.	No incentive compensation.
Garrison's	All managers described annual written performance evaluation based on targets and goals.	Incentive compensation based on corporate performance only.
Scitron	All managers described annual written performance evaluation based on goals.	Incentive compensation based on business-unit performance.
Engineering Software, Inc.	All managers described extensive written performance evaluation based on goals.	Incentive compensation based on corporate performance and individual performance.
Puraire, Ltd.	Managers described written performance evaluation based on goals and targets.	Incentive compensation based on individual and corporate performance (none recently).

Exhibit 1-3 Job Titles of Managers Interviewed

	Companies with Performance Evaluation Schemes Clearly Described by Managers	Companies with Performance Evaluation Schemes That Managers Could Not Clearly Describe	Companies with No Performance Evaluation Reported by Managers
	Worldwide Computer Belton Foods Garrison's Scitron Engineering Software	Canadian Oil Dell Chemicals Communications Equipment Plastex Puraire	Stanga Steel Cancoil
Marketing and Sales Managers	International Marketing Manager[a] Sales Manager, International[a] Industry Marketing Manager[a] Industry Marketing Manager[a] V.P. Sales and Marketing[a] Product Manager V.P. Consumer Marketing V.P. Sales Division Marketing Manager Program Manager	Bulk Marketing Manager Marketing Manager Product Manager Retail Business Director V.P. Marketing Assistant V.P. Major Accounts Division Market Director	Regional Sales Manager Product Manager Director of Sales and Marketing Industry Marketing Manager
Production and Manufacturing Managers	V.P. Quality V.P. Product Manufacturing V.P. Product Manufacturing Plant Manager	Distribution Manager Regional Manufacturing Manager Production Manager	Plant Manager Manager of Engineering and Maintenance V.P. Steel Operations

	Distribution Manager V.P. Regional Manufacturing Manager Engineering Services V.P. Operations V.P. Operations V.P. Logistics Manufacturing Manager	Plant Manager Division Manufacturing Manager Purchasing Manager Manager, Distribution and Transportation V.P. Operations V.P. Technology	Manager Coke and Iron Production General Foreman, Steel Making
General Managers	Division Manager General Manager, Design Business-Unit Manager	Business Unit General Manager Division President Division President Division Director	
Staff and Financial Managers	V.P. Controller Corporate Controller Chief Financial Officer Director Corporate Accounting V.P. Controller Corporate Controller Division Controller	Business-Unit Controller Director of Planning and Financial Systems V.P. Division Controller Product Cost Coordinator Operations Planning Manager Assistant Controller Corporate Controller Division Controller V.P. Finance	Plant Controller V.P. Controller

[a]Not included in analysis. Please see text.

ing) at Garrison's (corporation names are disguised) described three activities: daily plant monitoring, tracking projects, and corporate management responsibilities. The first task was scored 1 because the manager specifically described the sources of data and the procedures he uses to monitor plant activities. The second activity was scored 2 because it was nonroutine and relied on occasional memoranda and informal communications. The third activity was scored 3 because no specific activities were described and information was sought as received or as needed. For this manager, the average score for specificity of tasks and activities would be 2, and his or her scores could be averaged with those of others at the firm to obtain a measure of specificity of production and manufacturing scores at Garrison or a corporate score.

In scoring task and activity descriptions, we decided to exclude data collected from the five managers interviewed at Worldwide Computers from further analysis for this report. All were high-level managers in marketing and sales, and during our interviews their functions were being restructured. Although from their experience at Worldwide, all described a well-defined performance-evaluation scheme, the new functional structure was different enough to make it doubtful that prior performance evaluation would influence descriptions of present tasks and activities. The major focus of the present activities described by all managers was the restructuring project. Consequently, almost all the activities they described were vague, tentative, and incomplete because they were still struggling to define new functional and job-specific activities. The analysis reported hereafter is based on data collected from sixty-six managers in the eleven other corporations where we conducted interviews.

Exhibit 1-4 shows the mean of specificity of task scores for managers at each of the corporations. These scores were calculated by taking the sum of task scores for all tasks and activities described and dividing it by the number of tasks and activities described by all managers interviewed at that company. Lower scores denote greater specificity in descriptions of tasks and activities. The average score for all managers in the performance-evaluation scheme group is calculated in the same way.

Exhibit 1-5 shows the mean specificity of task scores by job function within each performance-evaluation scheme group. These scores were calculated in the same manner as those in Exhibit 1-4.

Exhibit 1-6 is based on the scores reported in Exhibit 1-4 but

Exhibit 1-4   Specificity of Task Scores, by Corporation

With Well-Defined Performance-Evaluation Scheme		With More-Ambiguous Performance-Evaluation Scheme		With No Apparent Performance-Evaluation Scheme	
Belton Foods	1.77	Canadian Oil	1.68	Stanga Steel	2.37
Garrison's	1.89	Dell Chemicals	1.92	Cancoil	2.00
Scitron	1.83	Communications Equipment	1.88		
Engineering Software	1.80	Plastex	1.81		
		Puraire	1.63		
Average score for all managers	1.82		1.80		2.20

Exhibit 1-5   Specificity of Task Scores, by Job Function

With Well-Defined Performance-Evaluation Scheme		With More-Ambiguous Performance-Evaluation Scheme	With No Apparent Performance-Evaluation Scheme
Marketing and sales	1.69	2.04	2.25
Production and manufacturing	1.67	1.57	2.13
General managers	1.44	1.62	—
Staff and financial managers	2.05	2.18	2.29

Exhibit 1-6   Specificity of Task Scores by Corporations, Classified by Incentive Compensation Scheme

Incentive Compensation Based on Individual and Corporate Performance	
Belton Foods	1.77
Engineering Software	1.80
Puraire (none recently)	1.63
Incentive Compensation Based on Business-Unit Performance	
Canadian Oil	1.68
Scitron	1.83
Incentive Compensation Based on Corporate Performance	
Dell Chemicals	1.92
Stanga Steel	2.37
Communications Equipment	1.88
Plastex	1.81
Garrison's	1.89
No Incentive Compensation	
Cancoil	2.00

classifies corporations according to the incentive compensation schemes managers described for us.

Further analysis of the data was not considered justified because of caveats that must be attached to them:

1. Neither the corporations nor the managers interviewed were randomly selected.

2. By statistical standards, numbers in classification cells are not large.

3. The naive scoring scheme employed and its subjectivity are recognized.

4. Other factors that might affect specificity in managers' descriptions were not systematically observed or studied in detail (such as available job descriptions).

The findings presented here must be read with these caveats in mind.

Findings

The data collected in the interviews during this field study offer limited support to a conclusion that a well-developed performance-evaluation scheme understood by managers helps them describe their tasks and activities more specifically. Data in Exhibit 1-4 show no apparent differences in task description between corporations in which performance evaluation schemes are well defined (all managers describe the scheme in similar words) or more ambiguous (managers describe the scheme in different words but all are aware of its existence). Managers in the nine corporations with performance evaluation schemes, however, were more specific in describing their tasks and activities than in the two corporations with no apparent system for evaluating performance.

Variation in specificity of distribution scores by job function was also observed, and mean scores for task and activity descriptions are shown in Exhibit 1-5. General managers and production managers were generally more specific in describing tasks and activities than were managers in marketing and sales, and staff and finance. This greater specificity may be inherent in the work performed in the function (defined and repetitive versus undefined and varied) or in the ease with which performance can be measured and evaluated, as we will discuss below.

Finally, mean scores on task and activity specificity for corporations with individual or business-unit-based incentive compensation can be compared to those in companies with corporate performance-based schemes in Exhibit 1-6. These data may support an affirmative answer to our second research question, but we are not willing to conclude that they do. If this difference were supported by further research it could also provide support for management-by-objective or pay-for-performance schemes based on measures of individual performance.

Discussion

Our findings appear to support the conclusion that a scheme for individual performance evaluation increases managers' specific understanding of their jobs and the specific tasks and activities that comprise those jobs. Additional evidence is that we found such schemes in various forms at ten of the twelve corporations we contacted and visited, demonstrating that those organizations have concluded that performance evaluation schemes produce benefits that exceed the cost of developing, maintaining, and administering the scheme. As we have seen, corporations have many purposes for performance evaluation schemes, but the benefit of specifying job functions and expectations recurrently seems to be available regardless of the scheme for evaluating performance.

Our sample is not large enough to draw a conclusion about the manner in which an incentive compensation scheme is best used in conjunction with a performance evaluation scheme. In only three corporations did we find managers receiving incentive compensation that related to their individual performance, and in one of those no such payments had been received recently by any of the managers we interviewed. Despite the tendencies for greater specificity in task and activity descriptions in those three companies and two others where incentive compensation is based in part on business-unit performance, we can conclude only that more research is needed on how incentive compensation supports a performance evaluation scheme.

That nine of twelve corporations used corporate performance as a basis for their incentive compensation schemes, at least in part, and eight of these had performance evaluation schemes, verifies that the latter schemes must be seen as having important purposes other than individual incentive compensation. Performance evaluation schemes are not costless to create and maintain, and evaluations require time and discipline to prepare regularly. Identification of underperforming managers, management of career development, and motivation can all support corporate decisions to develop and maintain evaluation schemes. Reassurance of meeting expectations, recognition, rewards other than financial incentives, and promotion to greater responsibility are all reasons why managers may also like performance evaluation schemes. Developing these schemes in ways that will help managers understand their specific responsibilities, tasks, and activities seems riskless.

Further Evidence from the Field Study

On the absence of performance evaluation schemes. Considering the potential advantages in using performance evaluation schemes, we should perhaps be surprised that in two companies managers did not know whether such a scheme was in use. Our procedure does not allow us to say with certainty that managers are not evaluated in these companies. We relied only on the managers we interviewed to describe how their performance was evaluated, and they told us there was no performance evaluation. If they are evaluated but do not know it, presumably any positive benefits to them from these invisible performance-measurement schemes are lost.

The two corporations in which managers reported no performance evaluation schemes, Stanga Steel, Ltd., and Cancoil, Ltd., are not new, small, or unsuccessful. They have been highly profitable in some past years, although both appear to be in a more competitive environment now. Managers at Stanga Steel have received incentive compensation based on their salary level and corporate performance. One manager at Cancoil reported receiving some stock options, based on his organizational level and corporate performance, but he did not regard that as incentive compensation.

In these two companies, managers do not necessarily believe they are not evaluated. They know they must be. Salaries are adjusted periodically, and managers are moved to new positions. But they do not know the basis for these changes, nor does either corporation gain the benefit of a more explicit performance-evaluation scheme.

On focused managers. Eleven managers described all their tasks and activities so specifically that their mean score was 1. These focused managers and their companies and job titles are summarized in Ex-

Exhibit 1-7 Focused Managers with Mean Job-Specificity Scores = 1

Company	Identifier	Title
Canadian Oil	(FM1)	Division president
	(FM2)	Business-unit general manager
Belton Foods	(FM3)	Division manager
	(FM4)	Plant manager
	(FM5)	Distribution manager
	(FM6)	Manager engineering services
Communications Equipment	(FM7)	Division manufacturing manager
Plastex	(FM8)	Plant manager
Garrison's	(FM9)	Vice president logistics
Scitron	(FM10)	Business-unit manager
Puraire	(FM11)	Purchasing manager

hibit 1-7. Each is given an "identifier" for the following analysis. The focused managers are easily classified into three groups: business-unit managers (FM1, FM2, FM3, and FM10); plant managers (FM4, FM7, and FM8); and logistics and manufacturing support managers (FM5, FM6, FM9, and FM11). We analyzed these eleven interviews to determine what was more focused and specific than the other sixty managers we interviewed.

The business-unit managers and one plant manager (FM7) all regard themselves as running an entire business and see themselves as profit centers. They establish their expectations in terms of revenue (shipments) and expenses (costs) and profits for their unit. They have identified key indicators that will determine their success and they monitor these frequently—usually daily, often by walking around, and by personal contact with key subordinates. Contact with subordinates at different locations is frequent (telephone, facsimile, and electronic mail) and interactive. They monitor orders, units produced, shipments, backlogs, rejects, injuries, absences, downtime, competitive wage rates, material prices and shortages, and so forth, and they rely on systems and subordinates to notify them personally and immediately of changes, failures, or problems. All were very specific in describing their many tasks and activities.

The division president at Canadian Oil (FM1) was typical of this group. He manages a chain of discount-price retail gasoline stations. He monitors prices at each station and competitors' stations several times each day, and may change them hourly. Inventories, supply prices, and station conditions are likewise monitored continuously. He expects to hear immediately about safety problems, thefts, or damage to property. He sometimes visits or works at a station himself to help solve a problem there. For him and the other business-unit managers we must conclude that profit is a comprehensive and powerful focusing measure that is easily adapted to a performance evaluation scheme.

The plant managers (FM4, FM7, and FM8), one of whom we also included with the business-unit managers above, are similar. Their tasks are easily specified and progress on plans, objectives, and expectations is easily and continuously measured by them, their subordinates, and their superiors.

The logistics and manufacturing support managers (FM5, FM6, FM9, and FM11) are much like the focused plant managers. They are responsible for availability and delivery of material, conditions in plants, and shipment of product to customers. Each could describe to us the specific ways in which they get information they need, monitor activities as they are occurring, work around problems that appear, and monitor their own performance daily. Their improvement over time usually is easily expressed—such as fewer stock-outs, reduced cost of material handling, lower cost of freight—and relates easily to things that can be monitored daily. Again, we concluded that these focused managers had their personal performance-evaluation schemes, often related to or the same as corporate goals for their function, and these focused their management activities.

Not all business-unit managers, plant managers, or manufacturing support managers we interviewed made these lists as focused managers, and so it was not the job function that caused us to score them as we did. Instead we conclude that being able to express tasks, goals, and expectations clearly, in measures that relate to specifics that can be monitored continuously or frequently, focuses managers' descriptions and actions. Profit goals do that, as do production goals and their support. From this relation we concluded that performance evaluation schemes are likely to focus managers' tasks and activities best when they can be conduits between the expectations they create and actions that will lead to good performance.

By their absence from the focused manager group, marketing and sales managers and staff and financial managers support this conclusion. Expectations of growth in sales, development of markets, development of a new financial control system, or project analysis are much less amenable to descriptions of what should be done today and how to proceed if what was done previously did not have the desired effect. Sales calls, client contacts, spending on advertising, or added staff may not influence performance immediately, or ever. Hence, performance evaluation schemes are more challenging to develop for managers where linkage between action today may not be directly related to desired results. Our interviews confirm that few corporations have used performance evaluation schemes in a way that helps managers in marketing and sales and support functions to focus their descriptions of tasks and activities as well as do their colleagues who are managers of business units and plants.

Conclusions

Performance evaluation and incentive compensation schemes have several purposes, one of which is to focus managers' attention on tasks and activities that need to be done if expectations are to be achieved. Using interviews with sixty-six managers in eleven companies, nine of which use performance evaluation schemes, we conclude that these schemes appear to make managers more specific in describing their work. The effects of incentive compensation schemes are less clear from our work, but further research on both types of schemes appears justifiable.

Eleven "focused managers" identified in our interviews offer support for the conclusion that most effective performance-evaluation systems for helping managers understand what their tasks and activities should be will use measurables, including profit, which managers can relate to accomplishments toward expectations continuously or frequently.

Designers of performance evaluation and incentive compensation schemes should concentrate on developing short-term criteria and measurements that will lead to achieving long-term expectations. Under such schemes, managers would be able to focus on specific tasks and activities, knowing that long-term expectations would be met.

REFERENCES

Beer, Michael. "Performance Appraisal: Dilemmas and Possibilities." *Organizational Dynamics* (Winter 1981), pp. 24–36.

Flanagan, John C., and Robert K. Burns. "The Employee Performance Record: A New Appraisal and Development Tool." *Harvard Business Review* (September–October 1955), pp. 95–102.

Kaplan, Robert S., and Anthony A. Atkinson. *Advanced Management Accounting*, 2d ed. Englewood Cliffs, NJ: Prentice-Hall, 1989.

Latham, Gary P. "Job Performance and Appraisal" in C. L. Cooper and I. T. Robertson, eds., *International Review of Industrial and Organizational Psychology*. Chichester, Eng.: John Wiley, 1986.

Latham, Gary P., and K. H. Wexley. *Increasing Productivity Through Performance Appraisal*. Reading, MA: Addison-Wesley, 1981.

Levinson, Harry. "Management by Whose Objectives?" *Harvard Business Review* (July–August 1970), pp. 125–134.

Locke, Edwin A., and Gary P. Latham. *A Theory of Goal Setting and Task Performance*. Englewood Cliffs, NJ: Prentice-Hall, 1990.

Meyer, Herbert H., Emanuel Kay, and John R. P. French, Jr. "Split Roles in Performance Appraisal." *Harvard Business Review* (January–February 1965), pp. 123–129.

Odiorne, George S. *Management Decision by Objectives*. Englewood Cliffs, NJ: Prentice-Hall, 1965.

———. "The Trend Toward the Quarterly Performance Review." *Business Horizons* (July–August 1990), pp. 38–41.

Porter, Lyman W., Edward E. Lawler, III, and J. Richard Hackman. *Behavior in Organizations*. New York: McGraw-Hill, 1975.

CHAPTER 2

Performance Measurement and Appraisal: Motivating Managers to Identify and Reward Performance

Kevin J. Murphy

Introduction

THE key to any successful incentive compensation program is the system that defines performance and identifies high and low performers. Divisional or corporate-level profitability may serve as suitable performance measures for divisional managers or top-level executives. But, for most lower- and middle-level managers, performance measurement depends on subjective performance ratings assigned by direct superiors in the corporate hierarchy. The success of companywide incentive compensation programs therefore depends on managers' effectiveness in monitoring and appraising their subordinates' performance.*

A common malady in performance appraisal systems is managers' tendency to assign uniform ratings to employees regardless of performance. Medoff and Abraham (1980), for example, examined the distribution of performance ratings for more than 7,000 managerial and professional employees in two large manufacturing firms and found that 95% of the employees in each firm were crowded into two rating categories.[1] Forced-distribution rating systems—in which managers are forced to adhere to a specified distribution of performance ratings—mitigate managerial tendencies to assign uniform ratings but may generate important counterproductive side effects.

One example of a firm wrestling with managerial tendencies to assign uniform ratings is Merck & Co., Inc., a large pharmaceutical company headquartered in Rahway, New Jersey. From 1978 to 1986, managers assigned ratings on a scale from 1 to 5, based on absolute performance, and were unconstrained in the ultimate distribution of ratings. Employee ratings in each division were crowded together; only a few employees received the top rating 5, and even fewer received low ratings. Suggested salary revisions were tied to these relatively uniform performance ratings, leading to relatively uniform pay increases and undifferentiated pay.

Employee interviews conducted in 1985 revealed high levels of employee dissatisfaction over the 1978 performance appraisal system, as suggested by the excerpts reproduced in Exhibit 2-1. Employees generally agreed that rewards for excellent performance were not adequate: outstanding performers received salary increases, many of which were just marginally better than those given to average performers. Often, outstanding performance was not even clearly identified.

Merck executives, searching for a program that would better identify and reward top and bottom performers, introduced several changes in 1986, including a forced-distribution rating system. Although generally successful, this new program exacerbated some problems and created others, and the program was modified in 1989 to a flexible target system in which the targeted rating distribution varied with divisional performance.

This study is designed to describe, analyze, and evaluate the 1978, 1986, and 1989 Performance Appraisal and Salary Administration programs at Merck, covering approximately 7,000 domestic and 1,000 international exempt salaried employees. Merck enjoys a reputation for progressive personnel policies and aggressive pay practices, and therefore offers a promising laboratory for studying performance appraisal systems. With roots dating back three centuries, the pharmaceutical giant manufactures and markets more than 150 prescription pharmaceuticals and vaccines, and is the nation's largest provider of prescription medicines. *Fortune* magazine selected Merck as "America's Most Admired Corporation" for four straight years (1987–1990). *Fortune*'s 1990 rankings of 305 large corporations—based on a survey of nearly 8,000 senior executives, outside directors, and financial analysts—rated Merck first in innovativeness, shareholder value, product quality, and financial soundness. For the fourth year in a row, Merck was ranked highest in its ability to attract, develop, and retain talented people.

Exhibit 2-1   Excerpts from Employee Interviews on the 1978
Performance Appraisal and Salary Administration Program

"Managers are afraid to give experienced people a 1, 2, or 3 rating. It's easier to give everyone a 4 and give new people a 3."

"I could walk on water and spit gold quarters and my supervisor wouldn't give me a 5; he never got a 5 so why should I get one?"

"There is no way to get rid of the dead wood. They just hang in there with 3 − ratings and no one will move on them. Marginal people are draining our strength."

"What's the use of killing yourself? You still get the same rating as everyone else, and you still get the same 5% increase. It's demoralizing and demotivating."

"Charlie's been in that job for 20 years. He hasn't done anything creative for the last 15 years. Do you think my boss would give him a 3 rating? No way! Then, he'd have to spend the next 12 months listening to Charlie complain."

"Tell me this, how in the world can 83% of the people be exceeding job expectations while the company, as a whole, is doing just average? It just doesn't make any sense."

"I'm the one who carries this department, and yet I get the same increase as everyone else. It's just not fair."

"A lot of these people get to the top of the range and just sit there sucking up merit money, because the boss is afraid to give them anything less than an average increase. Where's the equity?"

"How can I rate my people objectively when the other directors are giving all their people 4s? A 3 isn't acceptable. I wouldn't mind if everyone played by the same rules, but they don't."

"I'll be honest. It's getting to the point where some of the best people are going to walk out of here unless they get recognized and rewarded properly. Now, who do you want to do the walking? Your best people or your worst?"

Quotations are excerpted from interviews with approximately 300 Merck employees conducted in 1985 by the Employee Relations Review Committee.

The 1978 Performance Appraisal and Salary Administration Program

Under Merck's 1978 Performance Appraisal and Salary Administration Program, managers rated employees on a scale from 1 to 5, with 5 designating exceptional performance and 1 indicating unacceptable performance. Pluses and minuses were allowed (exclud-

Exhibit 2-2   1984 and 1985 Rating Distributions under the 1978
Performance Appraisal and Salary Administration Program

Performance Rating	1984 Ratings		1985 Ratings	
	Number of Employees	Percentage Distribution	Number of Employees	Percentage Distribution
5	22	.33%	19	.28%
5 −	69	1.02%	77	1.14%
4 +	732	10.87%	709	10.53%
4	1,867	27.72%	1,849	27.46%
4 −	1,382	20.52%	1,427	21.19%
3 +	1,549	23.00%	1,607	23.86%
3	752	11.16%	694	10.31%
3 −	230	3.41%	200	2.97%
2 +	87	1.29%	97	1.44%
2	40	.59%	44	.65%
2 −	0	.00%	3	.04%
1 +	3	.04%	2	.03%
1	3	.04%	6	.09%

ing scores of 1− and 5+), thus managers effectively chose from
thirteen rating categories. The scale was *absolute*—the rating assigned
to an individual was to reflect only that individual's performance independent of other employees' performances.

Exhibit 2-2 shows the distribution of performance ratings assigned by Merck supervisors and managers in 1984 and 1985. Most
of the 6,736 employees (93%) received ratings from 3 to 4+ in 1984;
only 91 employees (1.4%) received 5 or 5− ratings, and only six
received the lowest ratings of 1+ or 1. The 1985 rating distribution,
virtually indistinguishable from the 1984 distribution, also shows that
most employees are crowded into a few rating categories. Moreover,
the companywide distribution depicted in Exhibit 2-2 overstates the
dispersion *within* divisions: some divisions would assign uniformly
higher ratings than others, making the overall distribution substantially more dispersed than divisional distributions.

An underlying hypothesis in this chapter is that the tight distribution of the ratings in Exhibit 2-2 in part reflects ineffective performance appraisal by self-interested managers and supervisors. Performance appraisals are typically conducted by the managers who work
closely with the employees every day, because these managers have
the specific knowledge required to evaluate their subordinates' performance. The time and effort line managers allocate to performance

appraisal partly depends on the rewards they receive for conducting appraisals relative to their rewards from engaging in other activities. Because performance appraisals are often a required but unrewarded managerial task, it is rational for managers to spend no more than minimal acceptable time and effort in evaluating subordinates' performance.

Moreover, managers bear a disproportionately large share of the nonpecuniary costs associated with performance appraisal, which leads them to prefer to assign uniform ratings rather than to carefully distinguish employees by their performance.[2] Careful performance appraisals are time-consuming, and it's much easier to assign uniform ratings than to assign and justify ratings that vary substantially from one employee to another. Managers also often have personal relationships with their direct subordinates, making employees' complaints and direct conflict with poorly performing employees particularly distasteful. Few managers relish giving poor or even mediocre ratings to popular but unproductive subordinates.

Salary Administration under the 1978 Plan

The uniformity of performance ratings suggested by Exhibit 2-2 affects employee incentives because both revisions in salary and probability of promotion are, in part, tied to performance appraisals. The basic procedure at Merck for determining salary remained intact throughout the period analyzed, and therefore it is useful to describe salient details of its salary administration system.

Salaries for exempt employees are based on a combination of job characteristics (as measured by "Hay points") and merit (as measured by performance ratings). Hay points are determined by individually evaluating each position in terms of the three "Hay factors"—know-how, problem-solving, and accountability. Numerical scores are assigned to each factor according to guidelines provided by Hay Associates, and the sum of these scores defines the Hay points for each position in the organization.

Hay points are converted to a "control point" (roughly an average monthly salary) using a salary-line formula. The 1986 salary-line formula was:

Control point = $1,502 + $4.69 × (Hay points).

Thus, a mid-level employee with 500 Hay points had a 1986 control point of $3,847 per month. The salary-line formula describes the hierarchic structure of wages in the organization, for higher corporate positions are associated with higher Hay points.

The employee's actual salary can range from 80% to 125% of the control point; actual salary as a percentage of the control point is called the employee's "compa-ratio." An employee with 500 Hay points and a compa-ratio of 90 would have a 1986 monthly salary of $3,462. An employee's compa-ratio goes up each time he or she gets a merit increase, and falls whenever the salary-line formula is moved upward (holding salaries constant).

Compensation for exempt salaried employees at Merck has traditionally ranked among the top 25% of large U.S. companies, contributing to high levels of employee loyalty as reflected in historically low turnover rates. Merck sets the salary-line formula so that employees with compa-ratios of 100 earn roughly 7% or 8% more than average compensation (for similar Hay points) in other large firms. The salary-line formula is revised annually on April 1, so that control points for a position (quantified by Hay points) approximates pay at the seventy-fifth percentile for similar positions in the sample of large firms. Salaries are not automatically adjusted when the salary-line formula changes; thus, individual compa-ratios generally decline every April 1, when control points are increased.

The maximum attainable compa-ratio is 125. Thus, salaries are effectively capped at 125% of the control point, and employees near the cap can receive only up to (but not more than) the cap. In practice, however, very few employees achieve and sustain compa-ratios exceeding 120. First, the salary-line formula is adjusted prior to salary revisions. Thus even employees hitting the cap in a particular year are likely to be well below the cap after the salary line changes on April 1. Second, employees with high compa-ratios are often strong candidates for internal promotions. Because it takes time to learn the skills required for a new position, the starting compa-ratio for a newly promoted employee is usually lower than the final compa-ratio in the prior position. The average starting compa-ratio for all employees promoted into positions in the 400–600 Hay-point range during 1984–1985 was 87.

Pay-for-Performance under the 1978 Plan

Salary revisions are linked to both control-point increases and performance ratings through guidelines established by the personnel depart-

Exhibit 2-3 Actual 1985 Average Salary Revisions for 6,734 Merck Employees under the 1978 Performance Appraisal and Salary Administration Program

1985 Rating	Number of Employees	Average 1985 Percentage of Pay Increase, by Compa-Ratio			
		Compa-Ratio 80.00–95.00	Compa-Ratio 95.01–110.00	Compa-Ratio 110.01–120.00	Compa-Ratio 120.01–125.00
5, 5 −	96	8.3%	8.1%	6.5%	4.4%
4+, 4, 4 −	3,985	6.5%	5.5%	4.8%	4.6%
3+, 3, 3 −	2,501	5.7%	4.0%	3.3%	3.5%
2+, 2, 2 −	144	4.3%	1.3%	0.0%	0.0%
1+, 1	8				

ment. Employees with higher ratings tend to get larger pay increases, and raises for a performance rating tend to be smaller for employees who have already attained a high compa-ratio. The recommended salary revision for an employee rated 4+, 4, or 4 − might be 5%–7% if her compa-ratio was in the 80–95 range, but only 3%–5% if her compa-ratio was in the 120–125 range.

Exhibit 2-3 shows the actual average pay increases received by 6,734 Merck employees in 1985, by performance rating and compa-ratio. Average pay increases ranged from 8.3% for high performers with low compa-ratios, to 0% for lower performers with high compa-ratios. The highest pay increases went to employees with high ratings but low compa-ratios such as strong performers relatively new to a position or employees rebounding from a string of bad years. Employees with ratings of 2+ or lower, with compa-ratios of 95 or higher received little or no increase in base compensation.

The average pay increases in Exhibit 2-3 are based on nearly 7,000 exempt salaried employees, serving in jobs with various Hay points. Exhibit 2-4 depicts hypothetical average salaries and pay revisions at the midpoint in each compa-ratio range for mid-level employees with 500 Hay points. Salaries for this hypothetical group range from $40,394 for an employee with an 87.5 compa-ratio to $56,551 for an employee with a compa-ratio of 122.5. Assuming that the ratings distribution for this group of employees approximates the population (Exhibit 2-2), 93% will receive annual pay raises of between $1,752 and $2,626. The premium for being in the top 1% of performers—earning a 5 rating instead of a 4—averages less than $900.

The data in Exhibits 2-2, 2-3, and 2-4 suggest two sources con-

Exhibit 2-4   Average 1985 Salaries and Salary Revisions for
Hypothetical Mid-Level Employees with 500 Hay Points, by
Compa-Ratio

1985 Rating	Average 1985 Percentage of Pay Increase, by Compa-Ratio			
	Compa-Ratio 87.50	Compa-Ratio 102.50	Compa-Ratio 115.00	Compa-Ratio 122.50
5, 5 −	$3,353	$3,833	$3,451	$2,488
4 +, 4, 4 −	$2,626	$2,602	$2,548	$2,601
3 +, 3, 3 −	$2,302	$1,893	$1,752	$1,979
2 +, 2, 2 −	$1,737	$ 615	$ 0	$ 0
1 +, 1	$ 0	$ 0	$ 0	$ 0
Average salary	$40,394	$47,318	$53,089	$56,551

tributing to ineffective incentives for Merck employees. First, the
1978 Performance Appraisal Program generally did not identify the
top and bottom performers in the organization. Second, the relatively
few employees whose performances were identified generally received
small rewards for superior performance and small penalties for low
performance. These two sources are inherently connected: increasing
the rewards and penalties in Exhibit 2-3 would probably have generated even *less* difference in the performance ratings in Exhibit 2-2,
for managers would face larger nonpecuniary costs of differentiating
among employees.

In March 1985, soon after his appointment as chief executive
officer, Dr. P. Roy Vagelos formed the Employee Relations Review
Committee, charged with reviewing and evaluating personnel policies
and practices at Merck. Over six months, the committee visited several companies noted for their personnel policies, and also interviewed
about 300 Merck employees from various ranks in Merck sites across
the United States and Canada. The committee concluded that many
of the complaints raised in the employee interviews (excerpted in
Exhibit 2-1) could be traced to the way in which employees were
evaluated under the current performance-appraisal program. Ultimately the committee made more than fifty recommendations in management training, recruiting practices, alternate work patterns, stability of employment, and communication. Late in 1986, as a result
of the committee's findings and recommendations, Merck revised its
performance review and pay practices.

The 1986 Performance Appraisal and
Salary Administration Program

The guidelines for the 1986 Performance Appraisal Program for exempt salaried employees are reproduced as Exhibit 2-5. The most important change—implemented to mitigate managers' tendency to assign uniform ratings—was a shift from an absolute rating system to a forced-distribution system, in which managers are forced to adhere to a specified distribution of performance ratings. Other major revisions included rating categories, performance categories, and timing of performance evaluations.

The revised rating categories and the targeted percentage of employees assigned to each category are reported as the first two columns in Exhibit 2-5. The old numerical thirteen-point scale (including pluses and minuses) was replaced by five rating descriptors: EX (Exceptional within Merck), WD (Merck Standard with Distinction), HS (High Merck Standard), RI (Merck Standard with Room for Improvement), and NA (Not Adequate for Merck). Under the targeted guidelines—strictly applicable only to groups with more than 100 employees—70% of employees would be rated High Merck Standard, which, according to Merck executives, designated performance that was average within Merck but above average for the industry. Five percent (but no more than 8%) of employees were to be rated exceptional, and 8% (but no fewer than 5%) were to be assigned Room for Improvement, designating performance below average but above the minimum acceptable level. Two percent of employees were to be given Not Adequate ratings, although managers could choose not to assign any of these lowest ratings. An optional sixth category was called PR (Progressing) designed for employees who were too new to the job to get a comprehensive evaluation.

Performance appraisals under the 1978 system were conducted throughout the year, although an employee would always be evaluated in the same month every year. Under the forced-distribution system, all employee appraisals were conducted within one month. The performance categories and definitions were also clarified and expanded. Under the 1986 plan, employees were rated on both qualitative and quantitative measures of their overall job performance, including their performance against five to seven planned objectives. Managers and supervisors were also rated on their *managerial performance*, including hiring, training and development, performance feed-

Exhibit 2-5 Performance Rating Definitions and Targeted Guidelines 1986 Performance Appraisal and Salary Administration Program

	Performance Ratings		Performance Definitions	
Rating	Distribution Target	Specific Job Measures Ongoing Doings	Planned Objectives	Management of People
EX Exceptional within Merck	5% (No more than 8%)	Far above Merck peers Capitalized on unexpected events to gain superior results	Made significant breakthroughs or exceptional achievements	Outstanding leader Exceptional development and recruitment of people Superior communications
Merck Standard WD with Distinction	15% (No more than 17%)	Clearly superior to Merck peers in most respects Took advantage of unexpected events to achieve unusually good results	Objectives met and many exceeded	A clear leader among Merck peers Top-quality people recruited and developed

Code	Rating	Distribution	Comparison to Merck peers	Objectives	Leadership / Communication
HS	High Merck Standard	70% (No fewer than 65%)	Comparable to Merck peers. Made use of unexpected events to achieve very good results	Objectives met	A very good leader. Hired very good people and develops people as well as peers. Very good communication
	Merck Standard	8%	Work is not quite as good as Merck peers'. Contended with unexpected events	Most objectives met. Some shortfalls	Adequate leader. Hires good people. Satisfactory communication
RI	Room for Improvement	(No fewer than 5%)			
NA	Not Adequate for Merck	2% (No minimum)	Work is not up to that of Merck peers. Did not fully cope with unexpected events	Missed significant objectives	Poor leader. Communication could be better
PR	Progressing	Not Applicable	Typically this employee is new to the company or in a significantly different assignment. Normally this rating would apply only during the first year in the new job.		

back and recognition, employee relations, communications, and affirmative action.

Costs and Benefits of Forced-Distribution Systems

Forced-distribution rating systems, such as the one implemented at Merck, discourage uniform ratings by making managers adhere to a specified distribution of performance ratings. These systems have a couple of obvious potential drawbacks. First, the targeted distribution may not adequately reflect the actual distribution of performances in a division, and in fact may be a worse approximation than the distribution assigned by the manager if no constraints applied. Second, although these systems raise the cost of assigning uniform rankings, they do not change the basic nonpecuniary costs associated with performance appraisals and do not guarantee that ratings will be assigned in accordance with performance. A few Merck managers, for example, attempted to randomize the rating procedure by following a bad rating in one year with a better rating in the next year; thus managerial preferences for assigning uniform ratings might be satisfied intertemporally instead of concurrently. Although rating randomization was not perceived to be a major problem under Merck's 1986 Performance Appraisal Program, it occurred frequently enough for top management to identify and label it the "it's-her-turn syndrome."

One context familiar to academics that highlights the potential problems with forced-distribution systems is "grading on a curve" in college courses. Guidelines specifying "A" grades for 20% of the students work fine if the twentieth percentile student is easily identified. But actual student test performance is often grouped in such a way that it might be easy to identify the top 15% or the top 25% of the class, but very difficult to identify the twentieth percentile student without making an arbitrary distinction among virtually indistinguishable students. The it's-her-turn syndrome may be less of a problem in academia than in other organizations, because students seldom take multiple courses with the same professor, giving little opportunity to smooth a student's grades intertemporally. Forced-distribution grading systems are predicted to be less successful where the professor and student have a long-run teacher–student relationship.

Assuming that the targeted distribution approximates the true distribution of individual performances, and that the manager's nonpecuniary costs are minimized by placing the division's best performers in the top categories and worst performers in the bottom categories, switching to the forced-distribution system will make performance appraisal more effective. Although the forced-distribution system gives the manager more incentive to identify and reward performance, it may also negatively affect the subordinate's performance.

Forcing managers to fit a specific ratings distribution implies that employees are evaluated by measuring their performance *relative* to that of other employees competing for positions in the same ratings distribution. Holmström (1982) argues that basing pay on relative performance may reduce risk for employees affected by a common outside factor beyond their control. Forced-distribution rating scales in academia protect students from systematically "hard" or "easy" graders. But Gibbons and Murphy (1990) argue that relative performance evaluation will have counterproductive side effects whenever employees can take actions that affect the observed performance of their fellow employees.[3] Relative performance evaluation may reduce team effort and cooperation, for example, by providing incentives to sabotage the performance of co-workers.[4] Employees rated under a forced-distribution system may also collude to lower team output, and talented workers may seek transfers to weaker divisions where their relative performance is likely to be higher.

The Employee Relations Review Committee stressed that the forced distributions would *not* apply to groups of fewer than 100 Merck employees. This policy makes sense because, by the laws of large numbers, the side effects of forced distributions are likely to be smallest in relatively large groups of homogeneous employees. First, the targeted distribution is more likely to approximate the true distribution in larger divisions. Second, incentives to sabotage or collude with co-workers are fewer in large groups, where individual employees have only slight influence on co-workers' average performance. Merck executives found little evidence of systematic sabotage among employees competing for higher ratings, but suggested that sabotage *may* be a problem when a few employees compete for a promotion.

Pay-for-Performance under the 1986 Program

The 1986 Salary Administration Program differed from its predecessor by recommending compa-ratio targets and increased differentiation in salary revisions across rating categories. The suggested 1986 salary guideline, which recommends salary revisions and intervals between raises by rating and compa-ratio, is reproduced as Exhibit 2-6. Suggested 1986 raises for employees with HS ratings and 100 compa-ratios, for example, were 6% to 8%, occurring approximately 13–15 months after their previous raise. Although a range of suggested increases was arrived at for all employees, supervisors could recommend no increase when appropriate. The suggested rate of adjustment to new compensation levels is fastest for high-rated employees with low compa-ratios (who could receive raises every 12–13 months), and slowest for lower-rated employees with high compa-ratios (who might wait 16 months or longer between raises). The compa-ratio targets, reported in the bottom panel of Exhibit 2-6, indicate hypothetical long-run compa-ratios for an employee maintaining the same performance for several years. An employee consistently rated as WD would have a long-run compa-ratio target between 100 and 120.

Exhibit 2-7 shows the actual distribution of performance ratings and average salary revisions for 1988, the second full year under the new system. The 404 (6.6%) employees assigned ratings of EX received average pay raises that were substantially higher than those received by the median (HS) employee, 11.3% compared to 5.1% for employees with midrange compa-ratios. In contrast, as shown in Exhibit 2-3, the 96 (1.4%) employees receiving 5 or 5 − ratings under the old program in 1985 received pay raises less than 3% higher than the median employee: 8.1%, compared to 5.5% for employees with midrange compa-ratios. Exhibit 2-8 compares the frequency distribution of salary increases in 1985 and 1988, using data from Exhibits 2-3 and 2-7. The frequency distributions reveal a substantial increase in both pay differentiation and the implicit relation between pay and performance at Merck. More top and bottom performers were being identified, and the rewards (and penalties) for superior (and unsatisfactory) performance were substantially increased.

Discretionary Award Program

After introducing the new Performance Appraisal and Salary Administration Program in 1986, Merck executives quietly and informally instituted a Discretionary Award Program designed to further reward superior performers. Never announced as a formal program, the first year's cash bonuses came as a surprise to almost 2,500 recipients (representing about 40% of eligible salaried, exempt employees).

Exhibit 2-6 Suggested Magnitude and Timing of 1988 Salary Revisions 1986 Performance Appraisal and Salary Administration Program

Performance Rating	Suggested Merit Increase Percentage			
	Compa-Ratio 80.00–95.00	Compa-Ratio 95.01–110.00	Compa-Ratio 110.01–120.00	Compa-Ratio 120.01–125.00
EX *Exceptional within Merck*	13%–15%	12%–14%	9%–11%	to maximum of range
WD *Merck Standard with Distinction*	9%–11%	8%–10%	7%–9%	—
HS *High Merck Standard*	7%–9%	6%–8%	—	—
RI *Merck Standard Room for Improvement*	5%–7%	—	—	—
NA *Not Adequate for Merck*	—	—	—	—

	Compa-Ratio Target	Suggested Timing Since Last Increase			
		Compa-Ratio 80.00–95.00	Compa-Ratio 95.01–110.00	Compa-Ratio 110.01–120.00	Compa-Ratio 120.01–125.00
EX	115–125	12–13 months	12–14 months	14–15 months	—
WD	100–120	12–14 months	12–14 months	14–16 months	—
HS	90–110	13–14 months	13–15 months	—	—
RI	80–95	13–14 months	—	—	—
NA	—	—	—	—	—

Exhibit 2-7 1988 Average Salary Revisions under the 1986 Performance Appraisal and Salary Administration Program

1988 Rating	Number of Employees	Percentage Distribution	Average 1988 Percentage of Pay Increase, by Compa-Ratio				
			Compa-Ratio 80.00–95.00	Compa-Ratio 95.01–110.00	Compa-Ratio 110.01–120.00	Compa-Ratio 120.01–125.00 to maximum
EX	404	6.6%	12.9%	11.3%	7.6%	to maximum
WD	1,218	20.0%	9.1%	8.0%	6.1%	—
HS	4,267	70.0%	6.7%	5.1%	4.3%	—
RI	190	3.1%	3.5%	3.0%	—	—
NA	18	0.3%	0%	—	—	—

Exhibit 2-8   Frequency Distribution for Average Salary Increases for Merck Employees, 1985 vs. 1988

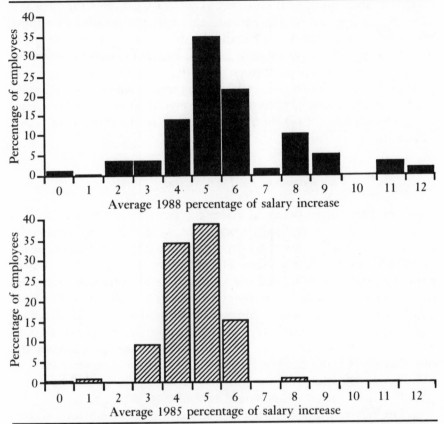

Note: Frequency distributions of actual annual increases are based on data in Exhibits 2-3 and 2-7, under the assumption that 25% of Merck employees have compa-ratios between 80 and 95, 50% between 95.01 and 110, 20% between 110.01 and 120, and 5% above 120. Salary increases for employees with compa-ratios exceeding 120 are assumed to be one-half the increase for employees with compa-ratios between 110 and 120.

Guidelines showing the targeted number of recipients by performance rating, and the suggested cash bonus payment (as a percentage of salary) by performance rating, are determined each year by top management. Discretionary awards in 1988 were given to all employees achieving EX and WD ratings, and to just under a third of employees with an HS rating. Cash bonuses for EX and WD employees in 1988 averaged about 10% and 6% of base salary, respectively, and bonuses for HS employees who received awards averaged about 4% of their base salary.

The first year's discretionary bonuses did not directly affect employee incentives, because employees were unaware of the program's existence until the first bonus checks were issued. But the prospect of receiving bonuses in subsequent years was an incentive to achieve high performance ratings. Overall, the discretionary bonus program increased incentives by substantially widening the gap between the rewards given to top performers and those given to mediocre and poor performers. Moreover, cash bonuses seem a particularly effective method of providing incentives, for the rewards are more flexible (and more easily taken away) than rewards given in the form of increases in base salary.

Two-Year Review of the 1986 System

Early in 1989, after being in effect for two full years, the revised performance-review and salary programs were evaluated by the human resource staff. Interviews were conducted with ten senior managers and eleven "focus groups" of employees at U.S. and European sites. The staff also tabulated the results from questionnaires returned by 251 managers and 5,413 covered employees. Fifty percent of the employees surveyed thought the new Performance Appraisal Program was better than the one it replaced, 25% thought it was worse, and 25% saw no differences in the two plans. Sixty-three percent saw the new Salary Administration Program as an improvement, and only 8% thought the old program was better. Almost a third (29%) were equally happy under either salary administration program.

The focus-group interviews generated many specific complaints and comments about the 1986 programs. Some managers in one European plant complained that the program demotivated staff. They felt that it had "too many objectives" and that "the salary link made discussions on performance improvement difficult." The focus-group interviews with employees, excerpted in Exhibit 2-9, revealed other specific positive and negative aspects of the revised programs.

The 1989 Performance Appraisal and
Salary Administration Program

The 1989 Performance Appraisal Program made two major modifications in the 1986 program. First, in response to requests for more gradations of performance within the High Standard category,

Exhibit 2-9   Excerpts from Employee Focus-Group Interviews About the 1986 Revised Performance Appraisal and Salary Administration Program

"HS category is simply too big. No way to show an employee he's at the high end or low end."

"One problem is that people are used to being rated against the job and its demands and expectations rather than against each other."

"On the positive side, the targeted distribution has forced managers to make tough decisions. It has produced frank and interesting discussions on performance."

"Shouldn't force distribution at the low end or high end. If you don't have a 'true' EX, don't be forced to give one just to fit the targets."

"Labels are a problem. People were in the middle before, but they didn't know it. It's the discovery that they're in the middle that is disquieting to them."

"The old program had more gradations. You could 'move someone through with small rewards.' Can't do that as well now."

"Competitive approach is valid. People aren't working in a vacuum. They are competing with peers—just like in the 'outside' world."

"We will have a future problem if we continue to get rid of people who aren't performing well. Very soon, we'll need to begin to get rid of people who are solid performers—but just not as good as others. This will cause a major morale problem in the workforce."

"Another problem is the labels. Get rid of them and go to a full ranking of people."

"Significant problem between line and staff people. When the division is doing very well in meeting its financial goals, most higher ratings are given to the line. There aren't any left over for staff people who may be performing just as well. More staff people get higher ratings during a bad year. Last year, many of staff performed superbly, but managers couldn't give them ratings that reflected that."

"A definite plus is having all appraisals done at the same time. This gives you the opportunity to compare performance of one employee with another and help you make decisions on each employee's performance."

"Forced distribution is inappropriate. Last year our group had the best year ever, but, because of the rest of the division's performance, higher ratings were 'used up.' How can you reward people in a situation like this where they deserve it, but are excluded from higher ratings because there are only so many to go around? It becomes very demotivational to people who performed extremely well."   *(Interestingly, this division didn't use its full quota of EX ratings)* that category was broken into three separate categories—Outstanding, Very Good, and Good. The number of employees assigned in these three categories was determined by the targeted distribution guidelines, but managers were given full flexibility in the distribution within these three categories.

Second, and more important, the plan allowed for differences in employee rating distributions depending on the employee's division performance for the year. Under the new plan, top management would rate divisional performance on an absolute scale as Exceptional (EX), With Distinction (WD), High Standard (HS), Room for Improvement (RI), or Not Adequate (NA). The distribution for employee ratings that supervisors use under the new plan now depends on divisional performance—the targeted percentage of workers assigned to the top rating category, for example, will be higher in better-performing divisions.

Beyond these two major changes, management promised to provide additional training in setting objectives and appraisal. Also, the employee performance ratings EX, WD, and RI were changed to emphasize their relativity. Exceptional (EX) was changed to Top 5% (TF), With Distinction (WD) was changed to Top Quintile (TQ), and Requires Improvement (RI) was changed to Lower 5% (LF). No changes were recommended in the Salary Administration Program; suggested salary increases would continue to depend on compa-ratio and performance ratings. The new subcategories in the old HS rank (Outstanding, Very Good, and Good) were to be treated as the same category for salary-planning purposes. The new performance appraisal guidelines are reproduced as Exhibit 2-10.

Forced-Distribution Systems with Flexible Targets

Although the 1989 Performance Appraisal Program at Merck has not yet been in effect long enough to determine its success, allowing the distribution to vary with divisional performance seems to mitigate several important problems caused by traditional forced-distribution systems. One inherent problem with forced-distribution systems is that the chosen distribution may not reflect the true distribution of performances. Merck's "flexible target" fixes this problem well enough that divisions with superior performance tend to have a higher percentage of superior performers. Flexible targets also promote collegiality and reduce incentives for sabotage, for individuals are implicitly rewarded for group performance and not strictly for relative performance.

Conclusion

The relationship between the firm's owners and the managers or supervisors who conduct performance appraisals is a subtle yet important variation of the traditional principal–agent relationship. Self-interested managers have little incentive to invest in performance evaluation, both because careful appraisals take time away from better-rewarded activities, and because managers face large nonpecuniary costs from disgruntled employees with mediocre or low evaluations. The agency costs associated with managerial preferences to assign uniform ratings are large, because uninformative performance appraisals preclude writing effective incentive contracts with other workers in the organization. Indeed, the difficulty in getting managers to reveal what they know about subordinates' performance may explain the relative paucity of successful incentive compensation systems in large organizations.

Performance appraisal systems can be made more effective by structuring incentives so that managers find it in their best interest to conduct careful and informative performance evaluations. One way to provide these incentives is to reward or penalize managers according to the combined output of their subordinates: a manager is more likely to identify and remove an unproductive employee when the employee's actions directly affect the manager's wealth. Structuring rewards in this manner is unlikely to eliminate ineffective appraisals, however, for the manager will naturally bear a disproportional share of the costs incurred by better performance appraisals.

Because managers have access to private information about the true performance of subordinates, they cannot simply be "told" to conduct more careful evaluations. But managers can be effectively told to differentiate among employees by making the managers' compensation, promotion, and continued employment conditional on observable characteristics of the evaluation, such as the distribution of assigned ratings. Therefore, because the manager's nonpecuniary costs are likely to be minimized by giving good ratings to the best

Exhibit 2-10 Proposed Guideline for Targeted Distribution of Performance Ratings 1989 Performance Appraisal and Salary Administration Program

Performance Rating for Employee	Rating Type	Targeted Employee-Rating Distribution, by Divisional Performance				
		Performance Rating for Division				
		EX *Exceptional*	WD *With Distinction*	HS *High Standard*	RI *Room for Improvement*	NA *Not Acceptable*
TF *Top 5%*	Relative	8%	6%	5%	2%	1%
TQ *Top Quintile*	Relative	20%	17%	15%	12%	10%
OU **Outstanding**	Absolute					
VG **Very Good**	Absolute	71%	75%	75%	78%	79%
GD **Good**	Absolute					
LF *Lower 5%*	Relative	1%	2%	5%	8%	10%
NA *Not Acceptable*	Absolute					
PR *Progressing*		Not Applicable				

Rating Definitions under Proposed System

Top 5%:
Those whose performance ranked among top 5% of peers.

Top Quintile:
Those whose performance ranked among top 20% of peers (i.e., those in the sixth to twentieth percentile).

Outstanding:
Performance clearly exceeded requirements of the position. Most planned objectives were achieved with results beyond established goals. Major accomplishments were made in addition to planned objectives. Quality and timeliness of results are consistently beyond the basic expectations of the job.

Very Good:
Results against planned objectives met and often exceeded goals. Performance was very satisfactory and was consistently at or above the level expected of a solid and seasoned employee.

Good:
Results against planned objectives generally met goals. There were no critical areas where accomplishments were less than planned. Any minor shortfalls in results were counterbalanced by solid accomplishments in other areas, so that the overall job met expectations.

Lower 5%:
Those whose performance ranked among the bottom 5% of peers.

Not Acceptable:
Those whose performance failed to meet important planned objectives; or did not have solid accomplishments in day-to-day performance; or did not adequately contribute to team effort; or otherwise failed to meet Merck standards.

Progressing:
Typically this employee is new to the Company or in a significantly different assignment. Normally this rating would apply during the first year in the new job.

Exhibit 2-11   Return on Assets for Merck and Its 10 Largest
Competitors, 1970–1988

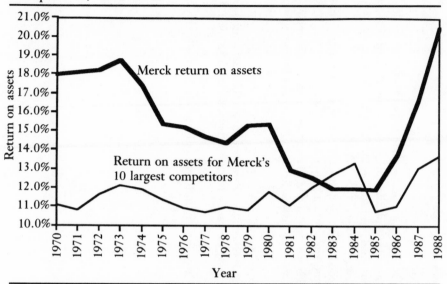

Note: Return on assets, defined as after-tax income plus interest divided by assets, obtained
from *Compustat*. The list of Merck's 10 largest competitors (as measured by sales, SIC code
2834) has generally varied from year to year because of takeovers, acquisitions, and different
rates of growth. The companies depicted in the graph (and the years during which they were
one of Merck's 10 largest competitors) are Abbott Laboratories (70–73, 75–88), American Home
Products (70–88), Baxter International (85–88), Bristol-Myers (70–88), Glaxo Holdings (87–88),
International Minerals & Chemicals (70, 71, 74–81), Johnson & Johnson (70–88), Eli Lilly &
Co. (70–88), Pfizer Inc. (70–88), Schering-Plough (82, 86), SmithKline Beckman Corp. (80–88),
Squibb (70–78, 84, 85), Sterling Drugs (70–79, 83), Upjohn (72–74, 78–84), and Warner-
Lambert (70–88).

performers and low ratings to the worst, the forced-distribution system adopted by Merck provides incentives for self-interested managers to differentiate among employees on the basis of their performance.

Providing better incentives to conduct performance appraisals
can increase the firm's value by generating better data on performance
by individual employees, which in turn improves the effectiveness of
the firm's promotion and incentive compensation systems. The 1989
Performance Appraisal Program at Merck has not yet been in effect
long enough for us to determine its success, but the intermediate
assessment seems positive. First, differentiation in employee ratings
has increased because managers have, in general, complied with the
forced-distribution guidelines. Second, the variation in rewards from

salary revisions and cash bonuses among employees has increased substantially. Third, Merck's return on assets, relative to that of its closest competitors, has increased dramatically since the 1986 plan was introduced (see Exhibit 2-11). Although not conclusive, these results suggest that the organization now has a more effective incentive structure.

NOTES

*This research is supported by the Managerial Economics Research Center, University of Rochester; the John M. Olin Foundation; and the Division of Research, Harvard Business School. Michael C. Jensen provided helpful comments. I am also grateful to Merck & Co. executives, especially Steven M. Darien and Judy C. Lewent, for sharing their time and experiences and providing access to data. The views expressed here, however, do not necessarily reflect the opinions of Merck management.

1. The first firm had four possible rating categories—Not Acceptable (assigned to .2% of employees), Acceptable (assigned to 5.3%), Good (74.3%), and Outstanding (20.2%). The second firm had six possible ratings—Unacceptable (0%), Minimum Acceptable (0%), Satisfactory (1.2%), Good (36.6%), Superior (58.4%), and Excellent (3.8%).

2. See Tirole (1986) and Baker, Jensen, and Murphy (1988) for related arguments.

3. Various aspects of the costs of relative performance are analyzed by Lazear (1989), Mookherjee (1984), and Dye (1988).

4. John Dvorak, *PC Magazine* editor (September 27, 1988) explains how a friend received his promotion: "He managed to crack the network messaging system so that he could monitor all the memos. He also sabotaged the workgroup software and set back the careers of a few computer-naive souls who didn't realize that someone was manipulating their appointment calendars. They would miss important meetings and be sent on wild-goose chases, only to look like complete buffoons when they showed up for appointments that were never made." Dvorak argues that stealing passwords and destroying important data are a trivial task for computer-literate employees.

REFERENCES

Baker, George P., Michael C. Jensen, and Kevin J. Murphy. "Compensation and Incentives: Practice vs. Theory." *Journal of Finance*, vol. 43, no. 3 (July 1988), pp. 593–616.

Becker, Gary S., and George J. Stigler. "Law Enforcement, Malfeasance, and Compensation of Enforcers." *Journal of Legal Studies*, vol. 3, no. 1 (January 1974), pp. 1–18.

Dye, Ronald A. "Relative Performance Evaluation and Project Selection." Unpublished paper, Northwestern University, 1988.

Gibbons, Robert, and Kevin J. Murphy. "Relative Performance Evaluation for Chief Executive Officers." *Industrial and Labor Relations Review*, vol. 43 (February 1990), pp. 30S–51S.

Hart, Oliver, and Bengt Holmström. "The Theory of Contracts." In *Advances in Economic Theory*, Truman Bewley, ed. Cambridge, Eng.: Cambridge University Press, 1987, pp. 71–155.

Holmström, Bengt. "Moral Hazard in Teams." *Bell Journal of Economics*, vol. 13, no. 2 (Autumn 1982), pp. 324–340.

Lazear, Edward P. "Pay Equality and Industrial Politics." *Journal of Political Economy*, vol. 97, no. 3 (June 1989), pp. 561–580.

Medoff, James L., and Katharine G. Abraham. "Experience, Performance, and Earnings." *Quarterly Journal of Economics*, vol. 95, no. 4 (December 1980), pp. 703–736.

Mookherjee, Dilip. "Optimal Incentive Schemes with Many Agents." *Review of Economic Studies*, vol. 51 (1984), pp. 433–446.

Tirole, Jean. "Hierarchies and Bureaucracies: On the Role of Collusion in Organizations." *Journal of Law, Economics, and Organization*, vol. 2, no. 2 (Fall 1986), pp. 181–214.

CHAPTER 3

Evolution of Performance-Based Management Incentives at the Fiat Group

Kenneth A. Merchant and Angelo Riccaboni

IN the United States, it is almost a management axiom that managers should receive cash rewards for their efforts. Compensation surveys have consistently shown that top- and mid-level managers in U.S. firms of all sizes are included in a short-term (typically annual) incentive plan and also often in at least one long-term (multi-year) incentive plan (e.g., Towers Perrin, 1989).

In most European firms, on the other hand, formal performance-based monetary incentives have traditionally not been an important part of management control systems. Some evidence shows that management incentives have gradually become more prevalent and carried more weight in the last couple of decades (e.g., "Europe's New Managers," 1982; Mosley, 1989). Rarely, however, is the public told how these incentives are structured and how they developed.

In this chapter, we report on a field study aimed at filling this void in knowledge by focusing on one European firm—the Fiat Group—the large Italian corporation engaged mainly in manufacturing and selling vehicles. Public knowledge of how incentives work in

We are grateful for the cooperation of personnel at the Fiat Group, especially Dott. Giuseppe Alessandria and Dott.ssa Maria Luisa Merlo, and for financial assistance from the Division of Research, Harvard Business School.

Italian corporations is almost nonexistent. Formal incentive compensation is not used in a high percentage of Italian firms, but its incidence is growing (De Martino and Marchettini, 1985; Galvani, 1990; Hay Group, 1990a). Surveys conducted by the Hay Group, the large international compensation consulting firm, show that the average variable pay for a broad sample of Italian managers has grown in the past five years from 12% to 15% of salary (Hay Group, 1990b); the average for top management is 25%.

Fiat was an appealing subject for studying how performance-based incentives are used in Italy. Fiat introduced its first formal management incentive system quite recently, in 1983, and so the study could trace the entire history of the company's experience with incentives. And Fiat is a prominent and complex organization: with 1989 revenues of 52 trillion lire,[1] it is the largest industrial group in Italy, excluding IRI, a state-owned group of companies.

The study was designed to describe Fiat's management-incentive systems and experiences and to generate ideas and hypotheses that might be used both in building a theory about the causes and consequences of management incentives in Italy and in motivating further research. The study is organized around three research questions:

1. Why did Fiat decide to implement a formal incentive system in 1983?

2. What factors influenced the implementation and refinement of the system?

3. What have been the effects of Fiat's formal incentive system?

The findings show that Fiat implemented a formal incentive system to replace a discretionary bonus system providing small cash awards to only a few senior managers; the new incentive system was integral to a major restructuring of the company's management systems; the present system is similar in design and effects to those in most U.S. firms, and it continues to evolve. Fiat managers' greatest present worry is that the company's incentives may be excessively short-term oriented.

Research Method

The study began with interviews with corporate personnel, planning, and finance managers. The interviewers gathered information on the firm's businesses, structure of the organization, and man-

Exhibit 3-1   Summary of Interviews

Role	Number of People Interviewed	Interview Hours
Top management	5	11
Corporate staff	4	16
Division managers	5	10
Other line managers	2	3
Operating group staff	3	8
Total	19	48

agement systems, including its formal performance-based compensation system. We collected as many internal documents as we could to corroborate the interview responses; we asked for specific data that would help us understand or document the incentive system's evolution and effects over its history; and we defined the characteristics of the line managers we hoped to meet for further interviews.

The line managers we interviewed filled roles at many levels and in diverse parts of the organization. The interviewees told us how the performance measures and incentives were designed in various parts of the organization, what the operating managers thought of the measurement and incentive system, and how it affected their behavior.

In sum, nineteen managers were interviewed for forty-eight hours. Exhibit 3-1 summarizes these interviews.

Background Information on the Fiat Group

Founded in 1899, the Fiat Group has grown to be the world's fifteenth largest corporation in revenues ("The World's [100] Biggest Industrial Corporations," 1989). Fiat operates in 52 countries and employs 286,000 people. In 1989, revenues were 52.0 trillion lire, and net income after taxes was 3.3 trillion lire. The company is publicly held, but the Agnelli family owns a controlling interest.

Although Fiat is an international company, it is particularly strong in Europe, where in 1988 almost 90% of its revenues were recorded (54% in Italy), 91% of its employees worked (78% in Italy), and 92% of its production plants were located. Fiat also has a significant presence in Latin America: 19,700 of its people (7%) work there.

Exhibit 3-2 presents a top-level organization chart of the Fiat Group. It is organized into sixteen operating sectors, which are composed of multiple profit centers called divisions or subsidiary companies. The sectors vary widely in size. The largest sector, automobiles, accounts for 55% of aggregate revenues. Although all are smaller than automobiles, the remaining sectors (among them commercial vehicles, tractors and construction machinery, aviation, telecommunications, publishing, and financial and real estate services) occupy important positions in their respective market segments, and some have leading positions worldwide.

The group's parent, Fiat S.p.A., is a holding company responsible for strategic management and control of sector activities. The parent company also provides administrative, fiscal, and legal support to the operating units. The Fiat Group operates with solid-line reporting throughout the financial organization; that is, financial personnel in the operating units have only a dotted-line reporting relationship with their line managers.

In the 1970s, Fiat suffered significant performance problems. Many factors contributed, including the oil embargoes and quadrupling of oil prices in 1973–1974, which created worldwide overcapacity in the automotive industry (especially in Europe); wildcat strikes and absenteeism; Red Brigade terrorism; and Italian inflation that soared above 20%. Fiat could not cope well with these factors because it had obsolete car models, productivity that lagged behind that of its competitors, and manufacturing facilities that badly needed modernizing. By 1980, Fiat bank debt totaled seven trillion lire, and the company's survival was at stake.

In the late 1970s and early 1980s, management began a corporate restructuring, which included:

1. Extensive cost reductions, including layoffs for about 15% of the workforce (an action unprecedented in the Italian postwar economy).

2. Creation of new operating companies in each sector and positioning of a substantially different middle-management team.

3. Strategic decisions to focus on core vehicle-production businesses and withdraw from some markets (most notably the United States and most of South America) to focus resources on European markets (Fiat's "natural backyard") and Brazil.

Exhibit 3-2 Fiat Group Organization Structure, June 1989

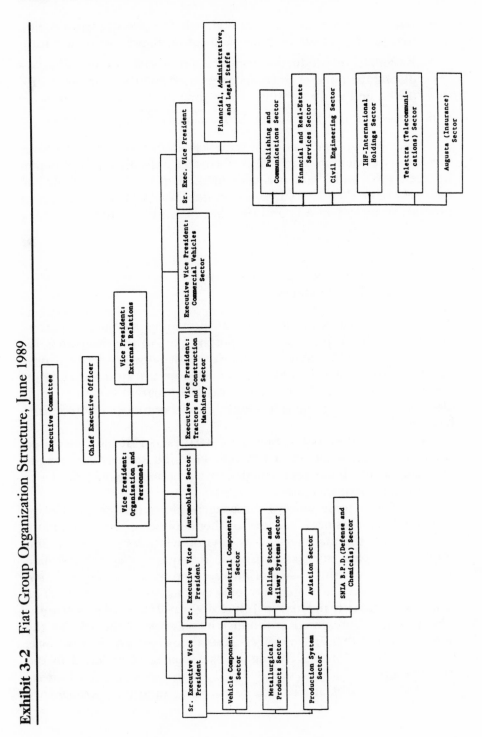

4. Large increases in share capital, which were used to develop new products and modernize and automate production facilities.

5. Rationalizing production facilities and procedures, including reducing the number of components used and the number of suppliers, and implementing just-in-time inventory procedures.

6. Implementing a formal performance-based incentive system.

Fiat's turnaround has been remarkable. In the 1980s, improvements were evident in nearly all performance indicators. For example, between 1981 and 1988, net sales more than doubled, net income increased more than 33-fold, excessive debt was paid off, absenteeism dropped from 16% to 6%, and time lost because of conflicts dropped from 4% to 1.5%.

Performance-Based Rewards for Fiat Managers

Fiat managers believe that providing significant performance-based incentives was an important part of the company's restructuring. Fiat offers managers three types of monetary performance-based rewards: salary increases, annual bonuses awarded through a formal management-by-objectives (MBO) program (for some middle- and top-ranking managers only), and occasional discretionary bonuses.

In the past few years, managers' salaries at Fiat have increased at an annual rate of between 10% and 13%. These increases include two components: increases mandated by the national managerial-labor contract and merit increases.

Italy has a trade union for managers (derived from the Fascist period in Italian history). A national labor contract specifies minimum conditions for the managers' work environment, compensation, and employee benefits (such as pensions). It requires that every Italian manager's salary be increased for inflation and seniority. The inflation adjustment covers managers for only a fraction of inflation.[2] The seniority increase mandated in July 1989 was 250,000 lire a month. This amount represented an annual increase of about 3% for the population of 3,880 Fiat managers, but the percentage increase was lower for the 521 relatively highly paid managers included in the MBO program.

Merit increases at Fiat are based on a subjective performance rating given by the manager's immediate superior. The ratings are made on a five-point scale, with a 3 representing minimum acceptable performance. The 1988 distribution of subjective ratings for Fiat managers was:

Performance Rating	Managers Receiving (%)
2	5%
3	40
4	45
5	10
	100%

These performance ratings are linked directly to specific merit salary increases. For one lower-level managerial job grade, the 1989 rating-to-merit-raise relation was:

Performance Rating	Merit Raise (% of base salary)
2	0%
3	5.8
4	7.5
5	8.6

But only 60% of Fiat managers received a merit increase for 1989. Those who did not were either already at or above the maximum salary specified for their job grade, among the 5% who received a 2 rating, or recently promoted.

The company's highest-ranking managers tend to receive higher ratings and higher merit raises than the managerial population as a whole. About 85% of the managers in the MBO program were given merit salary increases in 1989. Almost all in this select group had proven themselves over a number of years to be hardworking and effective.

The most significant performance-based incentive system used at Fiat is the MBO program. Designed for middle- and senior-level managers, MBO is the focus for the remainder of our discussion.

Fiat also provides one-time bonus awards to managers who deserve rewards not provided by any other mechanism (such as salary increase, MBO award). Only a few of these rewards are given each year. When such a special award is given, the amount is usually between one-half and one month's salary (4%–8% of annual salary).

Introduction of the Fiat MBO Program

Before the MBO program was implemented, Fiat gave some senior managers the opportunity to earn small bonuses—less than 10% of their base salary. These rewards were assigned by "personal bargaining"—a totally discretionary arrangement with no documentation attached.

The MBO program was one of the last elements in the major company restructuring program described above. Fiat introduced the program companywide in 1983 after experimenting with small samples of managers in the late 1970s and early 1980s. The program was intended to stimulate identification of management priorities (particularly financial ones) for the year, to direct managers' attention to those priorities, and to push everyone who remained with the company to move into a higher gear. Top Fiat managers felt that the old discretionary bonus plan could not create the desired changes.

The new program came as a shock because Fiat managers had little tradition of incentives and because salary increases for managers included in the MBO program were retarded. Salaries for these managers immediately fell 8% below where they would otherwise have been and below the salaries of managers and specialists at the same job grades who were not included in the program. (Inflation was then running at 17%–20% in Italy, and so it was not necessary to reduce nominal salary scales.)

Despite the shock, managers' resistance to the new program was minimal for several reasons. First, the top thirty-five managers in the company were closely involved in designing the program. Their involvement improved both the program's design and their acceptance of it. Second, Fiat had experimented with incentive programs before full implementation and had learned some valuable lessons, as about setting objectives. Third, some managers undoubtedly did not object to the new system because they were afraid of losing their jobs in this period of instability and downsizing. And finally, many managers realized that they were being given a chance to increase their compensation at a time when the company was not performing well; despite the slowing growth rate for base salaries, they soon learned that their bonuses more than compensated for the salary they lost. The incentives' value in the minds of Fiat managers was confirmed because the program was implemented at the beginning of a favorable economic period.

Characteristics of the MBO Program

Inclusion in the Program

All the "top managers" in Fiat are included in the MBO program except for eight managers at the most senior levels (CEO and executive vice presidents) who have individually tailored incentive schemes. These 521 highest-ranking managerial-level people (except for the top eight) include: 13 sector managers,[3] 161 other profit-center managers, and 347 other line and staff managers with significant responsibilities. Those in the MBO program are usually in organizational positions one or two hierarchic levels below sector manager. But in the large automobile sector, some managers four levels below sector manager are in the program.

The number of managers in the program has increased over the years; in 1983 only 314 were included. Expansion was caused both by corporate growth, generated internally and by acquisition of companies like Alfa Romeo, and by pressure from Fiat managers to be included in the program. Top managers expanded the program, of course, only because they judged it to be successful. They have no plan to push the program any lower in the management hierarchy, primarily because they are not convinced that any additional benefits generated would exceed the additional cost of incentive payments and program administration.

Bonus Potentials

The annual potential for cash bonus, as a percentage of base salary, is quite similar for all managers in the MBO program because the 521 managers are considered to be in one class: top managers. The highest-ranking 80 of the 521 managers are given the opportunity to earn annual cash bonuses of up to 32% of their salary for achieving predetermined goals.[4] The 441 lower-ranking managers in the program have the opportunity to earn a specific amount of lire, calculated as 30% of the midpoint salary of their job grade.[5]

The figures 30% and 32% for bonus potentials were chosen because they were higher than the bonuses allowed under the old program, and it was felt that managers should be given extra rewards because their risk had increased: they were being asked to generate substantially better results. The bonus potential has remained constant over the life of the program because corporate managers have judged that it has provided the desired motivation.

But one difference in payoff among the managers is significant. As a rule, 40% to 50% of the annual MBO award given to each of the thirteen sector managers in the program is added to the manager's base salary starting in the following year. These increases, which substitute for the sector managers' merit raises, accumulate without limit because Fiat has no salary maxima for sector managers. The value of this part of the reward can be huge because the salary increase provides an annuity that will be received until retirement, and it creates a higher base salary on which additional bonus awards can be earned in future years.

Performance Measures

The MBO awards are based on both financial and nonfinancial performance indicators. The criteria for evaluation and their weightings of importance are both tailored to a manager's specific situation.

1. Financial Measures

    At profit-center levels, the key financial measures are net profit before taxes (PBT) and net financial position (NFP). Profit is measured before taxes because top management judges that operating managers have little control over taxes. Managers at the corporate level set tax policies and approve all decisions affecting corporate taxes.

    The NFP is a measure of debt, defined as the sum of middle- and long-term financial debts, with both financial institutions and the Fiat Group. The measure was selected because by the early 1980s Fiat had built up dangerously high corporate debt (7 trillion lire) and because managers felt that Fiat's attention to asset and credit management was deficient. The company was cash rich in the 1960s and early 1970s, and the feeling grew that "the company's cost of capital was zero." The NFP measure has been retained even after Fiat's corporate debt has been sharply reduced because it is felt to reflect a key element in good management.

2. Nonfinancial Performance Indicators

Nonfinancial performance indicators of many types are used in the various Fiat operating entities. Such indicators include increasing sales in specific market segments; completing an acquisition, divestment, or reorganization; improving quality, asset management, or customer service; and introducing new products or processes.

Most nonfinancial performance indicators reflect areas of performance directly under the individual managers' control. But some cross-organizational indicators are used, particularly at functional organizational levels, to help overcome "selfishness." For example, managers who are part of a design-engineering-production team are sometimes given targets for customer service, production costs, or production defects.

3. Performance of Higher-Level Entities

All managers' MBO bonuses are also based partly on the PBT (and sometimes NFP) performance of entities higher than that for which they are responsible. First, the higher-level entity must achieve its threshold financial targets before anyone earns any bonuses. Then if these financial targets are met, a portion of each manager's bonus is based on the performance of the higher-level entity.

For sector managers, the relevant higher-level entity is the entire Fiat Group. If the Group fails to achieve its financial targets, these managers earn no bonuses regardless of how their individual sectors perform. Where bonuses are earned, 10%–25% of each sector manager's bonus is based on the performance of the Group.

For all other managers, the relevant higher-level entity is the sector. If the sector fails to achieve its PBT budget, these managers earn no bonus. When the sector does well, they earn 10%–20% of their bonuses based on sector (or sometimes division) performance.

4. Weightings of Importance of Individual Performance Measures

The weightings given the various individual performance measures vary significantly for the managers in the MBO program. For profit-center managers, financial performance measures are more important than nonfinancial measures. Before managers can earn any bonuses, profit-center PBT must equal or exceed a predefined minimum (threshold) level of perfor-

mance, regardless of the level of achievement in other performance areas (such as quality). Where bonuses are to be earned,
they are calculated with a weighting that has historically been
20%–40% PBT, 10%–20% NFP, and 10%–15% for each of
three or four other performance indicators, some financial (such
as inventory turnover) and some nonfinancial (such as quality).

For cost-center managers, cost is highly weighted. But because
cost is not a summary (bottom-line) measure of financial performance,
nonfinancial performance measures tend to be weighted more highly
in cost centers than they do in profit centers.

Performance Targets and Target-Setting

For most performance measures, three levels of target performance
are set as standards against which to judge actual performance. A
target level labeled 3 is set at a threshold level of performance that is
intended to require effort but is easy to reach.[6] A 4 reflects good
performance that requires further effort. A 5 reflects excellent performance at a level more challenging than the fourth level but still not
impossible.[7]

Exhibits 3-3 and 3-4 show representative samples of the combination of measures used as the basis for awarding MBO bonuses to a
profit-center manager and a cost-center manager, respectively. They
also show the weightings assigned to each specific performance indicator, the target levels for each indicator (defined in ranges of performance), and the calculation of the final weighted-average performance
rating based on the actual results.

The performance targets are set to equalize the managers' potentials for achieving targets. According to the corporate personnel department, all managers should have these probabilities of achieving
each target level:

Performance Level	Ideal Probability of Achievement
3 (threshold)	90%–99%
4 (good)	50%–60%
5 (excellent)	10%–20%

The three target levels are chosen during or immediately after
the annual budget is completed. Budgeting is a bottom-up process at

Exhibit 3-3   Sample MBO Targets and Evaluation of Results for a Representative Profit-Center Manager

Objectives	Weight	Budget	Target Scale			Result Achieved	Level	Score
			3 (Threshold)	4 (Good)	5 (Excellent)			
Sector performance								
Net profit before tax	0.10	109.5	105–120	120.1–130.0	>130	140	4.5	0.45
Net financial position		(29)	(30)–(10)	(9)–10	>10	(8)		
Profit center and individual performance								
Quantitative								
Net profit before tax	0.35	81.3	80–85	85.1–95	>95	80.6	3	1.05
Net financial position	0.15	29.5	28–35	36–40	>41	46.1	5	0.75
Nonquantitative								
Develop presence in Spain	0.20				X	no	0	0
Integrate functions with same sector functions	0.10				X	yes	5	0.50
Complete human-resource quality project	0.10				X	yes	5	0.50
Total	1.00							3.25

Exhibit 3-4 Sample of MBO Targets and Evaluation of Results for a Representative Cost-Center Manager

| Objectives | Weight | Budget | Target Scale | | | Result Achieved | Level | Score |
			3 (Threshold)	4 (Good)	5 (Excellent)			
Division net profit before tax	0.10	31.3	30–37	37–42	>42	44	5	0.50
Quality (scrap)	0.25	7%	8.3–8.0%	8.0–7.1%	<7.1%	7.9	4	1.00
Service (on-time deliveries)	0.25		70–75%	75–79%	>79%	74%	3	0.75
Projects (startup in Poland)	0.20			startup before December	startup before October	September	5	1.00
Install new production-control system	0.20		November	October	September	September	5	1.00
Total	1.00							4.25

Fiat. After receiving broad guidelines from corporate staff, operating managers prepare their budgets in the fall and present them at budget review meetings held in the last quarter of the year (October–December). Each entity has approved budget targets by January, and the formal MBO target letters defining the bonus contract are sent to the managers shortly after the audited figures for the preceding year's results are available, ideally in February.

With rare exceptions, the operating managers' budgeted core financial numbers (PBT and NFP) are accepted without revision and included within the threshold range of performance for MBO bonuses. At the sector level, budgeted PBT has been outside the threshold range only six times in the sixty-four sector-years in the period 1987–1990.

The few budget revisions that are made almost invariably lower profit targets to correct for optimism that a superior judges to be unwarranted or dangerous. A sector manager explained:

I revise budgets only when I judge the submission too ambitious. I have to be careful because I don't want to discourage [the managers] from setting high targets, but we've got to be realistic. In [one of his divisions], for example, we've got to restructure. It's hard to forecast this market, but in my opinion we'll never again reach earlier levels of performance. We need to be able to break even at very low activity levels. This will mean layoffs and factory closings. An optimistic budget would discourage us from taking the right actions; if we are too optimistic, we will do nothing. Consequently, I "invited" the manager to revise the budget.

Almost uniformly, the budgets and threshold targets are thus highly achievable. A corporate staff manager explained the rationale for this choice of design:

We are happy that it is highly probable that people included in the plan earn rewards. We don't want the managers to fail. Yes, people tend to be conservative in setting targets, and sometimes the budget is set at a level even lower than that at which we performed the prior year. But the [dominant] shareholder does not demand higher performance at that time. He believes that achievement of the budget results would be satisfactory [in the short term]. As it is, the system is stressed enough. We are coming from years of dramatic recovery, and we are convinced that the [MBO] system has helped. We feel no need for further stress.

The remainder of the MBO program target-setting (that is, the choice of the nonaccounting indicators to be used in assigning rewards, the weighting of importance to be placed on all indicators, and the performance ranges to be used in defining the other achievement levels of "good" and "excellent") is distinctly top-down. The manager's immediate superior bases these decisions on whichever factors are considered relevant. It was common knowledge within Fiat that superiors sometimes set higher 4 (good) and 5 (excellent) target levels when their subordinates submitted budget targets judged clearly to be undemanding.

The superiors do not always implement the ideal intended by the corporation. One sector manager felt that ideal probabilities for achieving the 3 (threshold), 4 (good), and 5 (excellent) levels of performance should be 95%, 75%, and 30%, respectively. His philosophy was that "Performance at a 3 level is a failure. A 4 level is fair."

Superiors are expected to discuss their choices and rationales with their subordinates, but they sometimes do not do so. One sector manager said:

Sometimes the target they send me as a 5 level of performance seems to have no foundation. They can't tell me how they came up with it, and they can't tell me how to improve my result to that level. It is very disturbing sometimes.

Award Schedules

The basic cash-award schedules are illustrated in Exhibit 3-5. The top line in the figure is for the 80 top managers; the bottom line is for the other 441 managers in the program. These schedules show that cash bonuses are awarded to all managers whose overall performance rating is 3 (threshold) or above. Performances falling below the 3 (threshold) level of performance are rated unacceptable: managers performing at that level earn no bonuses.[8] Those rated at the 3 (threshold) level are assigned a bonus of 12% of salary; those rated 4 (good) are given 18% or 20%; those rated 5 (excellent) are given 30% or 32%. The award curve is purposely kinked "to encourage people to strive for excellence." No extra bonus is promised for performance above the excellent level. This cutoff is set to prevent people from "running wild"—working for their own short-term benefit at the expense of the corporation's long-term good.

Rarely, when a *sector* performs significantly above the 5 (excellent) level, bonus awards to everybody in that sector can be increased. This extra award has been made to personnel in one sector each in 1985, 1987, and 1988. Each time, the sector performed 25% or more

Exhibit 3-5 Fiat MBO Program Award Schedule (cash award as a function of performance rating)

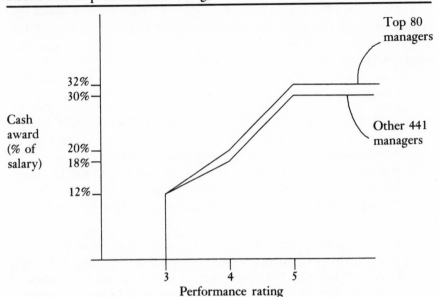

above the excellent level, and individual bonus awards were increased by 20%. But these parameters (the amount by which performance exceeds the excellent level and the amount of bonus increase) are not fixed program elements to which top management must adhere.

The Fiat management system also allows for recognition of *individuals* who perform outstandingly. They do so with promotions and the merit raises and one-time bonus awards described above.

Flexibility in Evaluating Performance

The MBO program is intended to be rigidly implemented. Fiat managers think that one year is a short enough period for managers to make reliable forecasts. They wish to hold managers accountable for their forecasts so that they will be motivated to anticipate events and try to work assumptions and estimates about uncertainties into their forecasts.

But evaluators are given some flexibility to help the system maintain its credibility. They are allowed to propose adjustments in exceptional cases where the planning assumptions proved grossly incorrect.

All proposed adjustments must be reviewed by a corporate personnel officer and the responsible central director. The adjustments are easier to justify to these reviewers if the risks and assumptions about the factors creating the need for the adjustment (such as interest rates, strike potential, exchange rates, timing of sale of assets) are specified when the budgets and targets are set.

Only a few adjustments are allowed each year. Here are two recent adjustments that were approved:

1. In 1989, the manager responsible for marketing Alfa Romeo cars in Italy was to be judged mainly on market share and the total volume of cars sold. But the Italian market grew so rapidly the factory could not keep up with demand, and market share fell while sales volume was increasing sharply. The division manager decided to rate the marketing manager just on the increase in total volume.

2. In 1988, the budget was not considered a good standard for judging the performance of the manager of Fiat Brazil. During that year the gap between internal inflation and the exchange rate rose sharply. This gap caused a significant loss in competitiveness for Fiat Brazil, which exports about 60% of its production with prices fixed in dollars. Superiors decided to evaluate this manager's 1988 performance subjectively because they judged this change unforeseeable.

Immediate superiors have some limited opportunities to use discretion in evaluations while avoiding the review procedures. They can exercise discretion at the margin, for if a subordinate's performance is just below the range needed to earn a rating, they may grant the higher rating. But they usually do so only if something happens to cause a manager's rating to fall below 3, not when the manager is already in the 3-to-5 range. And they can compensate for the negative effects of unforeseen uncontrollables by setting easier performance targets for the subsequent year, although these targets are also reviewed by top management.

The adjustments are intended to be in either the manager's or the company's favor, as circumstances dictate. But when they are in the company's favor, managers commonly become upset, as in this comment from a sector manager:

In 1988, I had a very good result, but [my superior] considered most of it uncontrollable. He adjusted my performance downward, and I was

Exhibit 3-6 Distributions of Fiat Managers' MBO Performance Ratings, 1983–1989

Performance Rating	1983	1984	1985	1986	1987	1988	1989
Less than 3.0	20%	6%	4%	13%	13%	10%	7%
3.0–3.3	9	7	5	3	6	5	10
3.4–3.7	10	5	7	5	9	10	11
3.8–4.2	23	34	27	22	19	25	21
4.3–4.8	26	38	39	37	37	44	45
4.9–5.0	12	10	18	20	16	6	6
	100%	100%	100%	100%	100%	100%	100%

very angry. It is hard to determine in any business year what is ordinary and what is extraordinary. Is a drop in the market extraordinary? If we lose an order, is that extraordinary? The discussion is endless.

Actual Results

Exhibit 3-6 presents the distributions of the managers' MBO performance ratings since 1983. Wide dispersion appears in the average ratings across the managerial population. Fiat corporate managers are pleased with this dispersion because it shows that discriminations about performance are being made. A small but noticeable proportion of the managers (10% in 1988) did not qualify for MBO bonuses, and even fewer performed at (or above) the highest target level.

Corporate system designers are uneasy because average performance ratings are becoming too high. In recent years the corporate rating average has ranged between 4.2 and 4.5, and in some sectors has been even higher. In the automobile sector performance has averaged 4.7 over the last several years. These levels are somewhat higher than the corporate ideal described above. Corporate managers recognize that the company has been performing well, but they want to make sure that the system is not becoming too generous because the objectives are too easy to achieve.

The Exhibit 3-6 distribution is also slightly broader than the ideal intended. It shows that the proportion of managers who rated below 3 averaged 11% over the six years, which is slightly higher

Exhibit 3-7 Performance Ratings for Sector Managers Remaining in Their Positions for the Period 1987–1989

Manager	MBO Performance Rating		
	1987	1988	1989
1	4.9	4.9	4.8
2	2.5	4.1	3.4
3	4.6	4.9	4.9
4	4.8	3.8	3.4
5	4.2	4.2	4.8
6	4.8	4.5	4.2
7	4.6	4.3	4.4
8	4.0	4.5	4.6
9	4.0	4.2	4.7
10	4.7	4.4	4.4
11	4.2	4.2	4.3
12	3.5	4.4	3.6

than the 1%–10% defined as ideal. It also shows that the proportion of managers scoring 4 or above was 76%, compared to the 50%–60% defined as ideal.

Exhibit 3-7 shows the distribution of performance ratings over the period 1987–1989 for the twelve sector managers who remained in their position for those three years. The exhibit shows that ratings for some managers vary considerably over the years. This variance, in a sustained period of favorable economic conditions, is evidence that the MBO awards are variable compensation; they are not just a component of fixed compensation.

Effects of the MBO Program

The effects of the MBO program are impossible to separate from those of the other elements in the restructuring begun in the late 1970s, but it is clear that the whole restructuring program has been a great success. Exhibit 3-8 shows key performance data for the Fiat Group since 1981, the first year in which reliable consolidated

Exhibit 3-8　Financial Data for the Fiat Group for Pre-MBO Years 1981–1982 and Post-MBO Years 1983–1989 (monetary amounts in billions of lire)

	1981	1982	1983	1984	1985	1986	1987	1988	1989
Net sales	20,312	20,619	21,985	23,813	27,101	29,337	38,435	44,308	52,019
Net income	90	137	253	627	1,326	2,162	2,373	3,026	3,306
Corporate net financial position[a]	(7,035)	(6,169)	(5,401)	(4,043)	(2,364)	(706)	180	2,349	2,121
Cash flow	966	1,142	1,471	2,142	2,966	3,946	4,674	5,559	6,429
Capital expenditures	818	1,316	1,453	1,486	1,433	2,879	3,437	3,394	3,423
Research and development expenditures	410	500	556	669	820	955	1,361	1,590	1,824
Employment (000)	302	264	244	231	226	230	271	277	286
Fiat common-stock index[b]	281.9	289.7	579.3	870.4	2,408.9	6,037.5	3,559.8	4,084.7	4,838.6
Italian stock-market index[b]	293.5	252.1	283.9	341.7	678.3	1,112.2	756.0	888.6	1,032.4
Consumer price index[c]	261.5	304.3	349.7	386.8	420.1	445.9	466.3	489.5	521.6

[a]Financial assets less financial liabilities.
[b]January 2, 1975 = 100.
[c]1975 = 100.

data became publicly available. All indicators show that performance has improved markedly over this period.

Fiat managers think the MBO program contributed significantly to this success. They think the program is an improvement over the previous incentive system, with its small, totally discretionary bonuses, primarily because it has forced managers at many levels in the organization to have direct discussions about objectives and accomplishments. In so doing it has helped managers at all levels to decide on their highest priorities and to focus on them.

Fiat managers have seen little downside to the MBO program. They worry most that the program may be generating incentives that are excessively shortsighted, but they have no firm evidence that poor decisions have been made. (This question is discussed further below.)

Corporate managers acknowledge the potential for operating managers to engage in games designed to increase their bonuses at the expense of the corporation's good, but they have seen little evidence of such games. They attribute the absence of gamesmanship to:

1. The control provided by solid-line reporting throughout the financial organization.

2. The sense of responsibility that the managers, who are mostly longtime Fiat employees, have to the corporation. One manager said, "It's not part of the Fiat culture to play tricks with the numbers. We have a loyalty to the company."

3. The sustained period of good performance, which has decreased managers' incentives to boost performance. The only significant examples of games that we found involved "taking a bath"—loading expenses into a down period. But the manager of the sector that included the divisions where the baths occurred was unconcerned. He said, "I'm not averse to [baths]. When we have had several bad years, it's good to have a clean-up."

Continuing Evolution of the MBO Program

Although the core of the MBO program has stayed intact for its eight years, a few refinements have been made. Decisions were made about:

1. How many managers to include in the program. The number has grown to 521, as discussed earlier.

2. How precisely to measure the intermediate points on the 3–5 performance scale. The decision was to measure each area of performance in increments of 0.1.

3. How to weight financial measures of performance. When the MBO program was started, this weighting was 60% for sector managers and their first level of reports. This weight was later reduced to 50% (as shown in Exhibit 3-3), and it is now being reduced to 40%.

4. How to measure NFP. Until recently, only *year-end* NFP had been measured. Late in the 1980s, Fiat began using a monthly average NFP, as well as year-end NFP, in some entities to reduce managers' temptations to engage in end-of-year window dressing. Year-end NFP was not dropped entirely because the year-end balance sheet figures are included in the annual reports and thus have more external visibility; end-of-month NFP cannot be measured in all entities; and managers, accustomed to using year-end figures, have resisted the change.

Planned Changes

Some of the most significant changes in the MBO program since its initial implementation were planned for 1990 and 1991. These include attempts to make the program more long-term oriented, more focused, more objective, and more timely.

1. More long-term orientation

Fiat managers' most significant worry about the MBO program is that it does not strike an appropriate balance between short- and long-run interests. Corporate managers know that some MBO objectives can be achieved in ways that do not serve the company's long-term objectives, and though they have no clear proof that any managers have acted inappropriately, they are uneasy, as a manager in corporate personnel said:

We have relied on the managers' sense of responsibility. Virtually all of our managers are here to stay; they have long tenure within Fiat. This lifetime employment, which is almost a reality, has substantially protected the system. However, this is not enough.

But corporate managers do not want to eliminate the attention to the short run that the MBO program has successfully brought about. An officer in the corporate control department stated, "I don't feel that managers are excessive in their orientation to the short run, but I do feel that they don't put enough emphasis on the long run." In other words, the feeling is that the short-run–long-run balance is not quite right.

To shift the incentive balance more toward the long run, corporate managers plan to make two changes in the MBO program. First, they will emphasize nonfinancial targets more. If they have not done so already, most managers will be asked to identify specific long-term development programs, and interim indicators of progress toward completing these programs will be included among the MBO objectives. Managers will also be asked to relate some nonfinancial targets directly to the company's total quality plan, a major corporate initiative begun in 1989.

Second, they may give some higher-level managers, probably sector managers and the managers reporting directly to them, long-term (multiyear) incentives either as part of the MBO program or in a separate program. Experiments with three-year objectives were to be conducted in 1990 within the organizations of three executive vice presidents. These long-term rewards will be earned only when the three years are over, but annual partial payments will be based on interim indications of progress toward the long-term goal.

Third, they may soon introduce a stock option plan for a few high-level managers (including sector managers). Fiat has not had an option plan until now because corporate managers judged the administrative costs to be greater than the benefits. They felt that the benefits are limited, primarily because corporate performance is substantially uncontrollable by any one manager and because most Italian managers do not believe that stock prices reflect true underlying economic values. But corporate managers are reconsidering an option plan because they recognize that options provide another link between top managers' rewards and company results, and stock awards can often provide higher remuneration than cash awards.

2. Fewer objectives

Corporate managers worry that some entities set too many objectives (some as many as twenty), and that the lists may become even longer if managers add long-term measures to those with which they have become comfortable. They believe each manager should be asked to set only three to five objectives

Exhibit 3-9 Proportions of Objectives That Were
Nonquantitative for 11 Sectors, 1988–1989

Sector	1988	1989
Automobiles	27%	25%
Commercial vehicles	48	39
Metallurgical products	39	39
Vehicle components	38	31
Industrial components	35	15
Production systems	37	30
Civil engineering	37	33
Rolling stock and railway systems	44	50
Aviation	39	31
Telettra (telecommunications)	59	50
SNIA B.P.D. (defense and chemicals)	22	12

so that weightings are significant enough to keep managers focused on each item. Thus for 1990, corporate managers were to have instructed each manager to identify no more than six or seven performance indicators in three categories: economic results (such as PBT and NFP), problem-solving and development (one or two key strategic objectives), and total quality.

3. Increased use of quantitative measures

Corporate managers are also trying to increase the proportion of quantitative measures used for judging success so that the criteria for evaluation are more "transparent" and less judgment is required. Beginning in 1989, they instructed their managers to be as specific as they could and to use quantitative performance indicators wherever possible. The effect of these instructions has been mixed, as demonstrated in the averages for eleven sectors in Exhibit 3-9. Corporate managers believe that further improvements are necessary, and they plan to reemphasize this instruction for implementation.

4. Timing of objective setting

Corporate managers are trying to ensure that all managers receive their objectives early in the year, at least by February.

Presently, objectives are not given to managers until the prior-year payments are made because "It's a risk to think about the future without the evaluation of the past." And the prior-year payments are not made until the auditors approve the preceding year's financial statements because "Before sharing the pie, we must be sure we have produced the pie." Sometimes the audit or the superior–subordinate communication or both were delayed and managers did not receive their targets until March or April. It is recognized that these situations should be avoided.

An even greater delay occurred in the automobiles sector in 1989 because a late-1988 reorganization forced reanalysis of the performance possibilities. The letters detailing performance targets were not sent to managers in this sector until June. The only way to avoid this type of situation is to time the reorganization properly. But because the reorganizations are usually more important than the delay in communicating objectives, some delays of this type are inevitable.

Other Concerns

Other worries about the MBO program were voiced by one or more of the managers to whom we spoke. Although corporate managers have no firm plans to make changes addressing any of these problems, they are aware of these issues and side effects.

1. Shared versus individual objectives

   One worry is about the proper amount of individual, rather than shared, objectives, particularly at cost-center levels in the organization where interdependence is significant. Fiat managers recognize that shared objectives create a team focus, but they also recognize that with too much sharing of targets, individual initiative is lost. One manager said, "[With shared objectives] there are always individuals who pull and others who are pulled."

   Shared objectives seem not to have created major problems yet, but some Fiat managers fear they may do so during the next business downturn. Right now the whole team has been winning. But during a downturn managers will rightly tend to introduce greater discrimination to reward those who performed well during a period of scarce resources, leaving out the rest. The sense of teamwork may break down.

2. Rigidity or flexibility

Some managers feared that one year was too long to have fixed objectives. They pointed out that targets set at the beginning of the year that are not revised during the year can be demotivating if planning assumptions turn out to be inaccurate. Inflexible objectives can be demotivating if seen as either impossible to accomplish or excessively easy, depending on the direction of the forecasting error. Perhaps even worse, rigid objectives can push a manager into making incorrect decisions in an attempt to achieve the current-period targets or to position the entity for the succeeding measurement period.

3. Consistency in objectives

Some managers worried about the lack of consistency in nonfinancial objectives. One said, "Fashions come and go too quickly."

4. Administrative cost

And several managers mentioned the system's administrative cost. The large amount of paperwork, particularly in detailing the objectives, sometimes causes the administrative details, and even the program's substance, to be delegated to the office of the operating managers' controllers. When managers believe that objectives come from their superior's controller, rather than their superior, they tend not to take them as seriously.

Discussion

Fiat's experience with its performance measurement and incentive system suggests several tentative theoretical propositions and some questions worthy of further exploration.

Tentative Theoretical Propositions

1. "Cultural" differences between the United States and Italy may not greatly affect the incentive practices used in firms in the two countries.

The many factors that comprise Italian "culture" seem to have had little effect on Fiat's systems for measurement and incentive. The one major difference between Fiat's history of using management incentives and that of most U.S. firms is the relatively recent implementation of Fiat's MBO program. This finding supports what Catturi (1989) and Riccaboni (1989) have noted about the introduction of management control tools in Italian firms.

But in design, the Fiat MBO program is similar to the short-term incentive plans of most U.S. firms in many of these important ways (from surveys by Vancil, 1978; Abdallah, 1984; and Merchant, 1989):

- Performance evaluations are heavily based on financial (ac-counting) measures of performance, but some nonfinancial performance measures are also considered.
- Preset budget targets are a vital standard for evaluating performance.
  a. The budget targets are set so that they are highly likely to be achieved.
  b. Managers who fail to achieve their budget targets suffer severe penalties, including loss of bonuses and possibly loss of job.
- The range of performance that is linked with rewards is bounded at bottom and top.
- Some adjustments are made for factors that managers can-not completely control.
  a. The adjustments are made subjectively.
  b. They are controlled tightly and made sparingly.
- Tangible rewards are paid mostly (or exclusively) in cash.

The great similarities between the Fiat MBO program and the performance measurement and incentive systems in most U.S. firms suggest that the factors that comprise both national (Ital-ian) and corporate (Fiat) "culture" seem to have influenced the Fiat program's design very little.

Fiat managers even have most of the same concerns as do managers in U.S. firms: the MBO incentives are excessively short-term oriented. This fear persists at Fiat despite a domi-nant shareholder group not greatly disturbed by short-run movements in the stock market. But the uneasiness seems inher-ent in companies whose managers are asked to make develop-mental expenditures and in which incentive plans base rewards on annual (or more frequent) accounting measures of perfor-mance (or, even worse, cash flows). To strike a better balance between short and long term, Fiat managers are considering the same alternatives that U.S. firms use, including leading indicators of forthcoming profits and cash flows, multiyear objectives for middle- and upper-level managers, and stock options for the most senior managers.

2. Incentive systems should be implemented when prospects are bright.

The Fiat experience strongly suggests avoiding or perhaps even changing, incentive systems if a downturn is expected. Because Fiat started its MBO program as a sustained period of good performance began, managers readily accepted it. Dott. Ruggero Ferrero, an executive vice president, turned this part of the Fiat experience into a management principle: "Never implement such a plan [when you're headed into] a crisis situation." Implementing and administering the program were also easier because few major changes such as reorganizations came up in the 1980s. In getting a new incentive program under way, timing seems not to be emphasized in the literature on strategies for implementing change (e.g., Kotter and Schlesinger, 1979; Huse, 1980; Argyris, 1985).

3. Providing proper incentives is a necessity in a corporate restructuring, but some other features characteristic of LBO or MBO restructurings may matter less.

The Fiat experience demonstrates how much weight an incentive system carries in a corporate restructuring. Unquestionably, Fiat's success up to the 1960s had caused it to lose focus and generate fat. When Fiat corporate managers realized what had happened, they started the restructuring with a high, even knowingly exaggerated, emphasis on short-term financial measures to direct the operating managers' attention. Short-term performance was necessary for survival. Fiat's restructuring program immediately generated improvements, and improvement continued all through the 1980s. Fiat corporate managers agree that the MBO program was critical in redirecting operating managers' attention.

Improved incentives greatly helped Fiat's restructuring, but most other features that Baker and Wruck (1990) describe as important in a leveraged or management buyout (LBO or MBO) restructuring were not. Fiat was not monitored and advised by a private LBO firm; its operating managers did not own significant amounts of its stock; it did not have a heavy debt load with restrictive debt covenants (at least for the first several years after the restructuring program was begun); and it did not make the middle-management team wealthy.

4. Limiting managers' potential for bonuses may indeed be worthwhile.

The Fiat example clarifies perhaps the outstanding reason for limiting managers' bonus potentials, which most firms do (Merchant, 1989) despite economists' calls for greater potential for incentive (e.g., Jensen, 1989; Baker and Wruck, 1990). Those who designed Fiat's incentive system report that the MBO program has already attracted the managers' attention, and they worry that foreseeing greater rewards, managers might be tempted to maximize their current-period bonus in destructive ways—by making short-term decisions or by managing earnings—even though most senior- and middle-level Fiat managers are long-term employees with strong loyalty to the company.

Managers' utility functions may therefore consist of two main impulses: a selfishness component that induces managers to act in their own self-interest, and a "conscience" that induces managers to do what is right—to act in the company's best interest—even at some cost to themselves.[9]

Management-incentive systems appeal to selfishness. They are most effective when performance is measured and feedback and rewards are provided quickly (see Merchant, 1989, Chapter 3; Locke and Latham, 1990, Chapter 8). If a company's short-term measures perfectly reflect individuals' contributions to its performance, its incentive systems can reinforce the motivation generated by conscience. But because perfect measures of performance are not available at managerial levels, the company must use imperfect measurement surrogates for changes in shareholder value such as accounting earnings. If the rewards based on these measures are substantial, selfishness may dominate conscience, and the corporation will feel the full brunt of weaknesses in measurement. These failings can be alleviated but not eliminated by using better performance measures (such as leading indicators of performance rather than just accounting earnings).

5. Worrying about the longer perspective is a sign of a maturing incentive system in a growing business.

The eight-year Fiat experience probably suggests conditions that many recently restructured firms (such as LBO and MBO firms) may look forward to in the next decade. Those that wish to grow, or even maintain their market position, will find that their incentives are excessively short-term oriented. In a business that has not been run efficiently, improvements in short-term efficiency and asset management are not a great challenge because effective management incentives are easy to implement. Good performance measures provide timely feedback and rewards. But corporations ambitious for something other than stability and decline must give their managers incentives for both short- and long-term performance, and they must balance these incentives appropriately. This balancing requires a far more complex incentive package.

Questions for Further Study

The Fiat experience also suggests some questions worthy of further study.

1. Where does it make sense to use performance-based incentives and where not?

   Fiat has no plans to expand its MBO program beyond the 521 managers already included because it believes the cost of doing so would be greater than the benefit. The direct incentive costs are reasonably easy to estimate. But what affects the costs of administration? And what affects the benefits? The key factors may be the effectiveness with which individual performance can be measured and the accuracy with which performance targets can be set.

2. Do some conditions create natural biases in setting objectives?

   Fiat managers are concerned that MBO performance ratings may be higher than the ideal. This tendency to be lenient in setting objectives may be caused by a natural conservatism in forecasting bias during a sustained period of favorable economic conditions and success. The opposite may occur during bad times. The question to explore is: Do changes in aspirations lag behind changes in economic possibilities?

   A natural bias toward easier targets may also affect non-quantitative objectives. Fiat managers achieved most of their nonquantified targets and thus were generally rated at 5 (excellent) in these areas. Is this a natural tendency in setting objectives? Do superiors use nonquantitative measures to exhibit "compassion" toward their subordinates?

3. What conditions make shared objectives useful motivators?

Shared objectives are assigned to create a spirit of cooperation, teamwork, and social (peer) control. But the benefit has its costs. Most notably, individuals' rewards reflect the quality of their individual behaviors imperfectly. When rewards are based on the performance of a large group (as in corporate profit-sharing), individual behaviors and rewards are almost entirely disconnected. Are shared rewards more likely to be effective in a small group? And are they more likely to be effective during good economic times than in down periods?

Conclusions

In this chapter we describe the findings of a field study that provides the first detailed, publicly available look at the performance measurement and incentive system used in an Italian corporation, the Fiat Group. The study shows that the Fiat incentive system is remarkably similar to those used in most divisionalized U.S. corporations. This finding suggests that the issues related to motivating Italian managers do not differ greatly from those involved in motivating U.S. managers. Because culture seems not to greatly affect the relationships studied here, we think this study suggests general theoretical propositions about designing and implementing measurement and incentive systems.

We suggest four general theoretical propositions in addition to the cultural issue.

1. Incentive systems should be implemented when corporate prospects are bright.

2. Providing proper incentives is vital to corporate restructuring, but restructuring can succeed without monitoring by a private LBO firm, without a heavy debt load, including restrictive debt covenants, and without providing lucrative rewards.

3. Limiting managers' potential for bonuses may be worthwhile.

4. A desire to create longer-term incentives is a sign of a maturing incentive system in a growing business.

We also suggest several questions that seem worthy of further study.

These results must be considered tentative, of course, because this study had significant limitations. In particular, we studied only one firm. And the whole period during which Fiat has used its MBO program has been one of sustained success. Some findings might have differed had the corporation passed through a recession.

This study does, however, provide the first solid evidence that we can use to build a theory of how incentives work in Italian firms. And if Italian cultural differences prove not to significantly influence management incentives and their effect on individuals, as the findings of this study suggest, then these data and findings will be useful in constructing theories with broader applicability.

NOTES

1. About U.S. $42 billion. One lire equals about .0008 U.S. dollar.

2. The inflation adjustment is set at a fixed amount, calculated with a formula designed to protect blue-collar workers from inflation. But the adjustment, defined as a fixed monetary amount, provides managers with incomplete protection because their salaries are higher.

3. Three of the sixteen sector managers have the rank of executive vice president and are thus excluded from the MBO program.

4. The thirteen sector managers (in this group of eighty) can also earn up to an extra 6% of salary based on the financial performance of the entire Fiat Group. This award is not an individual incentive because its size is not measurably affected by any one manager's efforts.

5. Defining the managers' bonus potentials in fixed-lire terms rather than as a percentage of salary is believed to facilitate communication of the program. But this definition is used only at the lower job grades, which include more than a few managers.

6. When the plan was first implemented, a rating of 1 was defined as "unacceptable," and a rating of 2 was defined as "poor." More recently, references to the 1 and 2 ratings were dropped. Any performance below 3 is referred to as "below threshold."

7. Sometimes not all three target levels are identified for all nonquantitative targets. For example, successful achievement of a task (such as implementing a new information system) may simply be rated at the 5 level.

8. Even more significant, managers whose performance is rated below the threshold two years in a row are fired, almost without exception. This was the fate of four managers (0.8%) in 1988 and six managers (1.1%) in 1989.

9. The strength of the conscience component of utility undoubtedly varies greatly among individuals. The company can probably do little to increase it in any individual except by trying to appeal to the manager's spirit of loyalty by building a strong corporate culture and, perhaps, by training in ethics designed to encourage managers to recognize their obligations to others.

REFERENCES

Abdallah, Wagdy M. *Internal Accountability: An International Emphasis*. Ann Arbor, MI: UMI Research Press, 1984.

Argyris, Chris. *Strategy, Change and Defensive Routines.* Boston: Pitman, 1985.

Baker, George P., and Karen H. Wruck. "Organizational Changes and Value Creation in Leveraged Buyouts: The Case of the O. M. Scott & Sons Company." *Journal of Financial Economics,* vol. 25 (1989), pp. 163–190. Reproduced with permission as Chapter 5 of this volume.

Catturi, Giuseppe. *Teorie Contabili e Scenari Economico-Aziendale [Accounting Theories and Business and Accounting Scenarios].* Padova: Cedam, 1989.

De Martino, Edoardo, and Piero Marchettini. "Executive Total Compensation in Italy—Current Situation and Future Trends." *Benefits and Compensation International,* vol. 15 (October 1985), pp. 2–7.

"Europe's New Managers: Going Global with a U.S. Style." *Business Week* (May 24, 1982), pp. 116–122.

Galvani, Raffaella. "Uno Stipendio Piu Bonus" ["Better Compensation"]. *Espansione* (March 1990), pp. 29–31.

Hay Group. *Evoluzione del Mercato Retributivo e Tendenze per Il Prossimo Triennio [Evolution of the Pay Market and Trends for the Next Three Years].* Milan: Hay Group, 1990a.

———. *Annual Pay Survey.* Milan: Hay Group, 1990b.

Huse, Edgar F. *Organizational Development and Change,* 2d ed. St. Paul, MN: West Publishing, 1980.

Jensen, Michael C. "Eclipse of the Public Corporation." *Harvard Business Review* (September–October 1989), pp. 61–74.

Kotter, John P., and Leonard A. Schlesinger. "Choosing Strategies for Change." *Harvard Business Review* (March–April 1979), pp. 106–114.

Locke, Edwin A., and Gary P. Latham. *A Theory of Goal Setting and Task Performance.* Englewood Cliffs, NJ: Prentice-Hall, 1990.

Merchant, Kenneth A. *Rewarding Results: Motivating Profit Center Managers.* Boston: Harvard Business School Press, 1989.

Mosley, Robert. "Main Trends and Developments: The Facts." *Making Europe Work.* London: Hay Group, 1989, pp. 3.1–3.12.

Riccaboni, Angelo. *La Misurazione Della Performance dei Centri di Profitto: Critica agli Strumenti Tradizionali e Nuovi Orientamenti di Indagine [The Measurement of Profit Center Performance: Analysis of Traditional Tools and New Research Trends].* Padova: Cedam, 1989.

Towers Perrin. *1989 Executive Pay Update: Worldwide Total Remuneration.* New York: Towers Perrin, 1989.

Vancil, Richard F. *Decentralization: Managerial Ambiguity by Design.* Homewood, IL: Dow Jones-Irwin, 1978.

"The World's [100] Biggest Industrial Corporations." *Fortune* (July 31, 1989), pp. 280–283.

CHAPTER 4

United Bank: A Case Study
on the Implementation of a
Performance-Related Reward Scheme

David Otley

Introduction

SYSTEMS of performance-related reward (PRR) for middle managers were the exception in the United Kingdom before 1985. Although payment for performance was common at both top and bottom of the organizational hierarchy, it was not used at all extensively in the middle. Senior managers at board level might well receive profit-related bonuses or participate in share option schemes;[1] production workers might receive bonuses for meeting production targets or be paid on a piecework basis. Salespeople too were often, but not always, rewarded by including a commission element in their remuneration. Junior and middle managers, however, would almost invariably receive a fixed salary; they would receive neither performance-related nor overtime payments.

Good performance was, of course, rewarded. By far the most important reward for managers was, and still is, the possibility of promotion. Promotion brings an increase in fixed salary which is often substantial and which once achieved is rarely taken away. But promotion is a poor method for rewarding excellent performance in a manager's present job, for it usually requires moving to a different job. Then too, although promotion-based rewards may encourage a

97

long-term emphasis, they do not readily permit stressing short-term targets.

Since 1985, a major trend in the United Kingdom has introduced payment schemes that give monetary rewards for achieving specific performance targets. By 1989, some 40% of U.K. middle managers were receiving some monetary payment for reaching performance targets. Introducing such schemes into a culture in which they were previously almost unknown provides an interesting and important research topic.

Banking is something of an extreme example, for performance-based rewards are alien to an environment that stresses loyalty and lasting relationships. In England and Wales (Scotland having a different legal system), banks operate nationally, and a few large banks dominate the market. Each major bank usually had a branch in every town of significant size, and a network of smaller branches in suburbs and rural areas. The bank's internal culture was very traditional, its tall managerial hierarchy consisting of many finely differentiated grades. Until the 1980s, business was conducted in a gentlemanly manner, restricting competition between major banks to the range and quality of services provided. Most customers would remain with the same bank for life, and most bank employees also remained with the same employer for their entire career. Movement of managerial staff between the major banks was, and still is, almost unheard of.

Since 1980, however, major changes have come, particularly in competition. Building societies have always been a major home for personal savings in the United Kingdom, offering competitive rates of interest for an essentially risk-free investment.[2] These societies were also the major providers of mortgage funds for purchasing homes, and had extensive branch networks. During the 1980s, banks began to compete with building societies in offering mortgage financing, initially to their own customers. Building societies retaliated by offering banking facilities, primarily attracting the considerable proportion of their investors who previously had not had a bank account. More recently they have provided credit cards, cash cards, and foreign-exchange facilities, broadening the range of competition, for example extending opening hours.[3] By 1990, the difference between a bank branch and a building society branch had become much less obvious to the individual customer. The whole transformation was fueled by the rising proportion of the population who owned rather than rented a home, the increased market penetration of personal banking, and the increased provision of credit in an expanding economy.

The clearing banks thus faced severe and increasing competition during the 1980s. Customer service became a more important factor in their operations. Whereas a restricted range of personal banking services had been provided to a select class of customers, a much wider range of services (such as mortgages, loan and credit facilities, foreign exchange, cash machines, insurance, share-dealing, and investment facilities) were now offered to customers who had no tradition of loyalty to one institution. This major shock to the system required all the banks to take steps to effect a change in organizational culture within their institutions. No longer were branch bank managers passive administrators who sought to avoid making mistakes; they were to become the front-line troops in a major competitive offensive.

Perhaps this assessment somewhat overstates the reality, but it does so just marginally. Nothing less than a major change in attitudes and a radical redefinition of the branch bank manager's role was required to meet the new marketplace. One mechanism chosen by some major banks to communicate the new job requirements to their managers was the performance-related pay system, whereby achieving preset performance targets brought monetary rewards.

Theoretical Perspectives

The introduction of performance-related reward systems can be seen as an extension of previous systems of budgetary and management control. It has been argued (Otley, 1987) that every management-control system is continually devising new answers to the same three basic questions, namely:

1. What are the dimensions of performance that are to be emphasized?
2. What are appropriate standards of performance to be set on each of these dimensions?
3. How are rewards to be tied to the achievement of these performance standards?

Banking's changing environment necessitated new strategies and business objectives, particularly development and delivery of new products to a wider range of customers. It was then a logical step to set targets at all levels in the organization to communicate these strategies to managers and motivate them to achieve those goals. Such tactics were adopted by all the major banks. United Bank chose to introduce a link between achievement of target and payment of a specific monetary reward.[4] This decision seems so radical within the traditional banking environment that it indicates how important it was to produce a significant shift in the bank's managerial culture.

A body of literature in budgetary control examines how overemphasis on imperfect performance targets generates dysfunctional consequences. Beginning with Argyris (1952), and extending through Hopwood (1972), Otley (1978), and Hirst (1981), these writers have studied accounting-based performance measures and the conditions under which dysfunctional behavior is most likely to be generated. Such behavior appears to be most likely when performance targets imperfectly reflect the manager's entire job, and when excessive reliance is placed on achieving such targets. For example, Hopwood identified a budget-constrained style of management, in which deviations from budget targets were treated as excuses (rather than explanations that might be accepted); this management approach led to a variety of dysfunctional consequences. But Otley's extension to the study suggested that these consequences would occur only when the targets themselves failed to cover the full range of a manager's responsibilities.

Most of this literature, however, has dealt with control systems incorporating no direct monetary reward associated with achieving a target. It seems likely that adding monetary rewards would increase the tendency to stress the short term at the expense of the long, and that dysfunctional behavior would be more likely to be observed. Alternatively, Merchant's (1989) work suggests that in such circumstances the performance targets themselves will be manipulated so that they are relatively easy to achieve: managers will be able to obtain reasonable bonus payments without being stretched to attain more demanding targets.

From a theoretical point of view, this study is designed to explore the ways in which target-setting and performance-related rewards have influenced managerial behavior in the U.K. banking environment. It is focused on the degree to which major aspects of a manager's job are captured in specific performance targets, and the way in which attaching monetary rewards to the attainment of such targets has emphasized short-term performance to the detriment of the longer term.

Performance-Related Reward
in United Bank

United Bank plc (UB) is a major British clearing bank having a branch network throughout England and Wales. The bank has eight divisions, one of which is our subject: the Domestic Banking (DB) division. The division operates the domestic branch banking network with support from other specialist divisions within the bank.

In 1987, UB introduced a system of performance-related reward (PRR), implementing it from the top down. Chief executives of divisions were included in the scheme from July 1987, senior managers from January 1988, and other management grades from July 1988. In summer 1988, managerial grades were reduced from ten to seven. Executive and senior managers were graded MA to MC, and the remaining management grades ran from MD down to MG. Within a bank branch are one or more managers on management grades, with more junior employees on staff grades below them. Although extending the scheme to staff grades is being considered, we shall primarily examine how the scheme can be extended to the lower management grades MD to MG, covering a salary range of £16,000 to £36,000 a year (on 1988 salary scales), although we refer occasionally to more senior managers.

The new pay structure's two major elements are merit increments based on an annual salary review, and bonus payments, based on achieving preset performance targets. Merit increments are a permanent increase in salary, which will be maintained into the future, whereas bonus payments are one-time awards with no commitment to continue payment in the future.

Merit Increments

The newly implemented PRR scheme has modified the previous salary review system, including formal consideration of individual performance into basic salary calculations. Salary reviews now take place only once a year, in April, and cover both overall individual performance and market comparability. Under this system, the salary rise

Exhibit 4-1   Merit Increment Matrix
(including 5% cost-of-living component)

Position in Salary Range (percentile)	Performance Evaluation Rating			
	Outstanding	Good	Fully satisfactory	Less than fully satisfactory
100				
80	5%–8%			
60	8%–10%	5%–8%		
40	10%–12%	8%–10%	5%–8%	
20				0%–6%
	12%–14%	10%–12%	8%–10%	

(merit increment) for an individual is defined with a matrix of possible percentage increments. Both an individual's present position on the salary range and an assessment of present performance are used to set an appropriate increment; managers at the lower points on an incremental scale are eligible for larger increments. Because this matrix includes an element allowing for general price inflation (a cost-of-living increase), a manager who receives no increment is effectively receiving a salary reduction. A typical matrix, assuming a 5% cost-of-living increase, is shown in Exhibit 4-1.

The rationale behind this part of the system is to allow above-average managers to rise up the salary scale more quickly than was possible before. Previously, increments would be earned by years of service, only exceptional managers receiving accelerated increments. Moreover, the new salary ranges for the grades now have much greater overlap, so that an outstanding manager in the MG grade can earn considerably more than a manager at the bottom of the MF grade, for example. The longer ranges and the overlap seem to help the bank retain outstanding managers in a specific job longer, whereas before, the only method available for rewarding outstanding performance was promotion to a new job because the pay range was so narrow. Conversely, managers who fail to perform up to expectations can progress only so far up the salary scale, gaining peak salary with fully satisfactory performance at the sixtieth percentile of the grade salary scale. Managers who perform well initially, but whose perfor-

Exhibit 4-2   Bonus Payments (as a percentage of annual salary)

| | Managerial Grades | |
Bonus Level	MA-MC	MD-MG
Below threshold	0%	0%
Threshold	5%	5%
On-target	15%	10%
Ceiling	25%	20%

mance subsequently deteriorates, can be held at a constant money salary until they are once more within an appropriate percentile band.

The Bonus System

Beyond the annual salary review, the PRR scheme introduced a once-only bonus for the first time. This payment rewards performance measured against preset performance targets, which are weighted together to give an overall measure of present performance. The period over which bonus payments are assessed is the calendar year, ending in December, making monetary payments in the following February or March. Three performance benchmarks are defined:

Threshold: The minimum level of performance necessary to obtain a minimum bonus payment. This grade is suggested as a financial result of perhaps 10%–15% below on-target performance.

On-target: Achieving a stretching but realistic target level of performance.

Ceiling: Achievement justifying payment of the maximum bonus; may be a financial result of about 25%–30% above on-target performance.

A bonus payment, expressed as a percentage of annual salary, is associated with each level of performance, and differs slightly between senior and other managerial grades, as shown in Exhibit 4-2.

The performance targets for managers are referred to as key objectives. Each manager's immediate superior is expected to set two to six key objectives for him or her. These objectives will be assigned numerical weights totaling 100% so that an overall performance measure can be computed. Key objectives are expected to be closely linked to the annual business plan for a manager's unit; they should relate to factors that a manager can directly influence or control; and they should include at least one financial objective, where possible.

Exhibit 4-3   Marking Key for Nonnumerical Targets

Performance Level	Mark
Unacceptable	1
Acceptable	2 (Threshold)
Fully satisfactory	3 (On-target)
Good	4
Very good	5
Outstanding	6 (Ceiling)

The objectives, however, are not necessarily expected to include every aspect of satisfactory job performance, because other factors will also be considered in the more subjective overall performance review.

Target-setting is evidently an important part of the bonus scheme. Targets are intended to be agreed on by managers and superiors at the start of the year and, as far as possible, to be objectively verifiable, reducing the subjectivity associated with this element of the PRR scheme. The three main types of target are:

Measurable: Targets with a precise numerical measure of achievement (e.g., sales or profit targets).

Testable: Targets which cannot be directly and routinely measured, but which can be subjected to tests such as opinion surveys (e.g., levels of customer satisfaction achieved).

Assessable: Targets for which achievement cannot be measured or tested, but which are subject to a superior's personal judgment (e.g., satisfactory completion of a project).

For each measurable target, the bonus percentage is determined by a straight-line calculation between the various performance levels defined. For nonnumerical targets, performance is rated with the marking scale shown in Exhibit 4-3. The mark is then translated into a bonus percentage, using the relevant weighting factor for the objective.

Research Methods

The effect of the scheme on managers was studied during calendar 1989, the first full year of operation. For all the managers involved, however, performance targets had been set for the period

July to December 1988, and had received a full annual bonus for their performance during the six-month period. In effect, the second year of operation was studied.

The bulk of the data collection was undertaken in summer 1989. Managers therefore had objectives that had been set for the full year, but were only six or seven months into the year when they were interviewed. Their performance for 1988 had been assessed, however, and they had received a bonus for 1988 that was paid in March 1989. It was expected that the scheme's teething problems would be overcome by this time and the managers would be fully aware of how it was intended to operate, but it was still early enough in the life of the plan for managers' assessments of its effect to have validity.

The research objectives were to obtain feedback from branch managers on the effect of introducing the PRR scheme, and to collect information on contextual features of their jobs in order to make a judgment about its effects and overall effectiveness. Information was gathered in three major ways. First, a sample of branch managers was interviewed, using a semistructured interview schedule; this format permitted many issues to be discussed and meant that factors individual managers felt were important could be followed up in detail. Precise answers to specific questions could not, though, be obtained from all managers. Second, a questionnaire was left with all managers interviewed to collect structured responses to a core of questions.[5] Finally, from the bonus summary sheet on which such information was recorded, we took information on the objectives set for each manager and how they were weighted.

A sample of sixty managers was selected nonrandomly to represent the bank as a whole. Four regions (referred to here as A, B, C, and D) were selected for their performance in 1988. Regions A and B had performed relatively poorly in 1988, although it was suspected that part of the reason was their targets, which had been set at quite stretching levels; regions C and D had performed relatively well in 1988, although senior management suspected that managers in region C had gotten better bonuses than they truly deserved. With help from the senior personnel manager in each region, fifteen managers were selected as representative of the managerial grades involved within the region. These included not only branch managers but also lending and administrative managers within branches and corporate account and lending managers outside of branches. Despite attempts to choose representative managers, those selected may not have included the very poorest performers: only two of the sixty failed to receive a

Exhibit 4-4   Managerial Grades

Grade	Number
MA	3
MB	4
MC	2
MD	14
ME	14
MF	15
MG	8
Total	60

bonus for 1988.[6] Nevertheless, they represented a wide cross-section of jobs and grades in the regions. In all, sixty managers were interviewed and fifty returned their questionnaires before the deadline set for analysis.

The managers had a mean age of forty-eight years, only five being less than forty. On average they had worked for the bank for thirty years, a pattern consistent with nearly all having joined UB directly on leaving school and staying with the bank for their entire career. At these grades, appointment of managers recruited from other banks was almost unheard of. Nearly 80% of the managers interviewed worked at branch level, 15% worked from a corporate banking group office, and 5% from a regional office. A representative sample was taken from all grades, as shown in Exhibit 4-4.

The average bonus received by the managers in each region was consistent with the method used to select the sample, as shown in Exhibit 4-5. The average bonus received across the DB division was 9.6% for grades MD to MG and 13.1% for grades MA to MC. The figures are thus consistent with the belief that regions C and D did well and region B did badly. The sample of managers selected for region A, however, did better than the regional average, although

Exhibit 4-5   Bonus Received in 1988

Region	Bonus Percentage
A	11.0%
B	7.6%
C	12.2%
D	12.6%

still not as well as the average for regions C and D. The main reason for this anomaly was that two managers had received exceptionally high bonus payments.

Results

Setting Targets

It is evident from the Tannenbaum influence scales (Q3) that target-setting was overwhelmingly done from the top down, and most influence by far was exerted by the head office. Regional managers were thought to exert some limited influence, but branch managers perceived themselves to have the least influence in target-setting. This perception caused some dissatisfaction because most managers desired a much more even distribution of influence, giving branch managers no less influence than managers at higher levels. A similar point of view was reflected in the participation scale (Q13), where managers indicated that although they voiced their opinions quite frequently, these opinions were not taken sufficiently into account. The overall measure of participation derived from this question (using six items selected by factor analysis) scored almost one point below the middle of a seven-point scale, indicating a very modest level of perceived participation. Certainly targets were seen as imposed, and that little account was taken of branch managers' own views and only a little attention was paid to an individual branch's circumstances.

It may be argued that in a business such as banking the case is strong for setting targets for the bank as a whole and then breaking these down into individual targets for operating units, because relatively reliable macroeconomic forecasts can be made. Some disaggregation may also occur, however, resulting in inappropriate targets being set for some branches, and unit managers certainly feel that their views are not being taken adequately into account. This dissatisfaction is reflected in the average score for satisfaction with target setting (Q1b; 2.62 on a five-point scale), which indicates that managers are generally somewhat dissatisfied with the way in which targets are set.

The results of target-setting do not, though, appear to be quite so adverse as those comments may suggest. The majority of managers (54%) thought their 1988 bonus payment was at least what they deserved. Of the remainder, a further half thought they were paid only a little less than they deserved, although the other half thought they received a lot less than they deserved. Although the setting of targets was heavily top-down, the outcome in bonuses was considered more or less satisfactory by 75% of those questioned.

Moreover, 70% of managers considered overall performance to be fairly evaluated, in the context of the previous year. This feeling may reflect an underlying culture of fair performance evaluation that has persisted from earlier periods, for a more general question (Q8f) indicated that 90% of managers thought the overall evaluation of their performance was mostly fair. But interestingly, this attitude is not reflected in the average interpersonal trust rating, which, at 3.44 on a five-point scale, indicates managers had only moderate trust in their superiors. Although superiors are seen as helpful and open to discussion, junior managers are not confident that they are kept fully informed or that decisions will take their own interests into account.

Therefore, we conclude that the target-setting process is open to significant distortions, causing some individual managers to receive inappropriate targets, and that mistrust and lack of open information flow are sufficient to produce at least the suspicion that targets are inappropriate. This interpretation seems to make a prima facie case that some dysfunctional behavior may be motivated.

The Targets Themselves

Within the DB division the targets that are set seem fairly comprehensive, for 70% of managers claim that they include most matters of importance. But this consensus may be no consolation for the 30% of managers who think significant items are not included in their targets. Remember, however, that the target system was not intended to be totally comprehensive, but rather to direct managers' attention to areas of present importance. The more subjective part of the evaluation scheme should consider these other aspects of performance.

Managers were set five to eight targets (mean = 6.1), three to six of which (mean = 4.5) were measurable rather than assessable or testable. Thus, whether targets were achieved was mostly a matter of objective fact rather than a superior manager's subjective judgment. At the start of the year each target was expected to have somewhat more than a 50/50 chance of being achieved. Halfway through the year, on average, this expectation remained unchanged, although the dispersion of expected outcomes had increased significantly, indicating greater certainty about the outcome, for good or for ill. Targets appeared mostly independent of each other, with only small positive correlations appearing between the likelihood of achieving different targets. Interestingly, additional targets (beyond six) were generally set at relatively easy levels.

It thus appears that targets are quite realistic, and managers perceive that they are more likely than not to be achieved. Because an average 10% bonus would be earned if targets were attained, this level of difficulty may appear to be quite modest. Despite their views on the likelihood that the target would be achieved, however, managers did not translate these directly into bonuses, for the average bonus expectation for 1989 was just under 8%, whereas the likelihood estimates suggested that it would be more than 10%. This disparity may reflect the bank managers' natural conservatism—they do not wish to count their chickens before they are hatched. Nevertheless, a strong correlation appeared between the likelihood that the target would be attained as perceived by managers and the amount of bonus they expected to receive in the present year ($r = 0.60; p < .001$).

These results reflect those of Merchant, in that targets appear to have been set at levels that will most often lead to on-target performance. They certainly were realistic in the initial year, when the average bonus earned by the same managers was 10.7%. Thus, despite (perhaps because of) the method used to set the targets, the targets themselves seem generally fair, and represent only a modestly demanding standard of attainment.

Perceived Effects of the Plan

The general impression gained from managers, and reflected in the responses to Q2, was that although the PRR scheme had produced only limited influence, it had no negative or dysfunctional consequences. The majority of managers felt the scheme had no effect *on themselves*, although 36% believed it had increased their effort slightly and 42% thought it had led to a small improvement in their performance. By contrast, most managers thought the scheme beneficially affected *other* managers. Eighty-four percent thought it had produced increased effort by other managers, and 86% thought it had slightly improved performance by those managers. Only two managers reported that they believed the scheme had negative effects, and these applied to managers other than themselves.

Exhibit 4-6   Items in Style Question

These statements describe some of the criteria by which a superior evaluates a subordinate's performance. Please indicate the extent to which you consider each of these criteria is used by your superior to evaluate your performance, as far as you are aware.

(a)   How well I cooperate with colleagues.
(b)   My long-term concern for costs and revenues.
(c)   How well I get on with my superior.
(d)   How much effort I put into the job.
(e)   My concern for quality of service.
(f)   Meeting branch (or unit) targets in the short term.
(g)   My attitude toward my work.
(h)   My ability to handle my subordinates.
(i)   How well I cooperate with other managers.
(j)   How well I cooperate with individuals outside the branch (e.g., clients).
(k)   How well I perform on my branch (or unit) inspection.

Reported levels of job-related tension were very low, with a mean score of 2.4 on a five-point scale. These scores are consistent with the view that a branch manager's job is well ordered, with little ambiguity (1.7 on a five-point scale), and relatively free of stress. One might argue that increased stress would improve motivation and performance. Target-related tension was just slightly higher, at 2.5 on the same scale. Pressure to achieve targets must be considerable, apparently, before adverse side effects appear.

Criteria for Performance Evaluation

The importance of various criteria in performance evaluation was examined, using a question similar in form to that used by Hopwood and Otley. This question, in eleven parts, based on preliminary discussions with senior managers, is shown in Exhibit 4-6. Respondents were asked both to score these criteria for importance and to rank them. The conclusions drawn from the average importance scores are very similar to those drawn from the ranking procedure. A great deal of importance was attached to subjectively assessable factors, in contradistinction to more measurable aspects of performance. The top three items were seen as (1) the effort a manager put into the job; (2) concern for quality of service; and (3) attitude toward the work. Meeting unit targets in the short term ranked only fourth, and long-term attention to costs and revenues sixth. Thus subjective assessment of qualities that are difficult to observe was generally ranked above more measurable factors, although most managers thought nearly all the items had some importance. When they were asked which items were more important, they thought all six top-ranked items required even greater importance, except for meeting short-term targets, which needed less emphasis. This interpretation may indicate that the target-setting scheme is actually achieving its objective of bringing specific short-run targets nearer the forefront of managers' attention.

A style measure was constructed by the same method as that of Hopwood (based on the relative ranking of "long-term concern with costs and revenues" and "meeting targets in the short term" if these ranked in the top three items). We considered including the four top-ranked items, because the scale had more items than Hopwood's, but this change would have affected only three cases. Also, it can be argued that only the most important items are relevant, however many alternatives are given. The distribution of responses is shown in Exhibit 4-7.

Factor analysis of the eleven-item scale yielded a four-factor result. Factor 1 included only subjectively assessable items such as effort, attitude, and cooperative abilities; factor 2 covered attention to quality of service and long-run costs; factor 3 included meeting short-term targets and performance on branch inspection; and factor 4 consisted of other cooperative factors. Three measures with these items were therefore constructed for further analysis.

Another question (Q5) explored the importance of target-related performance and the degree to which other factors were taken into account in assessing performance. These responses displayed a wide spread, the most consistent items being the need to supplement

Exhibit 4-7 Hopwood Style of Budget-Use Measure

Style	Description	Number of Managers
BC	Target-constrained (i.e., short-term only in top three)	13 (26%)
BP	Target-emphasis (i.e., both short- and long-term in top three; short-term more important)	8 (16%)
PB	Profit-emphasis (i.e., both short- and long-term in top three; long-term more important)	2 (4%)
PC	Profit-conscious (i.e., long-term only in top three)	7 (14%)
NA	Nonnumeric (neither in top three)	20 (40%)

target-related information with other information and allowing variances from target to be explained. Target-related information was considered significant in evaluation. A factor analysis of this scale produced three factors, the first of which seemed to mix different items; the other two picked up strong emphasis on the short term and the flexible use of target-related information. Measures were therefore constructed for these three factors. Again, the most consistent response expressed the importance of using target information flexibly, but variability was considerable.

It did not seem sensible to pursue Hopwood's distinction too far because most managers relied relatively little on target-related criteria. Comparing managers who used either short- or long-term target-related criteria, however (that is, BC, BP, PB, and PC groups; $N = 30$) and those who did not (that is, NA group; $N = 20$) revealed that the latter group had more education than the former ($p = .04$). They also had fewer years of service with the bank ($p = .07$), partly reflecting the longer time they had spent in school. The PRR scheme also appeared to influence these managers less, certainly not motivating them to put more effort into their work. They also had more trust in their superiors' decisions and felt that they were consulted more frequently in setting targets. It is difficult to avoid the view that the PRR scheme had yet to dispel the cosy, "club" atmosphere that such managers exuded.

Performance

Performance was assessed by means of two sets of questions. First, managers were asked to give an overall self-rating of their performance, both absolutely and relative to other managers, and also a rating of their unit's performance compared with that of other units. Perhaps it was to be expected, but few managers considered themselves less than adequate or below-average performers, although a few thought their unit was below average. All three measures were positively intercorrelated (at between 0.40 and 0.75; $p < .01$). Interestingly, only a small positive correlation appeared between managers' own self-rating of performance and the bonus payment they received in 1988 ($r = 0.24$; $p = ns$).

Second, managers were asked to complete Mahoney's self-rating question (Q11) in which eight dimensions of performance are rated together with importance scores for each activity. The item on staffing was omitted from further analysis because a significant proportion of managers indicated that this function was largely outside their control. Two summary measures were computed; the first added up the performance ratings on the remaining seven dimensions, the second weighted these by the importance score attached to each. The first measure correlated with all three overall self-ratings (0.48 to 0.57; $p < .001$), and most highly with the self-rating of overall performance. The weighted measure did not correlate with the other measures even when a logarithmic transformation was used. Only small correlations between the performance measures and the bonus payments were found, except for the weighted measure, which correlated reasonably well with the bonus expected for the present year (0.42; $p < .01$), although less well with the previous year's actual bonus (0.31; $p = ns$).

It would be easy to read too much into these measures; they are perhaps best used to indicate self-satisfaction with overall performance. They also reinforce the impression that overall performance was assessed by reference to a much wider range of criteria than the attainment of quantitative performance targets.

Education

One major factor that was found to influence managerial attitudes toward target-setting and the PRR scheme was their level of education prior to joining the bank. The sample of managers divided itself almost equally into those who had entered the bank at the minimum age for leaving school (age sixteen after taking O-level examinations) and those who had completed a further two years of education (after taking A-level examinations). The only four managers who had a degree are omitted from our comparison, although they are very similar to the A-level group.

In general, managers with less education perceived less job ambiguity ($p = .05$), and thought their regional managers exercised more influence on both setting branch targets ($p = .05$) and on achieving actual results ($p = .11$). Overall, they participated less in target-setting ($p = .10$) and felt they had less influence on the targets that were set ($p = .05$). But they were more confident that their superior kept them fully informed ($p = .02$) and were less likely to suffer from job-related tension ($p = .02$), particularly in feeling less stressed by heavy workloads, conflicting demands, and ability to influence their boss.

These managers, however, felt they performed better than their

more highly educated colleagues on both their own overall ratings
($p = .04$) and on the weighted performance measure ($p = .04$).
They felt their performance was evaluated more fairly ($p = .17$) and
expected a bonus in the present year some 2.5 percentage points
higher than their colleagues ($p = .07$). They also thought their performance depended more on their long-run attention to costs and revenues ($p = .07$), but also saw other factors as more important, including getting along with their boss ($p = .01$), their ability to handle
subordinates ($p = .02$), and cooperating with other managers ($p =
.001$). Finally, they perceived the PRR scheme as having a signifi-
cantly greater effect on the effort that other managers put into their
work ($p = .09$) and on their subsequent performance ($p = .10$).

The picture we come up with shows the less highly educated
managers existing more happily in the bank's hierarchic structure,
content to be told clearly what was expected of them. The PRR
scheme seems to have more strongly affected this group of managers,
encouraging them to work harder and to perform better. Conversely,
it seems to have less strongly influenced their more highly educated
colleagues, for whom the scheme raised issues they thought needed
to be discussed and gave them a desire to participate more fully in
target-setting, a desire mainly unfulfilled for most managers.

Effect of Age and Grade

More older managers than younger ones thought targets received
more emphasis, and also felt that the head office exerted much more
influence over their setting. This difference showed up especially in
the responses to Q5, in which every statistically significant difference
between age groups related to using targets as a means of affecting
performance. The PRR scheme thus seems to have most impact on
this older (beyond age forty-eight) group of managers. Although they
perceived that they had lower overall participation in target-setting
than younger managers, they believed they had more influence in two
areas: the final level at which targets were set and the contribution
their views made to setting branch targets. Older managers seem to
be formally participating in target-setting at only a low level, yet
believing their opinions were transmitted upward by their superiors
and taken into account in setting the final targets.

Another characteristic of the older management group was that
although they had received higher than average bonus payments in
1988 (11.5% as against 9.9%), they expected to receive lower bonuses

in the present year (7.2% compared with 8.7%). Although no measure of cognitive style was used in this study, we get a distinct impression that older managers feel the results they report are affected by many factors beyond their control, whereas their younger colleagues believe their own efforts have a more significant influence.

Dissatisfaction with the target-setting procedure was also linked to the grade of manager, the higher grades being significantly more dissatisfied ($r = 0.34$; $p = .01$). We compared the MD and ME grades (twenty-two managers) with the MF and MG grades (eighteen managers), and found that the higher grades of management felt subjected to significantly higher amounts of target-related tension ($p = .001$). Perhaps they thought their superiors were more target oriented than their junior colleagues, although they also believed that target-based information was supplemented by information in performance evaluation. Lower grades believed that such supplementary information should be used, but that in practice it was not. To no one's surprise, high-graded managers thought they performed better than did those in lower grades.

Overall Impressions

The initial impression, both from interviewing managers and the questionnaire data, is that the PRR plan has been generally successful in helping concentrate some managers' minds on short-term priorities. We have little evidence that the plan has produced untoward side effects; rather, it has helped managers focus on present priorities and identify short-term objectives on which they can have a positive influence. The general opinion appears to be that the plan has both increased and focused managerial effort, and has had a small but beneficial influence on performance. These effects, however, have been more pronounced with managers who had less education and with older managers; the scheme seems to have had less influence on the more educated managers and on younger managers. The procedure by which targets are set also caused dissatisfaction, particularly with the senior managers.

It may be, however, that the scheme's full benefit has yet to be extracted. The culture in the bank is changing, but it is a slow transformation. Targets seem undemanding, and most managers clearly achieve threshold performance and average on-target performance. Despite the few outstanding performers, the scheme does not seem to distinguish markedly among managers. Again, it is probably better to go slowly, but it appears that targets could require more stretching and make their achievement more rewarding. How much say managers should have in setting targets is another question that requires further consideration.

Regional Differences

As stated earlier, regions were selected for analysis based on their performance. Regions A and B had performed badly, and were thought to have been unfairly judged; regions C and D had performed well, but senior managers doubted that the region C rating was totally justified. On examining the comments and responses to questionnaires from managers, we saw that, although region A had indeed performed badly, managers felt this assessment reflected their performance reasonably well, though part of the reason may have been that the sample of managers from this region performed above average within the region. Similarly, region C differed from region D primarily in that targets were imposed more from on high; other aspects of performance were considered similar. Thus the most significant contrast was between region B (the poorest performer) and region D (the best performer).

Interestingly, managers' views of their own performance were remarkably similar between these two regions on all the performance measures used. Region B managers, though, were by far the most dissatisfied with the way in which performance targets had been set. They perceived that the head office's influence had been very high and the branch influence in setting targets had been negligible. Little consideration had been given to each unit's circumstances in setting their targets. The previous year's bonus was thought to have been unfair, along with performance evaluation generally. Notably, the scheme appeared to have least affected the effort managers put into their jobs or the performance that resulted from it. This weakness showed up particularly on one item of the job-related tension scale. In this region managers felt greatly stressed by "not being able to satisfy the conflicting demands of various people over you."

The clearest difference in response to the item (Q5f) "my superior is more concerned with actions which produce good short-term results than with long-term performance." This attitude was rated significantly above average in region B but well below average in region D. However, when one examines the importance ratings assigned various performance criteria (Q4), short-term targets received almost equal rankings (second or third) in all areas; regions B and D differed because "long-run concern with costs and revenues" was rated above it in region D and well below it in region B. This effect shows up in the measure of managerial style. Regions C and D displayed greater emphasis on targets than did regions A and B consistently on several measures. In regions A and B, however, managers felt they had made a more important contribution in setting targets.

In this context, Hopwood's concept about the relative importance of short- and long-run budget emphasis seems to have some justification. Good performance appears to be motivated by strong emphasis on meeting short-run targets coupled with a flexible attitude greatly stressing that short-term considerations should not be allowed to dominate long-term strategies. To the extent that region C is considered to have achieved good performance bonuses without performing very well, long-run attention to costs and revenues was well down the list of performance criteria thought to be used, although managers felt it should be given considerably more emphasis. Quality of service, which ranked first in all three other regions, was ranked only fifth in region C.

It therefore appears that several conditions needed to be met for the PRR system to produce the desired results. Managers needed to be involved in target-setting even if the greatest influence on the targets actually set came from higher levels in the organization. Using short-term targets could positively focus management's attention on results that needed constant attention, but achieving such results at the expense of other considerations was not justified. Attention to achieving targets needed to be balanced with attention to longer-run factors such as the quality of service provided customers.

Conclusions

In principle, the bank seems to have got it right, or at least not to have got it badly wrong. A scheme that provides a monetary bonus for achieving short-term targets gives positive direction and motivation. Longer-term aspects of performance also need to be monitored, though, and that can be done by the more subjective general appraisal of overall performance, which gives much more significant rewards in the longer term by means of promotion. Where the system works less than perfectly the cause seems connected to the methods adopted by some of the more senior managers in the system. Laying down targets from on high, even where these are seen as relatively easy to attain, does not seem to produce the required results. Nor, on the other hand, does a strong emphasis on numerous measurable targets. As in many things, balance is the answer, and some scope appears to be available for educating senior managers in using quantitative targets to motivate their subordinates to perform to the best of their ability. They need to be encouraged to direct their effort in appropriate directions rather than merely work harder.

These limitations, however, did not produce the problems reported by Hopwood (1972) for two reasons. First, quantitative targets seem to capture many of a bank branch's basic objectives despite branch managers' perceptions about the importance of effort, attitude, and quality of service.[7] Second, the emphasis on short-term targets was still only relatively low. All the indications suggest that considerably more emphasis could be placed on such targets before dysfunctional effects appear.

Implementing the scheme led to other relatively minor problems. The targets were not well tailored to the circumstances of some individual branches; here greater participation in target-setting would probably be beneficial. Targets sometimes required revision during the year, but general principles for doing so had not been developed. That measurable targets were easier to set for branch managers than for their colleagues in support divisions caused some dissatisfaction, for changing circumstances were more easily taken into account where target achievement was only subjectively assessable. Finally, branch managers were bothered that they received monetary bonuses whereas their staff did not. This situation was being remedied by extending the scheme to more junior staff in 1990.[8]

On balance, the PRR scheme's positive effects appear to considerably outweigh its negative influences. On the positive side, it has the general support of nearly all the managerial staff and is believed to have been useful in making the corporate culture more appropriate to the new environment in which the bank operates. It has helped managers focus on key short-term issues and has even helped encourage better cooperation within large branches as individuals realize how their work jointly contributes to achieving specific targets. On the negative side, some unfairness is perceived both between regions and branches within the DB division and between the DB division and other divisions in the bank. Targets have been unilaterally imposed, sometimes inappropriately, and most managers would have appreciated both more involvement in target-setting and in receiving feedback on their own performance in relation to others. But these negative factors seem relatively easy to overcome as implementation of the scheme proceeds.

As a first step, the PRR scheme has been a useful tool in helping the bank focus managerial attention on short-term performance in a number of crucial areas. It therefore assists an important cultural change toward values that emphasize attaining competitive standards for performance in a changing environment. The new pay scheme has moved toward reducing the number of hierarchic grades in the bank, although the cultural effect of this change seems to have been less pronounced. Perhaps the next stage will involve further breaking down hierarchic distinctions by more actively involving junior managers in setting their own targets as well as in achieving them.

NOTES

1. Stock option schemes are the U.S. equivalent.

2. Savings and loan institutions are the nearest U.S. equivalent.

3. British banks usually are open between 9.30 A.M. and 3.30 P.M., Monday to Friday. Building societies are open from 9.00 A.M. to 5.30 P.M., and also on Saturday mornings.

4. A pseudonym.

5. See Appendix to this chapter.

6. The bank staff were surprised that even two managers in the sample failed to earn a bonus. Fewer than 1% of the bank's managers failed to earn a bonus.

7. It is also possible that "quality of service" may be perceived more from a branch manager's point of view than from a customer's. No great evidence was found that customers' expectations had been coherently monitored.

8. One alternative being considered was allocating branch managers a lump sum of money, depending upon overall branch performance, to be distributed among the staff as they felt appropriate. Such a change would be a considerable alteration to the hierarchic culture in the autonomy granted branch managers, although how they would operate such a system within their branches is not clear.

REFERENCES

Argyris, C. *The Impact of Budgets on People.* Ithaca, NY: Controllership Foundation, 1952.

Armstrong, M., and H. Murlis. *Reward Management: A Handbook of Salary Administration,* 2d ed. London: Kogan Page, 1988.

Emmanuel, C. R., D. T. Otley, and K. A. Merchant. *Accounting for Management Control,* 2d ed. London: Chapman and Hall, 1990.

Hirst, M. K. "Accounting Information and the Evaluation of Subordinate Performance." *The Accounting Review,* vol. LXVI (1981), pp. 771–784.

Hopwood, A. G. "An Empirical Study of the Role of Accounting Data in Performance Evaluation." *Empirical Research in Accounting,* Supplement to *Journal of Accounting Research,* vol. 10 (1972), pp. 156–182.

Kahn, R. L., et al. *Organizational Stress: Studies in Role Conflict and Ambiguity*. New York: Wiley, 1964.

Merchant, K. A. *Rewarding Results: Motivating Profit Center Managers*. Boston: Harvard Business School Press, 1989.

Otley, D. T. "Budget Use and Managerial Performance." *Journal of Accounting Research*, vol. 16 (1978), pp. 122–149.

———. *Accounting Control and Organizational Behaviour*. London: Heinemann, 1987.

Read, W. H. "Upward Communication in Industrial Hierarchies." *Human Relations*, vol. 15 (1962), pp. 3–16.

Schiff, M., and A. Y. Lewin. "The Impact of People on Budgets." *The Accounting Review*, vol. XLV (1970), pp. 259–268.

APPENDIX

Summary of Questionnaire Items

The questionnaire included items aimed at eliciting managers' opinions on aspects of their jobs and the PRR scheme. It did not, however, seek measures of items such as task uncertainty, for these were considered very similar between managers for the types of post being considered. Job differences, to the extent that they exist, are assumed to be correlated with the grade of the manager. Each item in the questionnaire was aimed at these concepts:

Q1   These items were meant to establish the completeness of the PRR targets, satisfaction with the way in which they were set, and the fairness of the system in general.

Q2   This question sought opinions on the effect of the PRR scheme on the effort put into the job and the results achieved both on the individual and on other managers.

Q3   This is a standard Tannenbaum influence scale examining the influence that each level of management is perceived to have (and ought to have) on setting targets and on actual performance.

Q4   This question is similar to that used by Hopwood (1972) and Otley (1978) to measure style of budget use. It is adapted for use in this organization and is used in conjunction with the ranking requested in Q14.

Q5   An alternative to Q4, gathering information explicitly on the use made of targets in conjunction with other information.

Q6   A five-item Inter-Personal Trust measure.

Q7   A two-item Target-Related Tension item, similar to that used by Otley (1978).

Q8   A five-item Job Ambiguity scale, plus a one-item Felt Fairness of Evaluation.

Q9   This question was intended to establish the perceived difficulty of the targets set, by asking how likely the respondent thought it was that they would be achieved. The results of this question need to be interpreted, because it seeks a retrospective opinion on the start of the year and a current opinion seven or eight months into the year.

Q10 A fifteen-item Job-Related Tension scale derived from Kahn et al. (1964).

Q11 Mahoney's eight-item job-performance scale.

Q12 Three items measuring perceived overall performance on different scales, two specifically in comparison with other managers and units.

Q13 This question explores the manager's participation in setting targets against which his or her bonus will be assessed.

Q14 See question 4.

CHAPTER 5

Organizational Changes and Value Creation in Leveraged Buyouts: The Case of the O. M. Scott & Sons Company*

George P. Baker and Karen H. Wruck

THIS study documents the organizational changes that took place at the O. M. Scott & Sons Company in response to its leveraged buyout. Our findings confirm that both the pressure of servicing a heavy debt load and management equity ownership lead to improved performance. Equally important at Scott, however, and undocumented in large-sample studies, are debt covenants restricting

*We would like to thank everyone at the O. M. Scott & Sons Company and Clayton & Dubilier who gave generously of their time and made this study possible: Lorel Au, Richard Dresdale, Martin Dubilier, Richard Martinez, Lawrence McCartney, Tadd Seitz, John Smith, Robert Stern, Homer Stewart, Henry Timnick, Kenneth Tossey, John Wall, Craig Walley, and Paul Yeager. In addition, we would like to thank Kenneth French (the referee), and Robin Cooper, Robert Eccles, Leo Herzel, Michael Jensen, Steven Kaplan, Kenneth Merchant, Krishna Palepu, Richard Ruback, G. William Schwert, Eric Wruck, the participants in the Financial Decisions and Control Workshop and the Organization Behavior and the Theory of the Firm Workshop at the Harvard Business School, and the participants in the Conference on the Structure and Governance of Enterprise sponsored by the *Journal of Financial Economics* and the Harvard Business School for their helpful comments and suggestions. Support from the Division of Research, Harvard Business School, is gratefully acknowledged.

From *Journal of Financial Economics*, vol. 25 (1989), pp. 163–190. © 1989, Elsevier Science Publishers B.V. (North-Holland). Reprinted with permission.

how the cash required for debt payments can be generated, the adoption of a strong incentive compensation plan, a reorganization and decentralization of decision making, and the relationship among managers, the leveraged buyout sponsors, and the board of directors.

1. Introduction

1.1. A Brief History of the Company

In December 1986, the O. M. Scott & Sons Company (Scott), the largest producer of lawn care products in the United States, was sold by the ITT Corporation (ITT) in a divisional leveraged buyout. Scott, located in Marysville, Ohio, was founded in 1870 by Orlando McLean Scott to sell farm crop seed. Beginning in 1900, the company began to sell weed-free lawn seed through the mail, and in the 1920s, introduced the first home lawn fertilizer, the first lawn spreader, and the first patented bluegrass seed. In fiscal 1988, Scott had sales of $197 million and employed 792 people.

Scott was closely held until 1971, when it was purchased by ITT. Scott became a part of the consumer products division of the huge conglomerate, and operated as a wholly owned subsidiary for fourteen years. In 1984, ITT began a series of divestitures, prompted by a decline in financial performance and rumors of takeover and liquidation. Exhibit 5-1 presents a summary of ITT's financial performance and of the number of companies it bought and sold from 1978 to 1986. In January 1985, ITT announced that it would divest $1.7 billion in assets. The object of these sales was to "streamline ITT into a telecommunications, insurance, and high-technology company." On January 17, 1985, an article in *The Wall Street Journal* identified Scott as one of the businesses that "could be included among the certain companies" ITT wanted to sell. On November 26, 1986, ITT announced that the managers of Scott, along with Clayton & Dubilier (C&D), a private firm specializing in leveraged buyouts, had agreed to purchase the stock of Scott and another ITT subsidiary, the W. Atlee Burpee Company. The deal was closed on December 30, 1986, and represented 25% of ITT's total dollar divestitures for the year.

Clayton & Dubilier secured financing for the sale. Exhibit 5-2 describes the financial structure of Scott after the buyout. Bank loans

Exhibit 5-1   Financial Performance and Divestiture and
Acquisition Activity of ITT Corporation, 1978–1986[a]

Year	Units Acquired[b]	Units Divested[b]	Earnings per Share	Dividends per Share	Stock Return	Market Return
1978	2 [$198]	0 [$0]	$4.66	$2.05	−6.1%	9.0%
1979	9 [$35]	17 [$74]	2.65	2.25	4.1	22.3
1980	2 [$35]	17 [$564]	6.12	2.45	27.5	30.5
1981	4 [$13]	9 [$82]	4.58	2.62	11.2	−3.5
1982	3 [$38]	7 [$498]	4.75	2.70	19.7	20.2
1983	3 [$26]	11 [$126]	4.50	2.76	45.7	21.4
1984	NA	8 [$638]	2.97	1.88	−30.5	5.9
1985	NA	23 [$1,455]	1.89	1.00	31.9	27.9
1986	NA	12 [$597]	3.23	1.00	39.1	17.0

[a]Acquisition and divestiture activity as reported in ITT 10-K reports. NA indicates not available in these reports. Acquisitions for 1984–1986 were not reported by year, but the total amount is $208 million. Stock returns are annual returns. The market return is the CRSP value-weighted return.

[b]Number of units and value in $millions given in brackets.

and the sale of notes and debentures raised $190.9 million. Another $20 million was raised through the sale of equity: 61.4% of the shares were held by the C&D partnership, 20.6% by debtholders, 17.5% by Scott management and employees, and 0.4% by Joseph Flannery, a board member who had been involved in another C&D deal. Immediately following the buyout, Scott's capital structure consisted of 91% debt.

Large-sample studies of leveraged buyouts have documented median levels of post-buyout management equity ownership and leverage strikingly similar to those at Scott. Kaplan (1989), Muscarella and Vetsuypens (1989), and Smith (1989) analyze leveraged buyouts and post-buyout operating performance for samples of 76, 72, and 58 firms, respectively. Kaplan and Smith both document median post-

Exhibit 5-2 Financing of C&D's Purchase of Scott from ITT, December 31, 1986

Sources of Funds		
Bank revolving credit agreement ($137 million available)	$77,000,000	37%
Bank working capital loan	44,000,000	21%
Subordinated notes	50,300,000	24%
Subordinated debentures	19,600,000	9%
Common stock	20,000,000	9%
Total	$210,900,000	100%
Uses of Funds		
Purchase of Scott and Burpee	$151,000,000	72%
Repayment of indebtedness to ITT	52,600,000	25%
Transactions fees	5,000,000	2%
Working capital	2,300,000	1%
Total	$210,900,000	100%

buyout equity ownership by management of 22.6% and 16.7%, respectively, and median post-buyout leverage of about 90%.

Scott's operating performance improved dramatically following the buyout. See Exhibit 5-3. Between the end of December 1986 and the end of September 1988, earnings before interest and taxes increased by 56%. Over the same period, sales were up 25%. These increases were not caused by a reduction in spending on research and development, or spending on marketing and distribution: R&D spending increased by 7%, and marketing and distribution spending by 21%. Capital spending increased by 23% after the buyout. Largely through attrition, average annual full-time employment dropped by about 9%. Average working capital requirements were reduced by a total of $23.1 million over this same 21-month period, falling from 37.5% to 18.4% of sales. All three large-sample studies cited above find that over two to four years following the buyout, operating income increases by an average of 40%. Smith examines changes in accounting line items and finds no evidence that repair and maintenance expenditures are postponed, or that research and development expenditures are reduced. In addition, she provides evidence that firms manage working capital more closely after a buyout, documenting a significant reduction in both days receivables and inventories during the post-buyout period.

Exhibit 5-3   Financial and Operating Data for Scott ($000,000s)

	Pre-buyout Year Ended 12/30/86	Post-buyout Year Ended 9/30/88	Percentage Change
Income Statement			
EBIT	$18.1	$28.2	55.8%
Sales	$158.1	$197.1	24.7%
Research & development	$4.1	$4.4	7.3%
Marketing & distribution	$58.4	$70.7	21.1%
Balance Sheet[a]			
Average working capital	$59.3	$36.2	−39.0%
Total assets	$243.6	$162.0	−33.5%
Long-term debt	$191.0	$125.8	−34.1%
Adjusted net worth	$20.0	$38.3	91.5%
Other			
Capital expenditures	$3.0	$3.7	23.3%
Employment	868	792	−8.9%

[a]Balance-sheet figures are reported at the close of the buyout transaction. Adjusted net worth is GAAP net worth adjusted for accounting effects of the buyout under APB no. 16. In Scott's case the bulk of the adjustment is adding back the effects of an inventory write-down of $24.7 million taken immediately after the buyout.

1.2. Purpose of Our Study

By the objective measures used in the large-sample studies, Scott appears to be a typical buyout: its post-buyout leverage, equity ownership, and operating performance are close to the median values reported in those studies.[1] The authors interpret their results as consistent with an agency theory of the firm in which high leverage and managerial equity ownership lead to improved incentives and consequently improved operating performance. The studies do not, however, actually document any organizational changes resulting from an LBO. They cannot, therefore, explore the organizational links between buyouts and improved operating performance. Documenting these organizational changes is essential if researchers are to understand the mechanisms by which changes in a firm's financial structure affect organizational performance.

This study documents the organizational changes that took place at Scott in response to its LBO. The structure of the Scott organization and the way managers made decisions changed radically after the buyout. Our analysis of the data leads us to conclude that the organizational changes at Scott were a response to three factors: (1) the constraints imposed on the organization by high leverage, (2) changes in the way managers were compensated, and (3) changes in the way Scott's top managers were monitored and advised.

The factors that led to improved operating performance are examined in detail below. Each of the next three sections covers one of the factors crucial to organizational change at Scott: the constraints of high leverage, changes in incentives and compensation, and changes in the monitoring of top managers. Section 5 summarizes the organizational changes that took place, and section 6 presents our conclusions.

Our analysis focuses on the effect of each factor on the alignment of incentives across the firm's claimants. The combination of equity ownership and close monitoring by the board of directors aligns managers' interests with those of the firm's shareholders. The large debt burden and incentive compensation based on cash measures of performance give managers the incentive to operate the firm in a way that generates cash, while the debt covenants and equity ownership prevent managers from taking actions that would damage firm value in the long run.

1.3. Data Collection

The data used in this study are drawn from both public and private sources, including extensive interviews with C&D partners and managers at all levels of the Scott organization, confidential internal documents, prospectuses, ITT 10-K reports, and *The Wall Street Journal*. Exhibit 5-4 lists the titles of all the individuals we interviewed. The confidential data (both quantitative and interview quotations) presented in this study were released by the company for publication here. We had access to other data that are too sensitive for publication. Where applicable we describe the conclusions from our analysis of these data, though we are unable to publish the data themselves.

2. Constraints of High Leverage

2.1. Cash Requirements for Debt Service

Scott's senior debt consists of floating-rate working capital loans and borrowings against a $137 million revolving-credit agreement. A

Exhibit 5-4   Titles of the Individuals Interviewed as a Part of the Data-Collection Process

At O. M. Scott & Sons Company
President and Chief Executive Officer, Board Member
Chief Financial Officer
Assistant Treasurer and Head of Working Capital Task Force (now Treasurer)
General Counsel
Director of New Process Development
Vice President, Associate Relations
Assistant Vice President, Associate Relations
Manager of Contract Operations
Plant Manager

At Clayton & Dubilier
Chairman of the Board of O. M. Scott and Clayton & Dubilier Partner
Member of the Board, Liaison to O. M. Scott, Clayton & Dubilier Partner

group of six major banks, headed by Manufacturers Hanover Trust, provides this capital, as well as a standby letter of credit for up to $2 million. The interest rate on the loans is either the agent's reference rate plus 1.5% or LIBOR plus 3.5%, with interest periods of one, three, or six months, both at Scott's option. There is a repayment penalty of 2.5% if the loans are repaid with other than internally generated funds or the proceeds of a public equity offering. These loans are secured by substantially all of Scott's assets. After the buyout, Scott hedged some of its floating-rate obligations by entering into an agreement with lenders that limited the interest rate adjustment to a maximum increase of 2%. The rate of interest has averaged 10.25% over the post-buyout period. In addition to interest payments, the credit agreement includes a principal repayment schedule that requires the principal amount to be repaid by the end of calendar 1994.

Scott's subordinated debt consists of unsecured 13% notes to mature in 1996, and unsecured 13½% debentures to mature in 1998. The notes are senior to the debentures, but junior to the bank debt. The subordinated debt was originally sold to sixteen financial institutions. These institutions sold the debt to the public in February 1988. Sinking-fund payments are required for both the notes and the debentures. By maturity, two-thirds of the principal amount of the notes and three-fourths of the principal amount of the debentures will have been set aside.

The amount of cash required to service the debt was substantially greater than Scott's prebuyout cash flow. In the first year after the buyout, interest expense was $15 million; in the second year it was $18.5 million. Additional cash is required to pay down bank borrowings and make sinking-fund payments as follows:

1989: $ 7.9 million,
1990: $ 9.0 million,
1991: $ 9.0 million,
1992: $ 9.0 million,
1993: $ 9.0 million,
1994: $28.0 million,
1995: $22.0 million,
1996: $ 5.0 million,
1997: $ 5.0 million.

In 1986, the year before the buyout, Scott's *EBIT* (earnings before interest and taxes) was only $18.1 million. Exhibit 5-3 summarizes Scott's income statement and balance sheet before and after the buyout.

2.2. Debt Covenants

With so much pressure on the organization to generate cash, managers may be tempted to take actions that help service the debt but do damage to the value of the firm. Such actions are detrimental to all the firm's claimholders, including the debtholders. Debtholders are interested in the firm's ability to generate cash over the life of the debt agreement.[2] Debt covenants serve as a contract that restricts managers' ability to use value-reducing methods to generate cash or take other actions that reduce debtholder value.

If a firm defaults, managers are forced to negotiate with lenders to resolve the situation, or if no agreement can be reached to seek protection from creditors under Chapter 11. Resolution of a default or Chapter 11 generally involves replacing debt claims with equity claims, leading to a substantial dilution of the existing equity. A default is costly not only to equityholders, but to managers, since it may force them to surrender control of the company to a bankruptcy court. There is also a risk to managers of losing their jobs. Gilson (1989) finds that 44% of the CEOs of firms in financial distress lose their jobs as a part of the recovery process.

Restrictive covenants can also help control potential conflicts of interest between equityholders and debtholders. In highly leveraged organizations such as Scott the benefit to equityholders of taking actions that reduce debtholder wealth, for example paying themselves a liquidating dividend from the proceeds of a loan or making a "lottery-ticket" investment, can be large.[3]

The covenants in Scott's debt agreements are summarized in Exhibit 5-5. They restrict certain economic and financial activities and require the maintenance of certain levels of accounting-based measures of performance. With the exception of priority, the covenants of the subordinated issues are similar and are therefore discussed collectively. The accounting-based covenants are defined in terms of audited figures. Each year, Scott's financial statements are prepared in compliance with generally accepted accounting principles, and audited by Coopers & Lybrand. This is done to ensure the credibility of the reports to debtholders, to ensure the ability to continue to raise funds in the debt market, and to have an audited track record should the company be taken public again in the future.

Scott's bank credit agreement restricts the firm's investment and production decisions. Managers are allowed discretion in the choice of specific projects, but annual capital expenditures are restricted to specific dollar amounts set forth in a schedule. Scott can dispose only of assets that are worn out or obsolete and have a value of less than $500,000. No changes in the corporate structure, for example mergers or the acquisition of assets, are allowed. Hence, although Scott's credit agreement does not dictate production decisions, the firm is indirectly required to continue in the same economic activity. Cash dividends to stockholders are prohibited, as is the issuance of additional debt other than the debt securities outstanding at closing.

The subordinated debt covenants define restrictions on many of the same items restricted in the credit bank agreement, but the covenants are looser. Dividends, for example, are not prohibited, but a complex set of conditions must be met for dividends to be allowed. Similarly, control changes are not prohibited, but all subordinated debentures are required to be redeemed in the event of a change in control. Redemption also becomes mandatory if Scott's net worth falls below a specified level. Asset sales are not prohibited, but the covenants require that 75% of the proceeds from the sale of a business segment be applied to the repayment of debt in order of priority.

The overall effect of the covenants is to restrict both the source of funds for scheduled interest and principal repayments and the use of funds in excess of this amount. Cash to pay debt obligations must

Exhibit 5-5 Summary of Debt Covenants of Scott Borrowings to Finance the Buyout

	Bank Debt Restriction	Subordinated Debt Restriction
Economic Activities Restricted		
Sale of assets	• Only worn-out or obsolete assets with value less than $500,000 can be sold	• 75% of proceeds must be used to repay debt in order of priority
Capital expenditures	• Restricted to specific $ amount each year debt is outstanding	• None
Changes in corporate structure	• Prohibited	• Mandatory redemption if change in control • No acquisition if in default • Must acquire 100% equity of target • Must be able to issue $1.00 additional debt without covenant violation after acquisition
Financing Activities Restricted		
Issuance of additional debt	• Capitalized leases: max. = $3,000,000 • Unsecured credit: max. = $1,000,000	• Additional senior debt: max. = $15,000,000

	• Commercial paper: max. = amount available under revolving credit agreement	• For employee stock purchases: max. = $4,250,000 • Pre-tax cash flow/interest expense: min. = 1.0 for four quarters preceding issuance
Payment of cash dividends	• Prohibited	• Prohibited if in default • Prohibited if adjusted net worth <$50,000,000

Accounting-based Restrictions

Adjusted net worth[a]	• Specific min. at all times, min. increases from $20.5 million in 1986 to $43.0 million after 1992	• If adjusted net worth falls below $12.0 million, then must redeem $17.0 million notes and $5 million debentures, both at 103
Interest coverage	• Min. 1.0 at end of each fiscal quarter	• None
Current ratio	• Min. 1.0 at end of each fiscal quarter	• None
Adjusting operating profit	• Min. at end of each fiscal quarter, min. increases from $22.0 million in 1987 to $31.0 million after 1990	• None

[a] Adjusted net worth and adjusted operating profit are the GAAP numbers adjusted for accounting effects of the buyout under APB no. 16. In Scot's case the bulk of the adjustment is adding back the effects of an inventory write-down of $24.7 million taken immediately after the buyout.

come primarily from operations or the issuance of common stock. It cannot come from asset liquidation, stock acquisition of another firm with substantial cash balances, or the issuance of additional debt of any kind. Excess funds can be spent only on capital goods in accordance with the schedule, and cannot be spent on acquisitions or dividends to shareholders. Therefore, once the capital expenditure limit has been reached, excess cash must be either held, spent in the course of normal operations, or used to pay down debt ahead of schedule. Assuming the capital expenditure limits are set appropriately, the high leverage in conjunction with the debt covenants serves to reduce the free cash flow problem in a way that is not damaging to the long-run viability of the firm's operations.[4]

Additional bank agreement restrictions require Scott to maintain specific levels of consolidated net worth and the current ratio at all times. A required level of adjusted operating profit and interest coverage must be attained at the end of each fiscal quarter. These restrictions can be viewed as indicators of potential future problems. Even if Scott is currently able to service its debt obligations, the firm can still violate one of these accounting-based constraints. Such violation constitutes a technical default and brings managers and bankers together to renegotiate the terms of the loan.

The constraints imposed by the covenants can be relaxed at the discretion of the lender, though it is likely that the lender will be able to negotiate better terms in exchange. For example, if lenders can be convinced that a particular default was not the result of a financial problem, or that a new project prohibited by the covenants would increase firm value, they have an incentive to waive the default because it increases the value of their claim. In fact, despite the covenant that prohibits mergers and the acquisition of assets, Scott's lenders have recently agreed to allow Scott to acquire Hyponex, a garden and lawn products company, for $111 million.

3. Changes in Incentives and Compensation

3.1. Management Equity Ownership

The final distribution of equity in the post-buyout Scott organization was the product of negotiations between C&D and Scott management. ITT took no part in these negotiations, nor were Scott managers able to negotiate with C&D prior to the close of the sale. ITT sold Scott through a sealed bid auction, in which the winner would own 100% equity in the former subsidiary. Eight firms bid for Scott, and although bidding was open to all types of potential buyers, seven of the eight bidders were buyout firms. The parent was interested primarily in obtaining the highest price for the division.

Scott managers did not participate in the buyout negotiations, and therefore had no opportunity to extract promises or make deals with potential purchasers prior to the sale. Scott managers had approached ITT several years earlier to discuss the possibility of a management buyout at $125 million. At that time ITT had a no-buyout policy. The stated reason for this policy was that a management buyout posed a conflict of interest.

Each potential bidder spent about one day in Marysville and received information on the performance of the unit directly from ITT. Prior to Martin Dubilier's visit, Scott managers felt that they preferred C&D to the other potential buyers because of its reputation for working well with operating managers. The visit did not go well, however, and C&D fell to the bottom of the managers' list. According to Tadd Seitz, president of Scott:

To be candid, they weren't our first choice. It wasn't a question of their acumen, we just didn't think we had the chemistry. But as we went through the controlled bid process, it was C&D that saw the greatest value in Scott.

There is no evidence that ITT deviated from its objective of obtaining the highest value for the division, or that it negotiated in any way on behalf of Scott managers during the buyout process. C&D put in the highest bid. ITT did not consider management's preferences and accepted this bid even though managers were left to work with one of their less favored buyers. If ITT paid little attention to management's preferences in selecting a buyout firm, the distribution of common stock ownership after the sale clearly received no attention from the parent company.

Immediately following the closing, Clayton & Dubilier controlled 79.4% of Scott's common stock. The remaining shares were packaged and sold with the subordinated debt. C&D was under no obligation to allow managers equity participation in Scott, and clearly managers' funds were not required to consummate the deal. On the basis of their experience, C&D partners viewed management equity ownership as a way to provide managers with strong incentives to maximize firm value. Therefore, after Clayton & Dubilier purchased

Scott, it began to negotiate with managers concerning the amount of equity they would be given the opportunity to purchase. C&D did not sell shares to managers reluctantly; in fact, it insisted that managers buy equity and that they do so with their own, not the company's, money. The ownership structure that resulted from the sale can be viewed as the ownership structure that C&D felt gave managers optimal incentives.

Exhibit 5-6 presents the distribution of common stock ownership across investors and managers. There were 24,250,000 shares outstanding, each of which was purchased for $1.00. As the general partner of the private limited partnership that invested $14.9 million in the Scott buyout, Clayton & Dubilier controlled 61.4% of the common stock. The Clayton & Dubilier partners who are responsible for overseeing Scott operations own shares of Scott through their substantial investment in the C&D limited partnership. Subordinated debtholders owned 20.6% of the equity.

The remaining 17% of the equity was distributed among Scott's employees. Eight of the firm's top managers contributed a total of $2,812,500 to the buyout and so hold as many shares, or 12% of the shares outstanding. Tadd Seitz, president of Scott, held the largest number of shares (1,062,500, or 4.4% of the shares outstanding). The seven other managers purchased 250,000 shares apiece (1% each of the shares outstanding). As a group, managers borrowed $2,531,250 to finance the purchase of shares. Though the money was not borrowed from Scott, these loans were guaranteed by the company. The purchase of equity by Scott managers represented a substantial increase in their personal risk. Bob Stern, vice-president of Associate Relations, recalled that his spouse sold her interest in a small catering business at the time of the buyout; they felt that the leverage associated with the purchase of Scott shares was all the risk they could afford.[5]

Top management had some discretion over how common shares were distributed and, although C&D did not encourage it, issued shares to Scott's employee profit-sharing plan and other employees of the firm. Although they allowed managers to distribute the stock more widely, C&D partners felt that the shares would have stronger incentive effects if they were held only by top managers. As Craig Walley, Scott's General Counsel, described it:

We [the managers] used to get together on Saturdays during this period when we were thinking about the buyout to talk about why we wanted to

Exhibit 5-6 Owners of Common Stock of Scott after the Leveraged Buyout, as of 9/30/88[a]

	Number of Shares [000's]	Percentage of Shares Outstanding
Clayton & Dubilier private limited partnership	14,900	61.4%
Subordinated debtholders	5,000	20.6%
Tadd Seitz, President, CEO	1,063	4.4%
Seven other top managers (250,000 shares each)	1,750	7.2%
Scott profit-sharing plan	750	3.1%
Twenty-two other employees	687	2.8%
Joseph P. Flannery, Board Member	100	0.4%
Total	24,250	100.0%

[a] All shares were purchased by owners at $1 per share. Percentages don't foot because of rounding error.

do this. What was the purpose? What did we want to make Scott? One of our aims was to try to keep it independent. Another was to try to spread the ownership widely. One of the things we did was to take 3% of the common stock out of our allocation and put it into the profit-sharing plan. That took some doing and we had some legal complications, but we did it. There are now 56 people in the company who own some stock, and that number is increasing. Compared to most LBOs that is really a lot, and Dubilier has not encouraged us in this.

A group of eleven other managers bought an additional 687,500 shares (2.84% of the total) and the profit-sharing plan bought 750,000 shares (3.09%). These managers were selected for the right to purchase stock not by their rank in the organization, but because they would be making decisions considered critical to the success of the company.

The substantial equity holdings of the top-management team, and their personal liability for the debts incurred to finance their equity stakes, led them to focus on two distinct aspects of running Scott. One was the need to avoid even technical default on the company's debt, for although such default was unlikely to lead to liquidation, it very likely would have led to a reduction in the managers' fractional equity holdings (due to dilution in a debt-for-equity conversion), and thus a significant reduction in the managers' wealth. Thus the equity ownership served to bond managers to honor the debt covenants.

A second important effect of equity ownership was to encourage managers to make decisions that increased the value of the company, whether or not the violation of a debt covenant was imminent. Because managers owned a capital value claim on the firm, they had an incentive to meet debt obligations and avoid default in a long-term value-maximizing way. Short-sighted decision making would reduce the value of the managers' equity, and thus reduce their wealth.

Under this combination of incentives, value-reducing behavior will not occur unless the only way to avoid default is to make suboptimal decisions *and* the cost to managers of default is greater than the loss in equity value from poor decision making. Here, because default is so costly to managers, they may, for example, reduce investment in brand-name advertising, or cut back on research and development or the maintenance of plant and equipment to meet debt obligations. As evidenced in Exhibit 5-3, none of this type of activity was observed at Scott: the company's high leverage, combined with covenants and management equity ownership, provided managers with the incentive to generate the cash required to meet the debt payments without bleeding the company.

3.2. Changes in Incentive Compensation

Among the first things Clayton & Dubilier did after the buyout was to selectively increase salaries and begin to develop a new management compensation plan. A number of managers who were not participants in the ITT bonus plan became participants under the C&D bonus plan. The new plan substantially changed the way managers were evaluated, and increased the fraction of salary that a manager could earn as a bonus. While some of these data are confidential, we are able to describe many of the parameters of C&D's incentive compensation plan and compare it with the ITT compensation system.

3.2.1. Salaries

Almost immediately after the close of the sale the base salaries of some top managers were increased. The president's salary increased by 42%, and the salaries of other top managers increased as well. Henry Timnick, a C&D partner who works closely with Scott, explains the decision to raise salaries:

We increased management salaries because divisional vice-presidents are not compensated at a level comparable to the CEO of a free-standing company with the same characteristics. Divisional VPs don't have all the responsibilities. In addition, the pay raise is a shot-in-the-arm psychologically for the managers. It makes them feel they will be dealt with fairly and encourages them to deal fairly with their people.

In conversations with managers and C&D partners it became clear that C&D set higher standards for management performance than ITT. Increasing the minimum level of acceptable performance forces managers to work harder after the buyout or risk losing their jobs. Indeed, managers did work harder after the buyout; there was general agreement that the management team was putting in longer hours at the office. Several managers used the term "more focused" to describe how their work habits had changed after the buyout. Therefore, an increase in base salary may have been necessary to make managers equally well off before and after the buyout.

The increase in compensation also serves as remuneration for increased risk bearing. As reported earlier, Scott managers borrowed substantially to purchase equity in their company. Requiring managers to hold equity and using strong incentive compensation in addition increases managers' exposure to firm-specific risk. Because they cannot diversify this risk away, managers will require an increase in the level of pay as compensation.

Finally, C&D may have increased salaries because Scott managers are more valuable to C&D than they were to ITT. Consistent with this, managers at Scott felt that ITT was much less dependent on them than Clayton & Dubilier. One Scott manager noted: "When ITT comes in and buys a company, the entire management team could quit and they wouldn't blink." C&D was not, however, completely dependent on incumbent managers to run Scott. Several Clayton & Dubilier partners had extensive experience as operating managers. These partners were available to run Scott if necessary, and had on several occasions stepped in to run C&D buyout firms. They did not, however, have the specific knowledge about the Scott organization that incumbent managers had. If part of the value created by the buyout results from giving managers an incentive to use their specific knowledge about the firm more efficiently, then Scott managers would be preferred by C&D to its own operating partners. We believe that this is the case.

ITT had created a control system that allowed headquarters to manage a vast number of businesses, but did not give managers the flexibility or incentive to use their specialized knowledge of the business to maximize the value of the division. C&D relied much more heavily on managers' firm-specific knowledge, hence the incumbent management team was more valuable to the buyout firm. C&D was willing to pay managers more to reduce the risk of the managers quitting, and depriving Scott and C&D of this valuable knowledge.

3.2.2. Bonus

The bonus plan was completely redesigned after the buyout. The number of managers who participated in the plan increased, and the factors that determined the level of bonus were changed to reflect the objectives of the buyout firm. In addition, both the maximum bonus allowed by the plan and the actual realizations of bonus as a percentage of salary increased by a factor of two to three.

After the buyout, twenty-one managers were covered by the

bonus plan. Only ten were eligible for bonuses under ITT. The maximum payoff under the new plan ranged from 33.5% to 100% of base salary, increasing with the manager's rank in the company. For each manager, the amount of the payoff was based on the achievement of corporate, divisional, and individual performance goals. The weights applied to corporate, divisional, and individual performance in calculating the bonus varied across managers. For division managers, bonus payoff was based 35% on overall company performance, 40% on divisional performance, and 25% on individual performance. Bonuses for corporate staff managers weighed corporate performance at 50%, and personal goals at 50%.

At the beginning of each fiscal year, performance targets (or goals) were set, and differences between actual and targeted performance entered directly into the computation of the bonus plan payoffs. All corporate and divisional performance measures were quantitative measures of cash utilization, and were scaled from 80 to 125, 100 representing the attainment of target. For example, corporate performance was determined by dividing actual earnings before interest and taxes (*EBIT*) by budgeted *EBIT*, and dividing actual average working capital (*AWC*) by budgeted *AWC*, and weighting the *EBIT* ratio at 75% and the *AWC* ratio at 25%. The resulting number, expressed as a percentage attainment of budget, was used as a part of the bonus calculation for all managers in the bonus plan.

The plan was designed so that the payoff was sensitive to changes in performance. This represented a significant change from the ITT bonus plan. As Bob Stern, vice-president of Associate Relations, commented:

I worked in human resources with ITT for a number of years. When I was manager of staffing of ITT Europe, we evaluated the ITT bonus plan. Our conclusion was that the ITT bonus plan was viewed as nothing more than a deferred compensation arrangement: all it did was defer income from one year to the next. Bonuses varied very, very little. If you had an average year, you might get a bonus of $10,000. If you had a terrible year you might get a bonus of $8,000, and if you had a terrific year you might go all the way to $12,500. On a base salary of $70,000, that's not a lot of variation.

Exhibit 5-7 presents actual bonus payouts for the top ten managers as a percentage of salary for two years before and two years after the buyout. Exhibit 5-8 graphically illustrates these data. The new bonus plan gives larger payouts and appears to generate significantly more variation in bonuses than occurred under ITT. Average bonuses

Exhibit 5-7 Bonus Paid to Top Ten Managers at Scott as a Percentage of Year-End Salary, Listed by Rank in the Organization before (1985–1986) and after (1987–1988) the Buyout

	Before the Buyout		After the Buyout	
	1985	1986	1987	1988
	18.3%	26.6%	93.8%	57.7%
	14.0%	23.4%	81.2%	46.8%
	12.8%	18.8%	79.5%	46.0%
	13.3%	20.6%	81.2%	48.5%
	11.2%	19.4%	80.7%	46.8%
	10.5%	17.1%	76.5%	46.0%
	7.1%	10.8%	29.6%	16.6%
	6.1%	22.9%	78.0%	46.7%
	4.6%	6.3%	28.7%	16.8%
	5.1%	6.6%	28.4%	16.4%
Mean	10.3%	17.3%	65.8%	38.8%

Exhibit 5-8 Bonus Payoff Function under the Post-Buyout Incentive Compensation Plan for Three Levels of Management

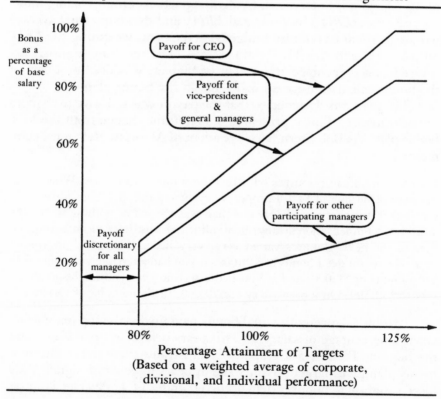

Percentage Attainment of Targets
(Based on a weighted average of corporate, divisional, and individual performance)

as a percentage of salary for the top ten managers increased from 10% and 17% in the two years before the buyout to 66% and 39% in the two years after, a period during which operating income increased by 42%. There also appears to be a bigger cross-sectional variation in bonus payout across managers within a given year. In the two years prior to the buyout, bonus payout ranged from 5% to 27% of base salary, whereas over the two years following the buyout, it ranged from 16% to 94% of base salary.

In addition to measures that evaluated management performance against quantitative targets, each manager had a set of personal objectives that were tied into the bonus plan. These objectives were set by the manager and his or her superior, and their achievement was monitored by the manager's superior. Personal objectives were generally measurable and verifiable. For instance, an objective for a personnel manager was to integrate the benefits package of a newly acquired company with that of Scott within a given period. An objective for the president of the company was to spend a fixed amount of time out of Marysville, talking to retailers and salespeople. At the end of the year, the manager's superior would evaluate whether the manager had achieved these objectives, and would quantify the achievement along the same 80–125 point range. This rating was then combined with the quantitative measures to come up with a total performance measure.

The weighted average of corporate, divisional, and personal target achievements was then used to determine total bonus payoffs. Exhibit 5-9 shows how payoffs were determined. If a manager achieved an 80% weighted average attainment of target goals, the payoff varied from about 30% of salary for the CEO to about 10% for lower-level managers. At 125% attainment, bonuses varied from about 100% to about 30%. Between 80% and 125%, bonus payouts as a percentage of salary varied linearly with target attainment. Below 80%, payments were at the discretion of the president and the board.

The combination of equity ownership by eight top managers, and a much more highly "leveraged" bonus plan for thirteen more, changed the incentives of the managers at Scott substantially. For those managers who held equity, the bonus plan, with its emphasis on *EBIT* and working capital management, served to reinforce the importance of cash generation. Those who did not hold equity, and were thus unaffected by the potential loss in equity value that would attend a violation of the debt covenants, were still induced to make the generation of cash a primary concern.

Exhibit 5-9 Bonuses for Top Ten Managers in the Two Years before and the Two Years after the LBO

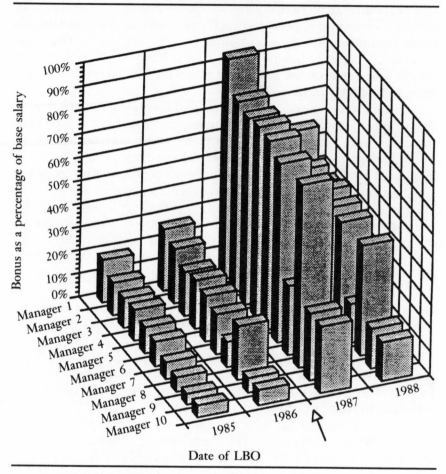

4. The Monitoring of Top Managers

4.1. Purpose and Composition of the Board

The purpose of Scott's board of directors was to monitor, advise, and evaluate the CEO. As Henry Timnick describes it:

The purpose of the board is to make sure the company has a good strategy and to monitor the CEO. The CEO cannot be evaluated by his management staff, so we do not put the CEO's people on the board. Scott's CFO and the corporate secretary attend the meetings, but they have no vote. The outside directors are to be picked by the CEO. We will not put anyone on the board that the CEO doesn't want, but we [C&D] have to approve them. We do not view board members as extensions of ourselves, but they are not to be cronies or local friends of the CEO. We want people with expertise that the CEO doesn't have. The CEO should choose outside directors who are strong in areas in which he is weak.

As the close of the buyout, Scott's board had five members. Only one, Tadd Seitz, was a manager of the firm. Of the remaining four, three were C&D partners; Martin Dubilier was the chairman of the board and voted the stock of the limited partnership, Henry Timnick was the C&D partner who worked most closely with Scott management, and Alberto Cribiore, the third C&D partner, was a financing specialist. The outside director was Joe Flannery, the CEO of Uniroyal, which had been taken private by Clayton & Dubilier in 1985. Later, Flannery left Uniroyal and became a C&D partner. He stayed on the Scott board, becoming an inside, rather than outside, director.

Over the next few years three new directors were added: one was an academic, one was a consumer products expert, and one, Don Sherman, was the president of Hyponex, the company acquired by Scott. The academic, Jim Beard, was one of the country's leading turf researchers. Henry Timnick described the process of putting him on the board.

Our objective was to find the best turf specialist and researcher in the country. We wanted someone to keep us up with the latest developments and to scrutinize the technical aspects of our product line. We found Jim Beard at Texas A&M. It took Jim a while to be enthusiastic about being on the board, and it took Tadd a while to figure out how to get the most out of Jim. After Jim was appointed to the board, we encouraged Tadd to have Jim out on a consulting basis for a couple of days. Now Tadd is making good use of Jim.

Seitz and Timnick were considering an individual with extensive experience in consumer products businesses to be the second outside director. They chose Jack Chamberlain, who had previously run GE's Consumer Electronics Division, Lenox China, and Avon Products. All board members were stockholders; upon joining the board they were given the opportunity to purchase 50,000 shares at adjusted book value. All the directors chose to own stock.

This board structure was typical for a C&D buyout. Martin Dubilier explains:

We have tried a number of board compositions and we found this to be the most effective. If you have too many insiders the board becomes an operating committee. Outsiders fortify the growth opportunities of the firm.

The board of directors met quarterly. A subset of the board, the executive committee, met monthly. The executive committee was made up of Martin Dubilier, Tadd Seitz, and Henry Timnick. In their meetings they determined policy, discussed personnel matters, and tested Seitz's thinking on major issues facing the firm. The board meetings were more formal, usually consisting of presentations by members of the management team other than Seitz.

4.2. The Operating Partner

In each of C&D's buyouts a partner with extensive operating experience serves as the liaison between the firm's managers and C&D. The operating partner functions as an adviser and consultant to the CEO, not a decision maker. Henry Timnick was Scott's liaison partner. He had been CEO of a division of Mead that was purchased through a leveraged buyout and had since worked with several of C&D's other buyout firms. Timnick spent several weeks in Marysville after the buyout closed. Following that he was in touch with Seitz daily by telephone and continued to visit regularly.

Timnick would advise Seitz, but felt it was important that Seitz make the decisions. When he and Seitz disagreed, Timnick told him: "If you don't believe me, go hire a consultant, then make your own decision." Initially, Seitz continued to check with Timnick, looking for an authorization for his decisions. Henry Timnick explains:

Tadd kept asking me, "Can I do this? Can I do that?" I told him, "You can do whatever you want so long as it is consistent with Scott's overall strategy."

This consultative approach to working with Scott managers was quite different from ITT's approach. Martin Dubilier explains:

ITT challenges managers not to rock the boat, to make budget. We challenge managers to improve the business. Every company takes on the personality of its CEO. Our main contribution is to improve his performance. All the rest is secondary.

Scott managers confirmed Dubilier's assessment. Meetings between ITT managers and Scott managers were large and quite formal, with as many as forty members of ITT's staff present. Scott managers found the meetings antagonistic, with the ITT people working to find faults and problems with the operating unit's reported performance. By meeting the formal goals set by ITT, Scott could largely avoid interference from headquarters. Avoiding such interference was an important objective. As Paul Yeager, CFO, describes it:

Geneen [then CEO of ITT] said in his book that the units would ask for help from headquarters; that the units came to look at headquarters staff as outside consultants who could be relied upon to help when needed. I have worked in many ITT units, and if he really thought that, then he was misled. If a division vice-president went to headquarters for help, in effect he was saying, "I can't handle it." He wouldn't be a vice-president for very long.

5. Organizational Changes and Changes in Decision Making

The organizational changes and changes in decision making that took place at Scott after the buyout fall broadly into two categories: improved working capital management and a new approach to product markets. These changes were not forced on managers by C&D. The buyout firm made some suggestions, but the specific plans and their implementation were the responsibility of Scott managers. Few of the changes in managerial actions represent keenly innovative or fundamentally new insights into management problems. As one observer noted: "It ain't rocket science." These changes, however, led to dramatic improvements in Scott's operating performance.

Management's ability did not change after the buyout, nor did the market or the assets they were managing. The only changes were in the incentive structure of the firm, as described in sections 2 through 4, and in the management control systems. According to Scott managers, the biggest difference between working at Scott before and after the buyout was an increase in the extent to which they could make and implement decisions without approval from superiors. ITT maintained control over its divisions through an inflexible formal planning and reporting structure. Changing a plan required approval at a number of levels from ITT headquarters, and a request for a change was likely to be denied. In addition, because ITT was shedding its consumer businesses, Scott managers found their requests for capital funds were routinely denied. After the buyout, Seitz could pick up the phone and propose changes in the operating plan to Timnick. These changes were likely to be accepted. This, of course, improved the company's ability to respond quickly to changes in the marketplace.

5.1. The Working Capital Task Force

Shortly after the buyout, a task force was established to coordinate the management of working capital throughout the company. The members of the task force were drawn from every functional area. The group was charged with reducing working capital requirements by 42%, or $25 million, in two years. They exceeded this goal, reducing average working capital by $37 million. The task force helped Scott managers learn to manage cash balances, production, inventories, receivables, payables, and employment levels more effectively.

5.1.1. Cash Management

Before the buyout, Scott's managers never had to manage cash balances. John Wall, assistant treasurer and chairman of the working capital task force, describes how cash was controlled under ITT:

Under the ITT system, we needed virtually no cash management. The ITT lock box system swept our lock boxes into Citibank of New York. Our disbursement bank would contact ITT's bank and say we need $2 million today and it automatically went into our disbursement account.

To control cash flow in its numerous businesses, ITT established a cash control system that separated the collection of cash from cash disbursements. Receipts went into one account and were collected regularly by ITT's bank; once deposited, these funds were not available to divisional managers. Cash to fund operations came from a different source, through a different bank account. This system allowed ITT to centrally manage cash and control divisional spending.

When Scott was a division of ITT, cash coming into Scott bore little relation to the cash Scott was allowed to spend. In contrast, after the LBO, all of Scott's cash was available to managers to spend. They needed to establish a system to control cash so that operations were properly funded, and to meet debt service requirements. Wall describes the process:

In the first six months after the LBO we had to bring in a state-of-the-art cash management system for a business of this size. We shopped a lot of treasury management systems and had almost given up on finding a system that would simply let us manage our cash. We didn't need a system that would keep track of our investment portfolios because we had $200 million borrowed. Finally, we found a product we could use. Under the LBO cash forecasting has become critical. I mean cash forecasting in the intermediate and long range. I don't mean forecasting what is going to hit the banks in the next two or three days. We could always do that, but now we track our cash flows on a weekly basis and we do modeling on balance sheets, which allows us to do cash forecasting a year out.

5.1.2. Production and Inventories

Between 1986 and 1988, the efforts of the task force increased the frequency with which Scott turned over its inventory from 2.08 to 3.20 times per year—an increase of 54%. During this period both sales and the number of products produced increased. Because Scott's business is highly seasonal, inventory control was always a management problem. Large inventories were required to meet the spring rush of orders; however, financing inventories was a cash drain. Scott's production strategy under ITT exacerbated the inventory problem. Before the buyout, Scott produced each product once a year. Slow-moving products were produced during the slow season, so that long runs of fast-moving products could be produced during the busy season. Before the spring buying began, almost an entire year's worth of sales were in inventory.

The old production strategy took advantage of the cost savings of long production runs, but under ITT, managers did not consider the trade-off between these cost savings and the opportunity cost of funds tied up in inventory. The cash requirements of servicing a large debt burden, the working capital-based restrictions in the debt agreements, and the inclusion of working capital objectives in the compensation system gave managers a strong incentive to consider this opportunity cost. As Wall explained it:

What the plant managers had to do was to figure out how they could move the production of the slow-moving items six months forward. That way the products we used to make in May or early June would be made in November or December. Now [instead of producing long runs of a few products] production managers have to deal with setups and changeovers during the high-production period. It requires a lot more of their attention.

Managing inventories more effectively required that products be produced close to the time of shipment. Because more setups and changeovers were necessary, the production manager's job became more complicated. Instead of producing a year's supply of one product, inventorying it, then producing another product, managers had to produce smaller amounts of a variety of products repeatedly throughout the year.

Inventories were also reduced by changing purchasing practices and inventory management. Raw material suppliers agreed to deliver smaller quantities more often, reducing the levels of raw materials and finished goods inventories. Through close tracking, Scott managed to reduce inventory levels without increasing the frequency of stock-outs of raw materials or finished goods.

5.1.3. Receivables and Payables

Receivables were an important competitive factor, and retailers expected generous payment terms from Scott. After the buyout, however, the timing of rebate and selling programs was carefully planned, allowing Scott to conserve working capital. Scott also negotiated with suppliers to obtain more favorable terms on prices, payment schedules, and delivery. Lorel Au, manager of Contract Operations, stated:

Within two months of the LBO, the director of manufacturing and I went out to every one of our contract suppliers and went through what a leveraged buyout is, and what that means. We explained how we were going to have to manage our business. We explained our new goals and objectives. We talked about things like just-in-time inventory, talked terms, talked about scheduling. Some suppliers were more ready to work with us than others. Some said, "Okay, what can we do to help?" In some cases, a vendor said, "I can't help you on price, I can't help you on terms, I can't help you on scheduling." We said: "Fine. Good-bye." We were very serious about it. In some cases we didn't have options, but usually we did.

The company succeeded in getting suppliers to agree to extended terms of payment, and was able to negotiate some substantial price cuts from major suppliers in return for giving the supplier a larger fraction of Scott's business.

Scott managers felt that the buyout put them in a stronger bargaining position vis-à-vis their suppliers. Wall states:

One reason we were able to convince our suppliers to give us concessions is that we no longer had the cornucopia of ITT behind us. We no longer had unlimited cash.

The suppliers understood that if they did not capitulate on terms, Scott would have to take its business elsewhere or face default.[6]

5.1.4. Employment

Scott had a tradition of being very paternalistic toward its employees and was a major employer and corporate citizen in the town of Marysville. Some have argued that an important source of cash and increasing equity value in buyouts is the severing of such relationships.[7] There is no evidence of this at Scott. Scott's traditional employee relations policies were maintained, and neither wages nor benefits were cut after the buyout. Scott continues to maintain a large park with swimming pool, tennis courts, playground, and other recreational facilities for the enjoyment of employees and their families. The company also continues to make its auditorium, the largest in Marysville, available for community use at no charge.

The company did begin a program of hiring part-time employees during the busy season, rather than bringing on full-time employees. This allowed Scott to maintain a core of full-time, year-round employees who enjoyed the full-benefits plan of the company, while still having enough people to staff the factory during busy season. Largely through attrition, average annual full-time employment has dropped by about 9% over the first two years after the buyout.

5.2. Approaches to the Product Markets

Scott is the major brand name in the do-it-yourself lawn care market, and has a reputation for high-quality products. Ed Wandtke, a lawn industry analyst and partner of All Green Management Consultants Inc., states:

O. M. Scott is ultra high price, ultra high quality. They absolutely are the market leader. They have been for some time. No one else has the retail market recognition. Through its promotions, Scott has gotten its name so entrenched that the name and everything associated with it—quality, consistency, reliability—supersede the expensive price of the product.

In 1987, Scott had a 34% share of the $350 million do-it-yourself market. Industry experts report, however, that the market had been undergoing major changes since the early 1980s. Indeed, Scott's revenue fell by 23% between 1981 (the historical high at that time) and 1985. The buyout allowed Scott managers the flexibility to adapt to the changing marketplace, ensuring a future for the company.

The do-it-yourself market was shrinking because an increasing number of consumers were contracting with firms to have their lawns chemically treated. Seitz had proposed that Scott enter this segment of the professional lawn care market for years, but ITT continually vetoed this initiative. Among the first actions taken after the buyout was the creation of a group within the professional division whose focus was to sell to the commercial turf maintenance market. Within two years, the segment comprised 10% of the sales of the professional division, and was growing at a rate of almost 40% per year.

Scott's position in the do-it-yourself market was challenged by the growth of private label brands that were sold at lower prices and a shift in volume away from Scott's traditional retailers—hardware and specialty stores—to mass merchandisers. Under ITT, Scott managers did not try to develop new channels of distribution. Timnick described it as too "risky" an experiment for ITT. The company's post-buyout acquisition of Hyponex gave Scott access to the private-label market. Wandtke argues:

With Hyponex, Scott will capture a greater percentage of the home consumer market. Hyponex is a much lower priced product line. It gives them [Scott] access to private labeling, where they can produce product under another label for a lesser price. . . . This will improve their hold on the retail market.

The acquisition of Hyponex represented a major response to the changes taking place in Scott's product markets. Hyponex was a company virtually the same size as Scott, with $125 million in sales and 700 employees, yet the acquisition was financed completely with bank debt. The successful renegotiation of virtually all of Scott's existing debt agreements was required to consummate the transaction. Because the new debt was senior to the existing notes and debentures, a consent payment of $887,500 was required to persuade bondholders to waive restrictive covenants. That such an expansionary acquisition was possible only two and one-half years after the buyout demonstrates the flexibility of the LBO as an organizational form. It also demonstrates the ability of the contracting parties to respond to positive NPV projects that might appear to be blocked by the post-LBO company's capital structure.

6. Conclusions

Our findings confirm the results of large-sample studies—that the pressure of servicing a heavy debt load and management equity ownership lead to improved performance. Equally important in the Scott organization, however, and undocumented in large-sample studies, are the debt covenants that place restrictions on how the cash required for debt payments can be generated, the adoption of a strong incentive compensation plan, a reorganization and decentralization of decision making, and the relationship between Scott managers, the Clayton & Dubilier partners, and the board of directors.

We attribute the improvements in operating performance after Scott's leveraged buyout to changes in the incentive, monitoring, and governance structure of the firm. Managers were given strong incentives to generate cash and were allowed more decision-making authority, but checks were established to guard against behavior that would be damaging to firm value. In the Scott organization, high leverage was effective in forcing managers to generate cash flow in a productive way largely because debt covenants and equity ownership countered short-run opportunistic behavior. Value was created by decentralizing decision making largely because managers were closely monitored and supported by an expert board of directors who were also equityholders.

We view this study as a first step toward the development of a theory of how organizations respond to radical changes in their financial structure and how these changes affect managerial behavior. Our results are applicable to organizations with other combinations of high leverage, management equity ownership, and active boards of directors, such as venture-backed high-technology firms or public companies that undertake leveraged recapitalizations. For example, if counterbalancing incentives are important, we should observe restrictive covenants and management equity ownership in leveraged recapitalizations. If it is important to couple a strong bonus plan with equity ownership to motivate managers, then why do we not observe such bonus plans in venture-backed startup companies? Further research can help us determine the relative importance of these factors and their interactions in determining optimal organizational forms.

NOTES

1. Scott's increase in capital expenditures appears atypical, given Kaplan's result that, on average, capital expenditures fall by 20% after a leveraged buyout.

2. This assumes that the value of the debtholder's claim on the organization as a going concern is generally higher than the value of the claim in liquidation. Jensen (1989) argues that in a highly leveraged firm this is likely to be true and that creditors will therefore tend to work out default situations rather than force Chapter 11 or liquidation.

3. The role of debt covenants in controlling the conflict of interest between debtholders

and equityholders is developed in Smith and Warner (1979). They classify the actions that equityholders can take to benefit themselves at the expense of debtholders as (1) asset substitution, (2) claim dilution, (3) underinvestment, and (4) dividend payout.

4. Jensen (1986) defines free cash as cash generated by the firm in excess of what is required to fund all positive NPV projects. The most valuable use of these funds is to pay them out to investors.

5. Scott refers to all its employees as "associates." Stern's position, therefore, is equivalent to vice-president of human resources or personnel.

6. Schelling (1960) supports the idea that increased bargaining power can occur as the result of a precarious financial situation. He states: "The power to constrain an adversary may depend on the power to bind oneself. . . . In bargaining, weakness is often strength, freedom may be freedom to capitulate, and to burn bridges behind one may suffice to undo an opponent. . . . [M]ore financial resources, more physical strength, more military potency, or more ability to withstand losses . . . are by no means universal advantages in bargaining situations! They often have a contrary value."

7. Shleifer and Summers (1988).

REFERENCES

DeAngelo, H., L. DeAngelo, and E. Rice. "Going Private: Minority Freezeouts and Stockholder Wealth." *Journal of Law and Economics*, vol. XXVII (1984), pp. 367–401.

DeAngelo, L. E. "Accounting Numbers as Market Valuation Substitutes: A Study of Management Buyouts of Public Stockholders." *Accounting Review*, vol. LXI (1986), pp. 400–420.

Gilson, S. "Management-Borne Bankruptcy Costs: Evidence on Executive Turnover during Corporate Financial Distress." Working paper, University of Texas, Austin, 1989.

Jensen, M. C. "Agency Costs of Free Cash Flow, Corporate Finance, and Takeovers." *American Economic Review*, vol. 76 (1986), pp. 323–329.

———. "Active Investors, LBO's, and the Privatization of Bankruptcy." *Journal of Applied Corporate Finance*, vol. 2 (1989), pp. 35–44.

Jensen, M. C., S. Kaplan, and L. Stiglin. "Effects of LBO's on Tax Revenues of the U.S. Treasury." *Tax Notes*, vol. 42, no. 6 (1989), pp. 727–733.

Jensen, M. C., and K. Murphy. "Performance Pay and Top Management Incentives." *Journal of Political Economy*, vol. 98 (1989), pp. 225–264.

Kaplan, S. "Management Buyouts: Efficiency Gains or Value Transfers?" Working paper, Graduate School of Business, University of Chicago, 1988a.

———. "Sources of Value in Management Buyouts." Thesis, Graduate School of Business Administration, Harvard University, 1988b.

———. "Management Buyouts: Evidence on Taxes as a Source of Value." *Journal of Finance*, vol. 44 (1989a), pp. 611–632.

———. "Management Buyouts: Evidence on Post-Buyout Operating Changes." Working paper, Graduate School of Business, University of Chicago, 1989b.

Kirkland, L. Testimony before the House Ways and Means Committee on leveraged buyouts (1989): 89–3.

Lehn, K., and A. Poulsen. "Leveraged Buyouts: Wealth Created or Wealth Redistributed?" In M. Wiedenbaum and K. Chilton, eds., *Public Policy Toward Corporate Mergers*. New Brunswick, NJ: Transaction Books, 1988, pp. 46–62.

Lichtenberg, F. R., and D. Siegel. "The Effect of Takeovers on the Employment and Wages of Central-Office and Other Personnel." Paper, Graduate School of Business, Columbia University and National Bureau of Economic Research, New York, 1989.

Marais, L., K. Schipper, and A. Smith. "Wealth Effects of Going Private for Senior Securities." *Journal of Financial Economics*, vol. 23 (1988), pp. 155–191.

Muscarella, C., and M. Vetsuypens. "Efficiency and Organizational Structure: A Study of Reverse LBO's." Working paper, Graduate School of Business, Southern Methodist University, Dallas, 1988.

Schelling T. *The Strategy of Conflict*. Cambridge, MA: Harvard University Press, 1960.

Schipper, K., and A. Smith. "Corporate Income Tax Effects of Management Buyouts." Working paper, Graduate School of Business, University of Chicago, 1988.

Shleifer, A., and L. Summers. "Breach of Trust in Hostile Takeovers." In A. Auerbach, ed. *Corporate Takeovers: Causes and Consequences*. Chicago: University of Chicago Press, 1988, pp. 33–56.

Smith, A. "Corporate Ownership Structure and Performance: The Case of Management Buyouts." Working paper, Graduate School of Business, University of Chicago, 1989.

Smith, C. W., and J. B. Warner. "On Financial Contracting: An Analysis of Bond Covenants." *Journal of Financial Economics*, vol. 7 (1979), pp. 117–161.

CHAPTER 6

Incentive Pay and Organizational Culture

Regina F. Bento and Lourdes D. Ferreira

1. Introduction

THE widespread adoption of compensation systems that link pay to performance has generated substantial attention from academics in the past two decades. Theories using either economic or psychological frameworks made some predictions about the characteristics of optimal incentive contracts, and the effects of implementing them on motivation and performance. The studies inspired by those theories have reached sometimes conflicting results that have puzzled academics and practitioners alike. In practice, conformity with theoretical prescriptions does not guarantee successful implementation, and deviance from them does not preclude success.

Here we introduce one other variable, the organizational culture, to explore how the fit (or lack thereof) between a plan's assumptions and the culture can help explain the apparently inconsistent choices organizations make about the design of incentive contracts, as well as what happens after implementation. We conducted a field study with

Support from the Division of Research of the Harvard Business School, the Accounting Circle of the University of Southern California, and the University of California at Riverside is gratefully acknowledged.

157

a university organization that was thoroughly reviewing the results of a pay-for-performance plan, implemented in 1987, for professional (nonacademic) managers. We interviewed people involved with the plan at different stages of its design and troubled implementation. In-depth interviews were held with representatives of the groups who had a stake in the plan, including plan designers, administrators, and participants. We also attended some of the meetings that the organization sponsored to evaluate the stakeholders' perceptions about the plan's effectiveness.[1]

We organize this chapter in this way: In section 2, we draw from the literature on organizational culture to construct a taxonomy of basic assumptions that may inspire the design of compensation plans and facilitate or constrain their implementation. The field study and the organization's experience with the new incentive pay plan are described in sections 3 and 4, respectively. We interpret the results in section 5 and, in the last section, discuss the theoretical and practical implications of our findings.

2. Compensation Plans and Organizational Culture

A major issue in designing a compensation plan is the trade-off between absorption of risk by the organization and providing performance-contingent incentives (Stiglitz, 1987). Thus we can represent possible compensation plans as the rectangle in Exhibit 6-1. The area above the diagonal line defines the amount of risk absorption and the area under the line refers to the corresponding amount of incentive provided; vertical lines represent how specific compensation plans imply different relative proportions of risk absorption and incentive provision (for example, Plans A, B, and C depict, respectively, a risk-free fixed-wage system, a base-building merit pay system, and a strongly performance-sensitive bonus system).

The choice of where the vertical line should cross the diagonal can be made or justified with economic or psychological theories. If, however, we probe deeper why, in a given organization, one theory is chosen over another, or why an assumption is interpreted as justified or not, we find that the choice of a specific combination of risk absorption and incentive provision embodies the beliefs and values held by the plan's designer(s). These, in turn, may be more or less aligned with the "basic assumptions and beliefs that are shared by the

Exhibit 6-1 Trade-off Between Risk Absorption and Incentive Provision in Compensation Plan Design

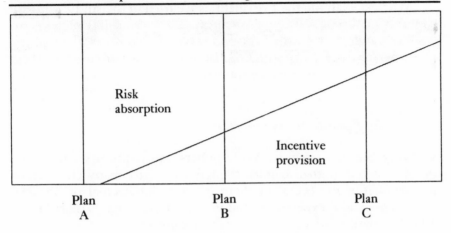

members of the organization, that operate unconsciously, and that define in a basic 'taken-for-granted' fashion an organization's view of itself and its environment" (Schein, 1985, p. 6)—in other words, the organizational culture.

It seems almost too obvious to propose that plan designers' basic assumptions and beliefs will influence design, or that those held by participants in a plan will influence implementation. Extensive search of the literature on both compensation and organizational culture, however, has revealed no study specifically considering how basic shared assumptions and beliefs (that is, culture) affect plan design and implementation.

Thus, when we found that economic and psychological theories could not provide a comprehensive understanding of our data, and that important cultural phenomena were at play, we had to construct our own analytical tools. We started by selecting from available taxonomies (Hofstede, 1984; Schein, 1985; Martin et al., 1983) the basic cultural assumptions that would be relevant for compensation plans. We then organized these assumptions into the five dualities they express.

According to Martin et al. (1983, p. 447), "a duality is an issue that cannot easily be resolved, because contradictory aspects of the issue are inevitably present and are simultaneously desirable and undesirable." When confronted with dualities, individuals and collectivities cope with the tension in the possibility of two opposing "truths" by forming basic assumptions that one side of the duality is "more true" than the other.

We next examine the five dualities we used in the study: equality versus inequality, certainty versus uncertainty, controllability versus uncontrollability, individualism versus collectivism, and materialistic versus personalistic foregrounding. In section 5, we discuss how these dualities were used to analyze the data.

A. *Equality versus Inequality*

A duality that has occupied philosophers and political scientists for centuries is that human beings, though they share many characteristics, still differ in several of them (such as intellectual or physical ability, education, experience, and interests). But what is more "true" of human nature: its equality or its inequality?

In time, members of an organization arrive at a deeply believed and shared answer to the question of equality versus inequality (Martin et al., 1983), which embodies core assumptions about human relationships (Schein, 1985). In the daily struggle to survive in the external environment and to solve problems of internal integration (Schein, 1985), they may take for granted the belief that people are intrinsically similar in their potential abilities or skills, and that differences are reducible by training and experience. An egalitarian culture thus forms and several ancillary beliefs, springing from the basic assumption of equality, may be translated in aspects of the organizational structure and process: the assumption that all members of the organization are worthy encourages a flat hierarchy, with small power distances, decentralized decision making, and small differentials in compensation and status among hierarchic levels (Hofstede, 1984).

On the other hand, members of a different organization may find that the opposite end of the duality more appropriately represents their reality. They construct a shared belief system, assuming that people vary widely in ability and skill; measuring and comparing these differences therefore become important in allocating positions, responsibilities, and rewards in the organization. This basic belief in inequality is likely to permeate other aspects of the organization—the scatter in talent and performance legitimizes large power distances, leading to tall, centralized hierarchies, with sharp differentials in compensation and status (Hofstede, 1984).

Beliefs in equality and inequality held by designers of compensa-

Exhibit 6-2 Impact of First Duality on Plan Design and
Implementation, First Duality: Equality versus Inequality

Issue	Equality Assumption	Inequality Assumption
Plan decision making	widespread participation by various stake-holders	centralized decisions by "elite" group
Link between pay and hierarchic structures	loosely related	closely related
Desired range of diversity in pay	small differentials	large differentials
Likelihood of differences in performance	homogeneous individual potentials leading to skewed distribution of outcomes	normal distribution of potential leading to normal distribution of outcomes
Performance measure	absolute	relative
Setting goals and monitoring performance	facilitated by small power distances	hindered by large power distances
Control focus	inputs	outputs

tion plans may affect various aspects of a plan's design and implementation, influencing not only where the organization will position itself (as in the diagram in Exhibit 6-1) but also the rules for decision and the criteria for providing incentives. This duality affects assumptions about the desired range of diversity in pay, the likelihood of differences in performance, how closely the pay structure should relate to hierarchic levels (Kanter, 1987), as well as other issues addressed in Exhibit 6-2.

B. Certainty versus Uncertainty

Although the first duality refers to the variability among human beings, a second duality has to do with optimal variability in the environment in which people operate. On the one hand, we can argue that the very reason for the existence of organizations, structures, habits, rules, and laws is to reduce variability to the levels of certainty required for rational human activity. On the other hand, we can argue that although certainty nurtures the human spirit, uncertainty is the

Exhibit 6-3 Impact of Second Duality on Plan Design and Implementation, Second Duality: Certainty versus Uncertainty

Issue	Certainty Assumption	Uncertainty Assumption
Primary aim in plan design	identifying and spelling out behaviors that will lead to desired outcomes	linking highly valued rewards to desired outcomes and letting participants figure out instrumental behavior
Security	plan nurtures feelings of security about position, rewards, progress	plan discourages feelings of entitlement to present position and reward levels
Performance measure	tactical, operational	strategic
Control focus	inputs	outputs

hunger that keeps it moving. Human beings are driven by the unknown, the unchartered that is yet possible—if their environment becomes too predictable, their curiosity, creativity, and progress are stifled.

As an organization copes, over the years, with external and internal challenges, it learns that one side of this duality is more relevant for its ability to survive and grow, and builds a culture which seeks and values certainty, or which assumes and thrives on uncertainty. The former has a "high-certainty culture" (which Hofstede, 1984, calls a "high uncertainty avoidance" culture), where varied elements in the organizational structure and process are used to create a working environment with certainty, predictability, and order: highly structured activities, many written rules, standardization and specialization, attention to detail, emphasis on stability (low turnover, clear career paths). The latter has a "high uncertainty culture" (Hofstede calls it a "low uncertainty avoidance" culture), with less structuring of activities, few written rules, plurimorphism and generalism, emphasis on creativity and flexibility, and labor turnover seen as beneficial.

The certainty versus uncertainty duality reflects assumptions about reality and truth (Schein, 1985) and is the source of basic value judgments that underlie plans for performance evaluation and compensation, affecting elements of the diagram in Exhibit 6-1. Exhibit 6-3 suggests some of these influences and their direction.

C. Controllability versus Uncontrollability

Basic assumptions about variability in the environment relate not just to its being seen as desirable or undesirable. They also address another important duality: Is the variability in the environment mainly caused by factors that are controllable by individuals and organizations, or by factors mostly beyond their control?

This duality is crucial in the individual's and the organization's way of attributing causality, interpreting events, and allocating responsibility, blame, and reward. It relates to the psychological construct of internal and external locus of control (Rotter, 1966) and, for organizations, it inspires assumptions about the relationship between humanity and nature, the organization and its environment (Schein, 1985; Martin et al., 1983).

In a culture that assumes individuals and organizations are able to control their own destiny, the emphasis is on formulating aggressive strategies, a "can-do" attitude, a tendency to see human resources as the key variable in creating or changing environment. By contrast, if individuals and organizations are seen as basically unable to control what happens to them, the emphasis is on adaptive strategies, on flexibility, on minimizing an event's negative consequences and maximizing its positive consequences. The key variable in survival and growth then becomes the ability to predict and monitor trends in the environment—this organization is not oriented toward action but toward information.

The management control literature has also struggled with the implications of this duality for performance evaluation and compensation (see review of literature and evidence presented in Merchant, 1987 and 1989). In designing plans for performance evaluation and compensation, controllability beliefs are crucial in providing a rationale for decisions on issues such as those involved in the diagram in Exhibit 6-1. Exhibit 6-4 summarizes some of these issues and how they are affected by different positions in the controllability duality, including how assumptions stemming from it can influence the choice of formula-driven versus subjective performance measures and rewards (Merchant, 1989).

D. Individualism versus Collectivism

A fourth basic duality is about the relevant unit of analysis in humanity's interaction with its environment: Is it the individual or the collec-

Exhibit 6-4   Impact of Third Duality on Plan Design and Implementation, Third Duality: Controllability versus Uncontrollability

Issue	Controllability Assumption	Uncontrollability Assumption
Expected effect of motivation on results	large (people have control over results and, if motivated, can exercise it in the "right" direction)	limited (desire to achieve results is not sufficient condition for success)
Causes of success or failure	controllable, internal (individual, group, or organization)	limited or no control, external (environment)
Performance measure	absolute	relative (assuming homogeneous effect of exogenous factors)
Control focus	inputs or outputs	planned inputs plus adaptive behaviors, or outputs adjusted for uncontrollables

tivity? How an organizational culture positions itself on this duality will influence its beliefs about motivation, the relationship between individual and organization, and the ethical choice when individual and collective goals conflict.

In highly individualistic cultures (Hofstede, 1984), people are perceived as driven by self-interest. These cultures assume that a person's involvement with an organization is primarily calculative (Etzioni, 1975), that policies and practices should allow for individual initiative, that organization members should defend their own interests, and that their best source of security is their market value.

In collectivist cultures (Hofstede, 1984), people are seen as deriving important benefits from identifying with a group or organization whose interests they should be ready to put ahead of their own and with which they are morally involved; policies and practices stress loyalty and a sense of duty; employees expect the organization to look after their interests and derive security from their specialized knowledge about the circumstances of their organization and a complex web of favors given and received.

Individualistic or collectivist assumptions in designing and imple-

Exhibit 6-5 Impact of Second Duality on Plan Design and Implementation, Second Duality: Individualism versus Collectivism

Issue	Individualistic Assumption	Collectivist Assumption
Organization's responsibility toward employees	limited (survival of the fittest)	moral obligation to shield employees from risk
Source of correction for possible unfairness in evaluation or compensation	market mechanisms	multidimensional criteria, recognition of services rendered to collectivity
Type of employee the plan seeks to attract and retain	people who are risk-taking, mobile, cosmopolitan, enterprising	people who expect personal security and stability even when making risky decisions on behalf of the organization
Basis for assigning, attributing, and rewarding attainment of goals	individual	group

menting evaluation and compensation plans permeate ethical implications, as in the diagram in Exhibit 6-1. They directly influence several issues in performance evaluation and compensation, as addressed in Exhibit 6-5, including the adequacy of using individual or group-based measures and rewards (Mohrman, Jr., Resnick-West, and Lawler, 1989).

E. Materialistic versus Personalistic Foregrounding

This final duality is inspired by the phenomenon referred to in gestalt psychology as "foregrounding and backgrounding": when confronted with a picture composed of several elements, we tend to perceive one or more of them as the foreground and the remaining ones as the background. This perceptual organization of the world, albeit unconscious, involves complex interpretation, whereby relationships among the elements are summarily established and judgments of relative importance are implicitly formulated.

By analogy, when we look at organized human activity, we may see people and their relationships as the foreground, and material contexts, actions, and outcomes as the background; or we may perceive material reality as foreground and people as the background. That both the personalistic and materialistic elements of reality are potential candidates for foregrounding creates a basic duality for the observer; resolving this duality, which ultimately leads to the foregrounding of personalistic or materialistic elements, implies forming some basic assumptions fundamentally important for life in work organizations.[2]

For example, in organizational cultures characterized by materialistic foregrounding, the emphasis is on task, outcomes, growth, efficiency, speed, winning; job stress is perceived as part of the game, conflict is acceptable, and work demands take precedence over personal life and relationships; when people hear an expression like "workforce reduction," the issues that come to mind are cost reduction, becoming "lean and mean."

In a culture that stresses personalistic foregrounding, on the other hand, the focus is on process, on people and relationships, on "being and becoming" rather than on "doing and achieving"; the preoccupation is with the quality of work life and with avoiding negative spillover of work demands into private life and relationships; the expression "workforce reduction" raises apprehension about real people losing their jobs and the effect of this event on their lives.

The materialistic versus personalistic duality directly influences which plan for compensation designers choose to signal to plan participants and what they try to get participants to focus on. For example, this duality affects the choice between a competitive or a cooperative emphasis in plan design (Nalbantian, 1987), as well as other issues presented in Exhibit 6-6.

3. The Field Study

The research method and site selection for our study were driven by theory. Our initial objective was to examine an incentive compensation plan from a dual perspective, drawing from economic and psychological theories, to capitalize on our different backgrounds. Both theories suggested the need for analyzing the plan from the multiple standpoints of different interest groups (plan designers, administrators, participants). Economic theories explicitly assume that

Exhibit 6-6   Impact of Fifth Duality on Plan Design and Implementation, Fifth Duality: Materialistic versus Personalistic Foregrounding

Issue	Materialistic Assumption	Personalistic Assumption
Source of motivation	monetary incentives, needs for accomplishment	interpersonal relationships, flexible mix of monetary and nonmonetary rewards
Instrumental behaviors	competition, striving	cooperation, mentoring
Mechanisms for encouraging instrumental behaviors	relative measures of performance, forced spreads in evaluation, zero-sum tournament models for allocating rewards	absolute measures of performance, group-based evaluations and rewards, "face-saving" procedures to preserve harmonious relationships
Measure of personal worth	contribution to attaining specified outcomes for the organization	stable personal characteristics and skills, roles played in social system

the very reason for an incentive contract is to align the presumably divergent interests of principals and agents. Psychological theories typically address the choices made by plan designers and administrators who are trying to anticipate, influence, or understand the behaviors of plan participants. The need to understand these different perspectives led us to choose a field study method that would give us a chance to probe, in depth, how the different constituencies perceived the plan, its objectives, and its consequences.

While we were selecting a site, we learned that a major California university was reevaluating its incentive compensation plan for managers because its stakeholders had reached a stage of explicit confrontation. Inspired by Kurt Lewin's observation that the best moment to learn about a system is when it is undergoing crisis and change, we concluded that this site was particularly suitable for our study.

Moreover, the "age" of the plan was ideal for the type of study we had in mind. On the one hand, its relatively recent implementation allowed us to talk with plan designers, administrators, and participants who could still recollect the details of the previous system, the initial discussions about choosing a plan design, objectives, and problems in implementation. On the other hand, the plan had been in effect long enough for two full cycles of performance reviews, so that plan participants had enough experience on how the plan affected their work and had formed their own attitudes about which aspects of the plan they liked or disliked.

The public university system selected for the study is state-supported and has several campuses.[3] The incentive compensation plan we examined—the Managerial Merit Pay System (MMPS) affects about 14,500 (full-time equivalent) professional managers, systemwide, who fulfill a critical role in administering the university, for they have general management responsibility over its main "operating" units.

Interviews were conducted with MMPS designers, administrators, and participants. The questions probed their perceptions about design and implementation of the plan, and its influence on employees' satisfaction and performance. The interviews lasted an average of one to two hours, and, although they followed a basic set of areas of inquiry, they were unstructured enough to promote a free flow of ideas and information. At least one of the authors was present at all interviews, and most interviews were conducted by both authors.

We also collected and reviewed documents from different phases of the plan's life cycle, from the early design drafts and discussion memoranda to the latest report on the results of a post-implementation study conducted by a special task force to evaluate the effectiveness of the MMPS plan. We further examined correspondence on the need for improving the plan's implementation and the recent opinion surveys the university had conducted to elicit the views of participants in the plan.

In spring 1990, the university sponsored several meetings between plan administrators and participants to assess the plan's effect. Because of serendipitous timing we could observe, at first hand, the dynamics of the interactions, often colored by emotion, between these two groups.

4. The MMPS Performance Evaluation and Compensation Plan

In 1985, the statewide university system established a steering committee of high-ranking university officials to review the university's personnel programs for all managerial and professional staff (faculty excluded). One of the committee's main objectives was to reorganize personnel positions into a uniform system of job classification, and to make recommendations for implementing a merit-based compensation plan for each of the job groups.

Linking financial rewards to superior performance was perceived as one of the strengths of the private sector, and the university administrators viewed performance pay as a way to depart from the traditional public sector approach to compensation. That approach emphasized adjustments in pay range based on cost-of-living changes and merit "step" salary increases within pay ranges that eventually led to "topping out"—that is, reaching the top of one's salary range, beyond which additional compensation could be achieved only by promotion. Nowhere in the plan's design was there an explicit preoccupation with correcting poor performance. The plan's stated objectives were to provide incentives to high performers, emphasizing promotional opportunities and internal recruitment, so that qualified professionals with advanced levels of independent judgment, analytical skill, and technical expertise would be attracted to key managerial positions in the university, and kept from moving to the private sector.

The steering committee hired a nationally known, prestigious compensation consulting firm to assist in restructuring the personnel programs. The consultant's recommendation for a four-tier personnel system (MMPS being one of them) was approved by the council of chancellors early in 1986. A new task force of high-ranking officials from all campuses was created to recommend a specific plan for implementation. For the MMPS, the task force recommended that superior performance be more highly rewarded than seniority, which had mostly determined compensation levels under the previous plan.

Until 1987, when the new performance-based compensation plan was implemented, each job level comprised five salary "steps" totaling a 25% salary range. Annual salary increases allowed an individual to move from one step to the next until he or she reached the highest step within the job level. By 1987, about 65% of managers who would later, under the new plan, participate in the Managerial Merit Pay System, had already reached the highest pay step within their job levels. For them, merit-based salary increases could come only with promotion to a higher job level. The only other possible source of an increase in annual compensation was the cost-of-living adjustment (COLA), as authorized by the state of California.

The task force considered the MMPS plan's main objective to be correcting this lack of monetary incentives for superior performance.

Under the new plan, the pay ranges were widened to provide more opportunities for pay increases within job grades. Under MMPS, positions with similar duties and responsibilities (comprising more than 200 job titles) were grouped in a six-grade salary structure, each grade corresponding to a 50% salary range. The midpoint in each salary range was set at a pay level 10% higher than the midpoint for the immediately lower job grade. Adjustments of salary ranges were to be determined by the president of the university, in accordance with the maximum limits set for payroll allocations by the state government.[4] Range adjustments—presumably reflecting changes in cost of living, competitive market conditions, and so on—could increase the potential for within-range salary advancement, without necessarily representing salary increases to each individual in the range.

Individual salary increases for MMPS managers (not to exceed 25% of current salary) could result from promotion to a higher grade, from within-grade equity adjustments, or from within-grade merit pay. Promotion to a higher grade resulted in pay increases varying from 0% to 15% of current salary (or more, if necessary to bring it to the minimum of the new range). Equity increases could be granted to correct individual equity problems, subject to approval by the university chancellor. Merit increases consisted of within-grade salary advancements intended to motivate and reward performance.

These merit-based, within-grade salary advancements were particularly important because the salary of a newly appointed MMPS manager would typically start between the minimum and the midpoint of the salary range for his or her grade. Such pay increases followed the guidelines defined in the MMPS Manual:

Within-grade salary advancement is based primarily on merit. The amount of increase awarded to an MMPS manager is influenced by performance as it relates to current pay and assigned responsibilities, the employee's current position within the salary range, relative performance among employees in the review unit, and availability of funds. The funds available are established as a percentage of payroll, which is applicable University wide.[5]

At the end of each fiscal year, the MMPS manager would meet with his or her immediate superior to set individual performance targets for the following year, weighted by their agreed-upon importance. At the end of the evaluation period, the degree to which the various objectives had been achieved would be calculated, ranging from 1 (unsatisfactory) to 5 (exceptional); these numbers would then be combined, in a weighted sum, to yield an overall performance rating. This rate would subsequently be compared with the performance ratings of other MMPS managers in the organizational unit, resulting in a relative ranking that would affect their merit increases, so that the unit's average payroll increase would fall within the limits set by the university (midpoint control).

The new plan included some other features (which the designers informally called "warm fuzzies") such as a flexible work schedule (that is, no obligation to keep an eight-hour workday if one could accomplish the day's tasks in less time) and extended paid vacation time.

The implementation of the MMPS plan was marked by problems and discontent. An opinion survey was done on MMPS participants in spring 1990 on a campus where it had been in effect since 1987. The response rate was 60%, and 86% of the respondents indicated that they were dissatisfied with the plan.

Their responses and open-ended comments included several criticisms of the plan, including a major concern that it eliminated guaranteed cost-of-living adjustment (COLA) increases in annual base salaries. This unease was aggravated because increases in base salary under the previous plan had not kept up with inflation late in the 1970s and early in the 1980s, and also because comparison was possible with other technical job groups (not included in the MMPS) that continued to have guaranteed COLA increases. Besides eliminating guaranteed COLAs, the plan in fact allowed for only insignificant pay increases, because of severe budgetary constraints on possible annual fluctuations in compensation (such as the need for each academic unit to keep its average payroll increase within a maximum percentage).

The respondents also noted many difficulties in the evaluation of performance. The MMPS participants took great pride in the complexity of their jobs and resented the objective performance measures that could assess only the less-important features of their jobs. Some participants also perceived that the performance standards were too hard to achieve. Furthermore, many MMPS managers doubted their supervisors' ability to evaluate the subjective aspects of their jobs (supervisors often rotated every two or three years), and thought training programs would not correct this deficiency.

Academic units varied widely in the formal procedures they used in performance evaluation. In one unit, supervisors met formally with each plan participant at the end of the fiscal year to establish in writing the performance goals for the following year, and reviewed a carefully filled-out eleven-page questionnaire on attaining the goals for the ending fiscal year. In another unit, plan participants were not clear about whether they even had to fill out their own performance evaluation questionnaire, and relative rankings were based on subjective evaluations by the unit administrator. In some units, plan participants decided to take turns at being nominated for the special bonus.

The survey also revealed that some participants distrusted the plan's objectives. Several respondents pointed out that they believed the plan was designed to control personnel costs by reducing compensation paid to some participants without a corresponding reward to those who were evaluated as top performers.

5. Interpreting Findings with the "Cultural Lens"

This pay-for-performance plan can be very puzzling if one tries to understand it from the point of view of economic or psychological theory.

From an economic standpoint, it seems that there was no rational justification for making pay contingent on performance: having the organization absorb risk would have been more efficient than allocating it to risk-averse employees, for whom downward fluctuation of income was a direct threat to their standard of living, rather than simply a reduction in savings or postponement of discretionary consumption of luxury goods. Moral hazard was not important, because supervision and other corrective mechanisms were possible. Besides, moral hazard would not be controlled by meager and doubtful monetary incentives.

From a psychological perspective, the plan suffered from structural strains: that evaluation and compensation were based on comparative criteria, assuming a zero-sum tournament model, weakened the links among effort, performance, and outcomes, therefore violating expectancy theory (Vroom, 1964). Also, the size of the rewards did not compensate for the psychological costs imposed by the forced distribution of performance evaluations, or the stress imposed on peer relationships; furthermore, the way in which position in the range influenced the rewards belied the objective of relating outputs to inputs, as required by equity theory (Adams, 1965).

How can we explain, therefore, why a group of intelligent, rational people designed this plan and expected it to work? This question puzzled us (and many of the people we interviewed) until we looked at the picture with a "cultural lens." Viewing the elements of the plan and its implementation as cultural artifacts and rituals, and exploring the stories and metaphors our interviewees used as part of intricate systems for interpreting and representing reality, we could gradually bring the picture into focus—or, more precisely, into focuses, for we realized that two realities were at play.

The first reality was that of the plan's designers and administrators. When we tried to unearth the basic cultural assumptions under which they operated, their decision to adopt the plan became very logical and the seemingly disparate elements of the plan fell into place like pieces of a puzzle.

We can summarize the contours of this first reality as a logical chain of assumptions about the basic cultural dualities: materialistic versus personalistic foregrounding, certainty versus uncertainty, controllability versus uncontrollability, individualism versus collectivism, and equality versus inequality.

A. Assumptions Made by the Plan's Designers and Administrators

- Materialistic versus personalistic foregrounding (pre-MMPS scenario)
  When the plan's designers and administrators diagnosed the needs to be addressed by the new plan, their perception of the world was shaped by materialistic foregrounding: they saw a lack of monetary incentives for the many managers who had reached the top of their ranges, and perceived an atmosphere that needed challenge and aggressive pursuit of outcomes. What came to the foreground was incongruent with their vision of a businesslike context, where real managers operate.
- Certainty versus uncertainty
  Having diagnosed a need to change this foreground, the designers had to determine what was wrong with it; operating under the assumption that challenge does not thrive in conditions of certainty, they saw that they must increase the environmental uncertainty in the motivational and cognitive maps of the plan participants.
- Controllability versus uncontrollability
  How could such uncertainty be created? The assumption that

the organization had no control over the resources available to reward performance (that was in the hands of the state decision makers in Sacramento) precluded making uncertainty reside in the size of the pie to be divided.

- Individualism versus collectivism
Therefore, uncertainty should reside in individual entitlement to pieces of the pie. The assumption was that people are primarily motivated by the individualistic pursuit of their own interests and that the organization is not responsible for the well-being of its members, suggesting that a competitive model for entitlement to different-sized pieces of the pie was desirable and ethically justified.

- Equality versus inequality (horizontal)
This tournament model, however, requires the further assumption that although the motivational effects of the prize will be felt by all the contenders, the intrinsic differences in their ability, skill, and effort will result in outcomes sufficiently spread to enable meaningful comparability (as repeatedly symbolized by the use, in meetings and interviews, of the normal distribution to depict the spread of performance in the organization). In other words, the inequality assumption made it reasonable to conclude that using midpoint controls was compatible with performance-based pay (because people's performance follows a normal distribution, the money saved from lower rewards to poor performers should average out the money spent in higher rewards to good performers).

- Materialistic versus personalistic foregrounding (post-implementation)
The visualization of the consequences that could be anticipated from making pay contingent on performance and, moreover, on relative performance, was again influenced by materialistic foregrounding: one perceived a stable cost structure, where economically motivated agents struggled for prizes and did not worry about the antagonistic elements of vertical and lateral relationships.

- Equality versus inequality (vertical)
Finally, assuming inequality indicated the need for complex measurements of performance, to offset the lack of visibility that the high-power distances implied; defining several layers of decision making in evaluating performance and allocating rewards was justified in order to concentrate discretion in the hands of the

people "most qualified to make good decisions"—those higher up in the hierarchy; and the need to preserve wage differentials among hierarchic levels led to detailed interweaving of performance and positional criteria in allocating rewards, as well as to a base-building system of merit pay.

When the plan was implemented, however, the basic assumptions that were crucial for its legitimacy and workability clashed with the assumptions by the plan participants.

This second reality—characterized by diametrically opposed positions in all the dualities—rejected the plan just as the human body rejects incompatible blood in a transfusion. We next summarize the logical net behind the unintended effects of implementing the plan.

B. Assumptions of Plan Participants

- Materialistic versus personalistic foregrounding (pre-MMPS scenario)
  When looking at the pre-plan reality, the MMPS managers saw in the foreground a web of social relationships in which human beings cared for each other and were morally involved with the organization. Although compensation was supposed to have some basis in merit, most managers received glowing reviews and, in some departments, simply took turns in the relative allocation of rewards. In this personalistic foregrounding, the psychological and social benefits of the status quo clearly outweighed its possible efficiency costs.
- Certainty versus uncertainty
  The harmony sought in this personalistic foreground assumed stable and long-term relationships. Introducing uncertainty into the picture led to disorientation rather than motivation. ("Before, we could at least be sure that we would have a cost-of-living adjustment; now, we are not even guaranteed that and we don't know what to expect.")
- Controllability versus uncontrollability
  The MMPS participants, like the plan's designers and administrators, assumed they had no control over the size of the pie. Previously, however, they had believed in their ability to control their entitlement to pieces of the pie. When the plan was implemented, they realized this assumption was no longer true, and

resented it (there were numerous complaints about "uncontrolla-ble" elements in determining pay and stories of powerlessness).

- Individualism versus collectivism
  The MMPS participants shared collectivist values and felt per-sonally offended by the notion that they would sell their loyalties for "thirty pieces of silver" ("That's an insult").
- Equality versus inequality (horizontal)
  Plan participants also believed deeply in the basic equality among them, and felt that the normal distribution was entirely inade-quate as a metaphor, for it implied randomness in selection and large numbers (we were told in no uncertain terms how they felt about the "bell curve," and how variability in performance should be corrected by hiring and firing rather than by tricks of compen-sation).
- Materialistic versus personalistic foregrounding (post-MMPS im-plementation)
  When plan participants reflected on the consequences of tying evaluation and pay to comparative criteria, they primarily saw disruption in vertical and lateral relationships. Their personalistic foregrounding stressed the negative consequences of superiors having to tell subordinates they were really not too good (before, adjectives were free and everybody could receive a pat on the back), of people having to revise their self-image ("you're judged and found wanting") and losing face for being rated under their peers. The intended effects on performance outcomes were either negated by participants or regarded as not worth the personal costs.
- Equality versus inequality (vertical)
  Last but not least, a critical unintended consequence of the plan was that it jeopardized a cross-occupational assumption of equal-ity that was important for the self-image of the MMPS managers. They perceived the plan as implying that their involvement with the organization was calculated and therefore less "noble" and "professional" than the moral involvement they felt they shared with the faculty. Also, the new evaluation procedures accentu-ated the distance in power between faculty and the MMPS man-agers, because their rituals and requirements stressed the fac-ulty's lack of interest in and knowledge of what MMPS managers did, and how powerless the plan's participants were against the material consequences of being evaluated by an irresponsible boss (our interviews recorded numerous references to the feudal lord–

serf relationship—a good lord protects you, a bad one doesn't). The change in the equality versus inequality assumption between faculty and administration contributed powerfully to anger and resentment against the plan ("They think we are a bunch of dummies").

6. Theoretical and Practical Implications

The main theoretical implication of our field study is its exploration of how the plan's designers' and participants' assumptions about these dualities in organizations may explain: (1) the internal logic of the plan design, even when this logic is not apparent from current economic and psychological perspectives; (2) how the lack of congruence between the assumptions underlying the plan and those held by the organization's culture may hinder implementation of the plan and generate unintended consequences.

Future studies are necessary to investigate the implications of different combinations of basic cultural assumptions about design and implementation of plans. Hofstede (1984) suggests that the interaction between distance of power and uncertainty should help us understand choices about organizational structure; similarly, he examines how the interaction between uncertainty and "masculinity" influences motivation. Investigating how various possible cultural characteristics interact can provide a powerful theoretical framework to explain adoption of a compensation plan and help resolve some of the conflicting results in the recent literature about the effects of pay-for-performance schemes.

On research methodology, we share the recommendation made by Tosi and Mejia (1989) that compensation researchers should conduct more in-depth studies to understand how incentive plans are selected—this kind of study is not possible if one uses only the variables available in public data bases. We further suggest that understanding how culture influences compensation policies requires a period of immersion in that culture and intensive use of insider information.

A cultural perspective on pay could be particularly relevant in examining the fit between values enforced by compensation contracts and different cultures in the same organization. For example, the recent trends toward mergers and acquisitions, increased diversification in products and industry, and global markets suggest that more explicit treatment of the effects of culture on compensation is needed. This realization was shared, in fact, during a recent practitioners' meeting on trends in management compensation (Levine, 1989).

From a practical viewpoint, this study suggests that compensation specialists should conduct a cultural diagnosis as a first step in designing the plan. Then, as they contemplate alternatives in the incentive contract, designers should explicitly analyze the values or beliefs underlying these alternatives. Finally, they must consider the implications of how the plan's assumptions embody or violate the values of the current culture.

The procedure for matching culture to pay schemes is similar to the medical analyses needed before a successful blood transfusion. Improper fit between the values embodied in the compensation plan and the organizational culture may not be fatal, but may still cause some puzzling dysfunctions such as performance evaluations that rank every participant in the highest category, equity raises disguised as incentive pay, irrelevant rewards, or an underlying attitude inclined to make the plan fail.

To compensation consultants and other specialists whose advice is sought as the plan is being designed, the evidence in this chapter indicates that selecting and implementing compensation features are not just technical exercises. Plan designers would benefit if they followed the example of anthropologists, who approach another culture by first learning and understanding its elements. This learner's approach can lead to an incentive contract that will achieve its objectives because it is based on powerful cultural forces.

Our observations of the organization in this study indicate that involving all the stakeholders in the contract choices may be at least as important as the outcome of the final plan. During the plan evaluation meetings we attended, participants frequently mentioned their resentment at being informed in detail of the new incentive plan *after* all significant decisions had been made. Communicating how the plan was supposed to work was effective in a cognitive, but not in an attitudinal sense: most participants fully understood the premises and features of the plan, yet strongly disagreed with some of its implications.

The stakeholders, including plan administrators and participants, would benefit from being involved in designing as well as implementing the plan. Whenever the values held by these parties diverge from the assumptions in a new compensation plan, consultants could facilitate contracting by encouraging everyone (especially the participants) to make their beliefs explicit. Consultants could serve as catalyzers, helping organization members identify their own blind spots. The consultant who has taken the time to understand the cultures can use the symbols, rituals, or metaphors that appeal to these cultures to facilitate communication.

Academics and practitioners should be aware that theories are not substitutes, but complementary goods. Adopting a cultural perspective should enhance the analytical, predictive, and practical power of economic and psychological theories on pay-for-performance. Ignoring the basic cultural assumptions of researchers, plan designers, administrators, and participants does not mean that they will not operate; rather, it means that each of these groups may be projecting onto the others its own cultural assumptions, only to be surprised when these do not hold in practice. Unearthing and addressing cultural differences may be, in fact, a necessary condition for aligning the interests of stakeholders by means of incentive compensation.

NOTES

1. For this study, effectiveness of the plan is defined as the subjective perception of the plan's designers, administrators, and participants about whether the incentive plan achieved its objectives.

2. The materialistic versus personalistic duality in foregrounding is related to basic assumptions about the nature of human activities (Schein, 1985) and has some interesting parallels with values that tend to be attributed to masculine and feminine sex roles. Though we acknowledge that this duality reflects the yang versus ying opposition in Oriental philosophies and Hofstede's (1984) "masculinity versus femininity" characterization of national cultures, we feel it is more appropriate to name the duality for what it entails, rather than for a debatable gender attribution.

3. Names and numbers are disguised to protect the organization's privacy.

4. In fiscal year 1989, for example, a maximum 4% limit was set for range adjustments.

5. The maximum percentage of merit increase in salary was also established during the budgeting process in California. In the 1989–1990 fiscal year, the total universitywide MMPS payroll was more than $200 million. The state government determined that state campuses could not increase their payroll costs beyond 6.2%. Under the 4% allowance for range adjustments in that year, the maximum merit increase was 2.2%.

REFERENCES

Etzioni, A. *A Comparative Analysis of Complex Organizations: On Power, Involvement and Their Correlates*. New York: Free Press, 1975.

Hofstede, Geert. *Culture's Consequences: International Differences in Work-Related Values*. Beverly Hills: Sage, 1984.

Kanter, Rosabeth. "The Attack on Pay." *Harvard Business Review* (March–April 1987), pp. 60–67.

Levine, Hermine. "Compensation and Benefits Today: Board Members Speak Out, Part I." *Compensation and Benefits Review* (1989), pp. 23–40.

Martin, Joanne, et al. "The Uniqueness Paradox in Organizational Stories." *Administrative Science Quarterly* (September 1983), pp. 438–453.

Merchant, Kenneth. "Disregarding the Controllability Principle." In *Accounting and Management: Field Study Perspectives*, W. Bruns, Jr., and R. Kaplan, eds. Boston: Harvard Business School Press, 1987, pp. 316–338.

———. *Rewarding Results: Motivating Profit Center Managers*. Boston: Harvard Business School Press, 1989.

Mohrman, Allan, Jr., Susan Resnick-West, and Edward Lawler III. *Designing Performance Appraisal Systems*. San Francisco: Jossey-Bass, 1989.

Nalbantian, Haig. "Incentive Compensation in Perspective." In *Incentives, Cooperation and Risk Sharing: Economic and Psychological Perspectives on Employment Contracts*, H. Nalbantian, ed. Totowa, NJ: Rowman & Littlefield, 1987, pp. 3–43.

Rotter, J. "Generalized Expectancies for Internal Versus External Control of Reinforcement." *Psychological Monographs*, vol. 80 (1966), pp. 1–28.

Schein, Edgar. *Organizational Culture and Leadership*. San Francisco: Jossey-Bass, 1985.

Stiglitz, Joseph. "The Design of Labor Contracts: The Economics of Incentives and Risk Sharing." In *Incentives, Cooperation and Risk Sharing: Economic and Psychological Perspectives on Employment Contracts*, H. Nalbantian, ed. Totowa, NJ: Rowman & Littlefield, 1987, pp. 47–68.

Tosi, Henry, and Luis Gomez-Mejia. "The Decoupling of CEO Pay and Performance: An Agency Theory Perspective." *Administrative Science Quarterly* (June 1989), pp. 169–189.

Vroom, V. *Work and Motivation*. New York: Wiley, 1964.

PART II

Performance and Organizations

CHAPTER 7

The Job as a Concept

Edward P. Lazear

FEW managers would deny that slots or jobs are well-defined concepts fundamental to the organization of a firm. And yet standard production theory has provided no technological role for the job. Indeed, it has ignored jobs altogether.

In this analysis I seek to enlarge our knowledge of jobs in two ways. First, I review the labor literature, pointing out the place the various theories assign to the job as a concept. Second, I apply a panel data set derived from studying a large organization to determine whether the job concept has any significance. Specifically, I ask whether assignment to a job affects real variables such as wages and turnover rates.

The key empirical findings are:

1. Changing jobs is the key to increasing wages. Individuals who change jobs are the ones who experience growth in wages.

2. Within-job heterogeneity is important. Individuals who remain on the job longer do worse than those who are promoted out early. Wages actually decline with job tenure, probably re-

This work was supported in part by the National Science Foundation. I am grateful to Edward Glaeser for excellent research assistance.

flecting the fall in the average worker's quality with length of time in the job.

3. The pattern of job-to-job turnover within the firm mimics the pattern often observed for movement between firms: turnover occurs most frequently at the beginning of the job and dies out with additional experience.

4. In almost all jobs significant hiring from the outside occurs. Although some jobs are more likely to be entry points into the firm than others, this firm has no strict ports of entry.

The Theory of Jobs and Its Historical Relevance

The concept of a "job" is an important one. Does the person define the job or does the job define the person? This question lies at the heart of modern theories of the labor market. The traditional, institutional view emphasizes the job as the unit of analysis. Although some recognize that skills affect an employee's placement in a specific slot, this view tends to assert that workers can be substituted for one another and that individuals' allocation to jobs generally reflects luck or other factors.[1] The literature that most forcefully advances this view deals with internal labor markets.[2]

The other view, dominant since the 1960s, derives from the theory of human capital.[3] This view focuses on the supply-side approach, arguing that workers invest in productivity-enhancing skills, which they bring into the labor market. The job is unimportant. Wages and lifetime wealth are determined primarily by the individual's stock of human capital, although it is admitted that psychic aspects of the job (such as danger, dirtiness, and undesirable hours) also affect monetary compensation. Occupation and industry variables are secondary in this theory. In fact, jobs are never even mentioned.

The concept of a job has no place in standard production theory. Labor and capital are defined as continuous variables. Slots and other integer problems are ignored. When labor differentiation is discussed, it is generally about the skills or quality of the workforce, rather than the tasks to which the labor is assigned. The view reflected in this literature deviates significantly from the businessperson's concept of labor markets. Personnel managers and department heads are usually aware of their slot allocations. But some evidence suggests that jobs are often tailored to the individual at high levels in the firm's hierarchy. A job is created, for example, to accommodate a former CEO when a new person steps into the job.[4]

Tournaments

A growing body of analytic literature emphasizes jobs or slots. The most obvious example, and the one with which I am most closely associated, is the tournament model.[5] In this model, workers compete with one another for a limited number of slots. By beating his or her competitors, the winner obtains a coveted job and the higher earnings that go with it. In this theory, jobs are another name for wage categories, but with two key provisions.

First, assignment to the job is based on relative rather than absolute performance. The individual who gets to be boss is not the one who is good, but rather the one who is best (even if both are excellent).

A second and related provision is that the number of slots is fixed in advance. Wages are assigned to the slots, not to the individuals. The reason for this arrangement is that appropriate incentive effects are generated by relative comparisons.

The attachment of wages to slots means that employers are less able to renege on promises to pay high wages if a standard is met. In this case, because someone must receive the high wage, employers gain little by lying.[6]

Indeed, it is the fixed slots that distinguish tournament incentive structures from others based on relative performance. One reason for using a tournament is to difference out random factors or common noise. Workers who are risk averse do not like their compensation to vary with market conditions, over which they have no control. A tournament eliminates the effect of common external forces on compensation. If the economy is in a slump, it affects all salespersons equally. Rewarding salespeople on their performance relative to that of their peers thus eliminates the common noise of a recessionary economy.

Tournaments are not the only way to eliminate the effects of common noise. For example, paying workers on the basis of their performance relative to the group mean eliminates common noise. This scheme differs from the tournament, however, in that tournaments imply slots, whereas relative pay by itself does not. With tournaments, only one individual gets the first prize or top job. One and only one gets the second prize or second-best job, and so forth. With relative compensation, the structure of wages and positions evolves ex post, rather than ex ante. Tournament models emphasize relative performance, but also rely on jobs themselves.

Insurance

Tournament models are not the only reason to be concerned about the concept of jobs. Jobs are at the center of any discussion of insurance and worksharing. Firms may reduce hours during downturns without eliminating jobs (if only by variations in overtime), but layoffs are still an accepted part of the American work environment. Thus, a job may be defined as the right to work in a specified state of the economy. Cutting employment by reducing the number of heads means that there must be a fixed cost, either in production or in leisure, that makes it preferable to set up jobs of fixed length and vary the number of them according to the state of the economy. Fixed costs in production are easy to imagine. Setup time in the office or shop is required for many production processes. Transportation time to work is an obvious fixed cost that it pays to amortize. Similarly, leisure may have fixed costs. Few individuals go on four-hour ski trips because travel time, packing time, and time merely to switch gears are required. Although the number of slots varies with economic conditions, slots have a well-defined meaning.

The insurance literature places a great deal of weight on who holds a job.[7] Here, workers are regarded as interchangeable. Little emphasis is assigned level of skill or other characteristics in determining order of layoff. The individual who is laid off is drawn randomly from some distribution, and the investigation relates to the compensation of the two groups over the cycle. This approach resembles the institutional analyses, which treat workers as interchangeable and focus on jobs as the unit of analysis.

Hierarchies

The literature on hierarchies and on the structure of control in organizations is inherently cast in terms of jobs.[8] The hierarchy analyses are explicit in their use of jobs. Most assume that each position has a span of control over a fixed number of other positions. Thus, the shape of the pyramid is determined ex ante, although the size of the firm, the number of levels, and the quality of the workforce are endogenous.

Contemporary theories of control in organizations also assume that slots are crucial. Here the question is whether projects should be evaluated vertically or horizontally. In a vertical organization, only projects accepted at lower levels are evaluated by more senior individuals. But seniority implies that the job, rather than the incumbent, defines the activity. The individual who is supervisor is assigned responsibility for making decisions on approved projects. Someone is always in that role. The human capital approach would assign authority to individuals based on the skills that they possessed. Rather than assigning all authority in advance to one supervisor, authority would be determined only after the incumbent's qualifications were known.

Hedonics

Hedonic wage analysis also dignifies the concept of jobs. Proponents of this school of thought have emphasized the characteristics of the job. The focus is not on the individual's skills or attributes but rather on the attributes of the position itself. For example, some jobs have more variable employment schedules than others. It is well known that durables manufacturing is more procyclic than health care. Researchers have found as much as a 25% wage premium for working in the most cyclically sensitive industries.[9] The layoff pattern attaches to the job, not to the individual who holds it. Layoffs are not high in manufacturing because the individuals who work there enjoy losing their jobs. Layoff rates are high as a result of demand conditions which pertain to the industry and which consequently dictate the duration of jobs in the industry.

Similarly, jobs with significant safety hazards tend to pay higher wages as a compensation differential.[10] The higher wages are attached to the jobs because the jobs themselves are risky, not because the workers who hold them are clumsy. The hedonic wage literature is thus the best example of empirical analysis that focuses on the characteristics of jobs rather than workers.

This approach has permeated the business community as well. Consulting firms such as Hay Associates place a great deal of emphasis on jobs and their characteristics. Their surveys and resulting salary recommendations adjust for the skill requirements, technical know-how, accountability, and pleasantness of work associated with a job. Although the incumbent may help to define the job, such analyses are targeted on deciding the salary appropriate to the position rather than to the individual who holds it.

Investment

Even human capital theory offers a role for the concept of a job. Some jobs offer more opportunity for advancement than others. In some fields, young workers spend a great deal of time and effort acquiring human capital, which makes them more productive in later work years. In other fields, human capital is less important. One way to define jobs is by the opportunities for technological investment available to workers. Different career paths are available, but the opportunity for investment is fixed in advance, with the workers assigned to those paths determined in some maximizing fashion.[11] Unlike other theories that deal with job structures, human capital theory does not assert that the number of slots must be fixed in advance. If more investors show up at the door during a period, this theory assumes that the firm can accommodate them by creating more positions of the investment type. Jobs dictate, ex ante, the amount of investment that the incumbent undertakes. Individuals can choose the amount that they invest only by choosing the appropriate job.

One interpretation is that the opportunity for human capital investment is one of the characteristics of the job that enter the hedonic wage function. An alternative view is that jobs are unimportant in determining how much investment occurs. Workers simply alter the amount of time that they spend investing and working to suit their optimal investment profile, irrespective of job assignment.

Collection of Tasks

The final interpretation of a job is the most traditional one. A job can be defined as a collection of tasks. The tasks need not be hierarchic, nor need they be compensated in any specific way. In this sense, a job is defined as a partition of the firm's technology.

Some Specific Questions

It is somewhat of an overstatement to dichotomize theories into those which look at jobs and those which look at workers, but recent work in labor economics, especially empirical work, has paid little attention to jobs. This chapter is an attempt to remedy that oversight. The general questions are, "Do jobs matter?" and "Do firms behave as if they have some reasonably well-defined idea of slots in mind when they make decisions?" Because most empirical work follows from human capital models, such questions have been all but ignored in recent years. In the empirical section of this chapter, I address these general questions. But more specific questions can be asked as well.

Jobs and Wages

How does a worker's placement in a job affect his or her wages and lifetime wealth? Suppose that two otherwise identical individuals end up working different jobs in the same firm, purely by chance. Will their lifetime wealth levels differ? Does the job path matter, or does one's stock of human capital dominate the determination of wages? That is, do jobs determine wages or do the individual's characteristics determine wages? It has been argued that once occupation and industry are held constant, male-female wage differential is slight.[12] Is the same true for other human capital variables, such as education and prior experience?

A related question is important. Wages in one job may be higher than wages in another, but the job path of which the lower-wage job is a part may provide higher expected lifetime wealth than the typical path of which the higher-wage job is part. This result would be expected if human capital were important and if wages reflected the different levels of productivity associated with the investment period. Alternatively, steeper profiles that start lower could reflect an incentive mechanism, which underpays young workers and overpays old workers as an instrument of motivation.[13]

Jobs and Turnover

It is well known that the varying turnover rates of workers are a function of demographic characteristics and of tenure with the firm.[14] But jobs may have different turnover rates, independent of the incumbents. In fact, it may be argued that the job determines the turnover rate and that once this rate is held constant, no demographic effects remain. Demographic characteristics may be important in placing individuals in jobs, but demographics may have no independent effect on anything real.

Movers versus Stayers

Differences in job assignment may reflect heterogeneity in the population. One possibility is that individuals who start out in high-wage positions tend to remain in high-wage positions throughout their tenure with the firm, an example of a fixed unobserved effect. Some individuals may have higher levels of ability that are not held constant by the variables included in the regression. Alternatively, ability may be constant but some workers may be favored for varied reasons. It is quite possible that a worker once favored would tend to remain that way. Unfortunately, the data used here will not distinguish between unobserved heterogeneity, either in ability or treatment, and actual productivity-based reasons for different wages.[15]

Classification into Jobs

Comparing differences in job assignments raises the question of how those assignments are determined. A basic question is whether it is possible to explain job assignments systematically. Demographics, seniority, or past job assignments may be good predictors of future job assignments, but it is also possible that nothing predicts job assignments very well. If the latter description fits, it gives more credence to the hypothesis that individuals are alike and job assignments are gained by sheer luck. Of course, one can always argue that unobservables must make up for differences in observed ability, or individuals would not be assigned to the jobs. But if they did, one would still expect the measured ability variables to matter.

Careers

Another question is whether an interesting pattern of background variables affects assignment of jobs. Aside from the issues of whether race and sex matter (which are not our focus in this study), it is interesting to know whether "careers" occur within firms. An individual may move from assembly-line worker to foreman to supervisor and dead end there. Another may move from secretary to administrative assistant to manager I to general manager. It may be that production workers rarely become managers, whereas clericals have a higher probability of moving into the managerial track. These career paths would be interesting to document. As far as I am aware, they have not been studied.

Ports of Entry

One's casual impression is that very little hiring occurs at upper levels in management. Most individuals are promoted from within, implying that the firm has entry-level jobs. More concretely, the probability of having held another job in the company is expected to be positively related to the position of the job in the firm's hierarchy. But the exact relation is an empirical question. A weak result implies that the firm has no real "ports of entry." A stronger one implies that some jobs are prerequisites for others, a premise that is worth documenting.[16]

The Data

The data used in the analysis come from the personnel files of one large corporation. Data cover a thirteen-year period from the late 1970s through the 1980s. Because the data are from only one company, this analysis is closer to an econometric case study than to an empirical study claiming to represent the bigger picture. Still, the corporation is a large one, and we have no reason to believe it is idiosyncratic. Higher-level managerial employees are not included in the data set, and so all information about promotions and job mobility relates to individuals in jobs paying less than $100,000 a year in 1989.

About 100,000 people worked for the company at some time during the thirteen-year period. We have slightly fewer than .5 million records, each record consisting of an observation for an individual during one year. If all the employees in the data set had worked during all thirteen years, we would find about 1.3 million records. That as many as .5 million remain suggests that a significant number of individuals had relatively lasting careers with the corporation.

The sample is restricted to full-time employees. Some individuals are hourly employees and some are on monthly salary. When conversion was necessary, a monthly salary was computed for hourly workers by multiplying the hourly wage by 173.93.[17] The variables, definitions, and sample statistics are reported in Exhibit 7-1.

For confidentiality, descriptions of industry and occupation are deleted or disguised. As far as I can tell, they are not relevant to any of the statistical tests or conclusions. It is convenient to think of this firm as a manufacturer of durable goods. The firm is mature, having been in business for about fifty years. Management changed hands about halfway through that period. Output is somewhat sensitive to

Exhibit 7-1   Means and Standard Deviations

Variable	Description	Mean	Standard Deviation
SAL	Salary per month	2,182.22	1,137.32
ED	Years of education		
	(12 = high school completed)	12.35	1.73
COTEN	Years in company	17.13	8.77
JOBTEN	Years in job	12.34	8.28
CHG	Average number of job changes for each individual, 1977–1990	0.15	0.50
PROM	Average number of promotions for each individual, 1977–1990	0.08	0.30

business cycles in this industry. Workers are separated into hourly and salary categories. These correspond roughly to production workers and clericals, the latter including managers as well.

We find a number of advantages in using data on one company.

First, national panel data sets do not permit extensive analysis at the firm level. Thus, questions on subjects such as promotion paths or ports of entry simply cannot be answered using a panel data set.

Second, even when data sets include significant detail on individual firms, the results tend to average within-firm and between-firm effects. Unless we had many observations from each company, we would not be able to ascertain whether a positive correlation between promotions and wage growth meant that individuals who were promoted received larger raises or that companies in which promotions were common had steeper age-earnings profiles.

Third, most national data sets do not carry detailed information on job assignments within firms. For example, in the Panel Study of Income Dynamics, within-firm job changes were followed only in the data collected during the 1980s.[18] Significant career paths cannot be traced in national data sets of this kind.

Empirical Analysis

The distinction between human capital–based theories and job-based theories of the labor market is useful from the conceptual point of view. But distinguishing between the two theories is quite difficult empirically. Although my argument touches on human capital issues, the primary goal in our empirical analysis is to study issues in which jobs are the important explanatory variables. In the recent past this area has been neglected in favor of the now-traditional analyses of human capital and earnings.

Furthermore, most work on job mobility has been focused on changes between firms rather than within firms, perhaps because the data bases available lent themselves to this type of analysis. It is time to give movement from job to job within the firm at least some of the attention that has been paid to movement between firms, and to ask questions about the causes and effects of job movement among firms. The rate of interfirm job turnover sharply declines with experience on the job. Is this reduction observed for job changes within firms as well?

Jobs and Variation in Wages

We must determine the correlation between jobs and wage variation if we are to determine the role of jobs within the firm. One possibility is that jobs are simply another name for wages. If a different job were defined for each grade and step combination in the federal GS system, the result would be one wage for each job, for grade and step uniquely determine the compensation that the worker receives. Skill and experience probably matter in determining grade and step, but no salary variation appears within the grade-step category. Probably it is more accurate, however, to classify the job as a grade rather than a grade-step. Thus within each job we find as much variation as the different steps allow.

Job classifications such as these may be somewhat arbitrary, but they are useful tools for analyzing the individual and the firm. Choosing a meaningful definition of jobs within the firm is a crucial first step in analyzing my data set. The definition must help explain wage variation within the firm, and it must form a basis for considering issues of mobility, especially promotion and entry into the firm.

In the subject firm, jobs are assigned five-digit codes. As specificity increases, the job becomes synonymous with wage. This parallel is easily documented by looking at Exhibit 7-2, row 1. The R^2 that is reported comes from an analysis of variance; that is, a regression of individual monthly earnings levels on a series of job dummies. In the first row, each of the five-digit codes is considered as defining a different job, for a total of 791 jobs in the firm. At this level, the job is almost synonymous with wage. As the ANOVA results show, 95% of the variation in monthly earnings can be accounted for by the job

Exhibit 7-2　Monthly Earnings Variations (ANOVA)
Within Jobs versus Between Jobs

Level of Job Definition	R^2	Number of Jobs
5 digit	.958	788
4 digit	.923	371
3 digit	.814	134
2 digit	.791	45
1 digit	.373	5

Number of employees = 19,023.

Note: The analysis of variance reports the proportion of total variance removed by a regression of salaries on job dummies; that is, it shows the deviations from within-job salary means as a proportion of total deviations from the salary grand mean.

dummies. Thus, most of the variation in earnings is between jobs, not within jobs, when the job is defined by its five-digit classification.

At the other extreme, if the job is defined as the one-digit classification, with the other four digits possibly signifying level, location, or specific task or seniority within the job, then only five "jobs" are found within the firm and those five explain only 37% of the variation in wages. At the one-digit level, then, most of the job variation is within rather than between jobs. Of course, we could define job at the zero-digit level, leaving only one job in the firm! Then all the variation would be within the job and none between.

I have chosen the two-digit definition of the job for several reasons. First, moving from the two- to the three-digit definition does little to increase our power to explain variation in earnings. Second, what is gained comes at the cost of tripling the number of jobs. Because this condition would reflect many parallel jobs at the same levels, the two-digit analysis is a more reasonable choice. Furthermore, when mobility is considered, the two-digit level offers the advantage of larger cell sizes. Though admittedly arbitrary, the results shown below suggest that the two-digit job classification is a meaningful one.[19]

Wage Growth

A more direct way to examine the importance of jobs is to use the panel aspect of the data. This approach shows that job changes in a given year occur for some workers, but not for others. Yet all workers receive raises. In Exhibit 7-3, we examine the effects of job changes on earnings growth over the worker's entire career with the firm.[20]

Exhibit 7-3 Job Changes, Promotions, and Wage Growth
(Regressions: Dependent variable = average annual percentage
of change in real wages)

	1	2
Intercept	.0082	.0084
	(.0003)	(.0003)
Number of job changes	−.0114	.0044
	(.0006)	(.0003)
Number of promotions	.029	
	(.001)	
Number of years in	−.00129	−.00131
sample	(.00003)	(.00004)
R^2	.06	.04
N	33,290	33,290

Note: The sample size is larger than that of Exhibit 7-2 because it includes any individual who worked during the thirteen-year period.

In Exhibit 7-3, we look at average wage growth over an individual's career as a function of job changes. The results reveal that promotions positively affect wages, as we'd expect, for promotion is defined as a move from one job to another having a higher mean wage. Any job change other than a promotion is lateral or a demotion, and so the coefficient on such internal job changes is negative. Finally, the coefficient on the years in the sample is negative as well. The reason is best understood by considering the second specification, which suppresses the distinction between promotions and other job changes. For a specified number of job changes, an individual with more years in the sample has spent longer on each job. Such individuals are likely to be the losers—workers who have not been promoted. Thus, remaining in a job for a long time has adverse implications for salary growth.[21]

The results explain why the two-digit job definition is meaningful for this analysis. First, a significant amount of switching occurs. The average number of job changes is .17 per worker year. Second, most job changes are promotions. About two-thirds of the job changes in the sample are promotions. This proportion can also be observed when we see that the coefficient on job changes goes from negative to positive when we omit promotions from the regression. The result implies a positive (partial) correlation between promotions and job changes.

Finally, job change is the key to the story of wage growth in this

Exhibit 7-4 Annual Wage Growth (Dependent variable: percentage of real wage change between $t-1$ and t)

Variable	
Intercept	.012
	(.002)
Company tenure	$-.0011$
	(.0001)
Promotion	.191
	(.011)
Job change	.021
	(.009)
R^2	.005
N	228,000

Note: Exact N not available.

firm. Without job change, even at the two-digit level, column 2 of Exhibit 7-3 reveals that real wages would fall after about seven years of experience. (At seven years, the negative experience effect is larger than the intercept.) More accurately, individuals who are in the sample for more than seven years and who experience no job change are expected to see a decline in real wages each year. The most reasonable explanation for this decline is that these workers are not valuable enough to earn promotions. The longer an individual has been in the job without a promotion, the lower his or her expected quality as a worker. Exhibit 7-5 presents more evidence on this subject.

Another way to examine the same issue is by looking at annual changes in wages as a function of job change. In Exhibit 7-4, each two-year interval is treated as an observation. The form of the dependent variable is

$$\frac{W_{it} - W_{it-1}}{W_{it-1}} \tag{1}$$

where W_{it} is the wage for person i in period t.

Exhibit 7-4 confirms the findings shown in Exhibit 7-3. Individuals who won promotions got 21% (.19 + .02) higher average raises in that year than individuals who did not. (Remember that growth in Exhibit 7-3 refers to average wage growth over the entire career, whereas Exhibit 7-4 treats each year separately.) Individuals who experience job changes other than promotions still experience wage growth, but by an order of magnitude less.

Exhibit 7-5   Earnings Functions for Movers versus Stayers

	Movers	Stayers
Constant	7.239	7.063
	(0.042)	(0.014)
Education	.0085	.0088
	(.0030)	(.0010)
Tenure	.0117	.0152
	(.0006)	(.0002)
R^2	.10	.28
N	2,928	16,044

Note: Dependent variable in ℓn (monthly salary in 1989).

The average individual in the sample received .02 promotion per year. At worst, an individual might never receive a promotion. At best he or she may be promoted repeatedly until reaching the top job.

The problem with the analyses in Exhibits 7-3 and 7-4 is that they treat promotions as annual events independent of the past and future. The specification in Exhibit 7-4 ignores, for example, the effect of promotions on subsequent wages. This reading neglects the entire concept of a career path. It may be that future growth in wages, and indeed future promotions, are functions of past promotion. In the next section we investigate these issues.

Careers

One way to think about careers is to imagine two basic groups of workers—movers and stayers. Movers get promoted and move up the corporate ladder. Stayers never get promoted, but remain in their first job throughout their entire career with the firm.

We have various sensible ways of defining movers and stayers. I have chosen to define stayers as the group of workers who never changed jobs and movers as the group who changed jobs at least once during their career. Earnings functions are estimated separately for each group. Those regressions are reported in Exhibit 7-5.

From the earnings regressions in Exhibits 7-5 and 7-6, it is possible to predict the lifetime wealth of movers versus stayers. Of course, turnover behavior may differ across groups, as I document below. The wealth simulations are conditional on the assumption that the careers of workers last thirteen years. (The number thirteen is selected

Exhibit 7-6 Starting Log Wages

Year	Movers' Log Wage	Standard Error	Stayers' Log Wage	Standard Error	Diff. $(M - S)$	Standard Error
1979	12.05	0.033	11.97	0.009	0.08	0.035
1980	12.10	0.027	12.03	0.009	0.07	0.029
1981	12.18	0.021	12.14	0.008	0.04	0.023
1982	12.14	0.018	12.23	0.009	-0.09	0.021
1983	12.21	0.017	12.28	0.008	-0.07	0.018
1984	12.25	0.024	12.43	0.010	-0.18	0.026
1985	12.26	0.014	12.37	0.008	-0.11	0.016
1986	12.35	0.019	12.43	0.007	-0.08	0.021
1987	12.19	0.017	12.21	0.012	-0.02	0.021
1988	12.21	0.021	12.15	0.011	0.06	0.024
1989	12.27	0.025	12.15	0.013	0.12	0.029
Unweighted Average Difference					-0.016	0.080
Number of Observations	*Movers* 7,729				*Stayers* 20,675	

so that earnings can be estimated without extrapolating outside the period of the sample.)

Using the estimates from Exhibit 7-5, and assuming a 2% real interest rate, we can calculate wealth:

$$\text{Wealth} = \sum_{i=1}^{13} \frac{\hat{W}_{it}}{(1 + .02)^{t-1}} \tag{2}$$

where $\hat{W}_{it}$ is predicted from the appropriate Exhibit 7-5 regression and year 13 is taken to be 1989. The individual is assumed to have fourteen years of education and to have started in 1977.

The simulations reveal that movers have a thirteen-year wealth level of $235,875. The corresponding number for stayers is $203,675. Thus the wealth level of movers is about 16% greater than that of stayers. The difference in initial wages of movers and stayers is about 13%. Thus much of the difference in wealth is reflected in wages on the first job.

To get a sense of how important promotions are in the firm, it is useful to compare an individual who was promoted three times over a thirteen-year career with one who was never promoted. The estimates of wage growth and of the effect of job change on wage growth are taken from Exhibit 7-4. The calculation algorithm follows equation (2). The first promotion is assumed to occur at year 3, the second at year 6, and the third at year 9. The initial wage is assumed to be $1,500 per month.

Under these circumstances, the wealth for those promoted totals about $337,000, whereas for those not promoted it totals only $225,000. This is an enormous difference, equal to almost 50% of total wealth, and it suggests that tournaments may have had a large role in this firm's incentive structure. Of course, other explanations may be correct as well. Heterogeneity is the most obvious alternative.

We can find some evidence for heterogeneity. A strong test of heterogeneity implies that individuals are different when they join the firm, and these differences show up then and throughout. The first piece of evidence against this hypothesis is that even observable attributes such as education do little to predict starting wages in the firm. Education never enters regressions of log wage starting on year dummies, even when the initial job is not held constant.

In Exhibit 7-6, workers are separated into movers and stayers according to the definition given above. Starting log wage is computed separately for each group. In some years, the starting wage of movers is significantly higher than that of stayers, but in others the reverse is true. On average, over the full period, no significant difference appears between the starting wages of movers and stayers. If heterogeneity is an important determinant, it is nevertheless not clearly detected among workers at the outset and it is not reflected in wages.

This result is not especially surprising. Even if firms could identify the better workers at the time they were hired, selective offering of general human capital would tend to depress the starting wage of the ablest, so that no strong observable differences would at first be perceived. Interestingly, however, Exhibit 7-5 shows that the experience effect by itself is no larger for movers than for stayers. It is the move itself that captures the wage difference. This is consistent with the tournament view of promotions.

Turnover

External turnover can be defined as mobility between firms. Internal turnover refers to job changes within the firm. Although much work has been done on external turnover, very little attention has been focused on internal turnover and on the relation between internal and external turnover.

In this section, I merely report hazard rates for internal turnover. Exhibits 7-7 and 7-8 plot the probability of changing jobs within the firm by years of tenure.[22] In Exhibit 7-7, the absolute number of job changes is plotted against years of tenure. In Exhibit 7-8, the hazard rates of job changes are plotted.

From panel B, we can conclude that individuals with less than a year of tenure have about a 25% chance of changing jobs during their first year. By the time their tenure with the firm has reached approximately eleven years, the hazard rate for job change is less than 2%. This pattern of internal job change looks very similar to the pattern of job change between firms.

Job Paths

Let us now return to our main focus in this analysis. The key question is whether we can gain insight by looking at firm-based data and using the job as a unit of analysis that we could not gain from cross-section or panel data on individuals. Perhaps the most

Exhibit 7-7 Intrafirm Job Exit Rate: Levels

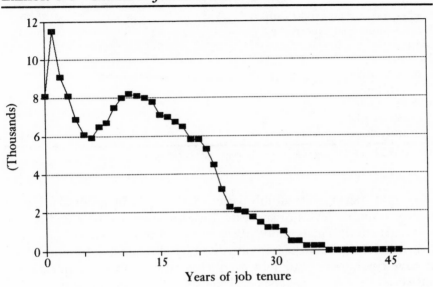

Exhibit 7-8 Intrafirm Job Exit Rates: Hazard

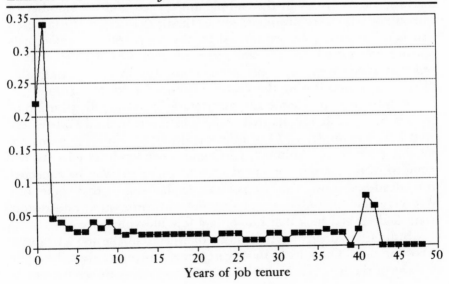

Exhibit 7-9 Promotion Export Analysis, Summary Statistics

Highest promotion export rate	1
Lowest promotion export rate	0
Mean	.13
Median	.03
90th percentile	.40
25th percentile	0
10th percentile	0
Number of jobs in analysis	44

Note: One job was lost because no one in it met the criterion of this sample.

important issues relate to job paths. Are some jobs necessary transit points to higher levels of success? This question can be asked in two ways: Are individuals more likely to be promoted out of some jobs than others? And are the individuals who hold the top jobs more likely to have come from some jobs than from others? The first question is answered by export analysis and the second by import analysis.

Export Analysis

At any time, each job category includes a set of incumbents, who may or may not be promoted to new jobs during the year. For this analysis, all the years in the sample are pooled and the number of individuals who were promoted out of their job category during each year is calculated. Jobs are ranked by the proportion of individuals who were exported. To prevent contamination by movement out of jobs that were eliminated, only promotions are considered. Individuals who separated during the year are dropped from the sample.

Exhibit 7-9 gives some summary statistics on the distribution of exports by jobs. It reveals that some jobs are true dead ends as expected. For example, CEO is a dead-end job, for no promotions are possible from there. Although CEO and other top-level jobs are not included in the sample, others at high levels might also be expected to be dead-end jobs. Another possible explanation is that some jobs have very few incumbents and that the zero promotion rate results from random bad luck that hits only a few individuals.

Still, it is surprising that more than 25% of the job categories export no one. The jobs in those categories, however, are only a few of those in the firm. Only 700 of 218,073 worker years were spent in

Exhibit 7-10   Regression of Job Export Rates
on Job Characteristics

Independent Variable	1	2
Intercept	− .94	.18
	(.55)	(.07)
Average salary	− .000076	− .00043
	(.000037)	(.00028)
Average tenure	.0105	.0034
	(.0061)	(.0044)
Production	.1084	
	(.0773)	
Education	.0792	
	(.0412)	
R^2	.09	.05
Number of jobs in sample	44	44

Note: Dependent variable = Promotion export rate.

these zero-export jobs. Thus, almost all jobs that account for significant numbers of workers export to other jobs.

Another way of throwing light on job exports is to examine whether the high-export jobs have characteristics in common. We do so by regressing the job's export rate on some job characteristics. Among the independent variables are average salary, average tenure of incumbents, hourly dummy, and production worker dummy. The results, reported in Exhibit 7-10, reveal that low-salary production jobs tend to have the highest export rates. If tenure with the firm enters at all, it enters positively. Jobs with experienced workers are more likely to export workers than jobs with inexperienced workers.

Note further that the education variable does affect the rate of promotion. Jobs with more highly educated workers tend to export more than those with less-educated workers. This result is consistent with most human capital analyses. But more interesting is that the other variables matter as much and perhaps more. This preponderance does not imply that human capital is less important than job assignment. It is plausibly argued that individuals who are assigned to the same job have the same human capital; those with low levels of education make it up in higher experience or unobserved ability. It is noteworthy, however, that job paths matter in a way that is not explained well by human capital variables. That some jobs and some job characteristics are more likely to lead to promotions than others

Exhibit 7-11   Feeder and Dead-End Jobs

Means	Feeder Jobs	Dead-End Jobs
Company tenure	17.3	16.8
	(.02)	(.02)
Job tenure	13.0	14.3
	(.02)	(.02)
Paid hourly	.61	.51
	(.001)	(.001)
Production	.92	.93
	(.001)	(.001)
Education	12.3	12.1
	(.004)	(.004)
Salary	2,214	2,136
	(2)	(2)
Number of observations	216,877	261,429

Note: The standard errors of the means are given in parentheses.

does not surprise us. But it is important because it suggests that useful ways of thinking about wage determination, namely by job selection, may have been unduly ignored in the past.

Import Analysis

It is possible to perform an import analysis that is symmetric with the export analysis shown above. Jobs could be ranked by the probability that the incumbent was in a lesser job during the previous year. It is more useful, however, to focus on selected jobs within the firm. Specifically, I want to consider the top jobs in the firm, as determined by a mean salary in the firm's top 2%, and to find out which jobs feed into those.

Let us now divide all jobs into feeder jobs and dead-end jobs. A feeder job is defined as a job included in the set that leads to top jobs. The dead-end jobs are other jobs in the current sample that have zero probability of being feeder jobs.

The characteristics of both jobs can be described. The means of some of the relevant variables are presented in Exhibit 7-11 by feeder or dead-end group. Because of the large sample sizes, the differences in characteristics of feeder and nonfeeder jobs are all significant but not very great. One might expect that production jobs would have fewer opportunities for promotion than clerical jobs. But the dead-end jobs are only a bit more likely to be held by production workers.

As might be expected, both salaries and levels of education are higher in feeder jobs than in dead-end jobs. Similarly, salaries are higher in feeder jobs. It is counterintuitive that the feeder jobs have a higher proportion of hourly workers and dead-end jobs have a higher proportion of salaried workers.

Of course, this approach may not capture the actual job path of the typical high-level worker. But it does seem to illustrate that mobility is quite even within this firm.

Although the characteristics of feeder and nonfeeder jobs seem to vary little, this characteristic does not imply that job assignment is unimportant. Recall that Exhibit 7-9 showed that some jobs have extremely high export rates, and others export almost no one. These differences may reflect the unobserved characteristics of workers assigned to the jobs. They do not, however, appear to greatly or consistently reflect the observable characteristics.[23]

Ports of Entry

It is natural to believe that hiring into some jobs is more likely than hiring into others. If firm-specific human capital were important, then individuals would be hired into low-level jobs and very few would be hired into the upper-echelon jobs. Beyond any theoretical significance of hiring patterns, it is interesting to determine whether hiring focuses on lower-level jobs. That is, are ports of entry important phenomena in the American corporation?

Here again, firm-based data are necessary, because the question cannot be answered by using national cross-section or even panel data sets. The current data set is ideal for addressing the issue. The approach used here is similar to that in earlier sections.

First, for each job category, we record the proportion of incumbents for whom the job is their first in the firm. They are the individuals who were hired from the outside. All jobs are ranked by those proportions. The numbers are reported in Exhibit 7-12. Only 1989 is used for this analysis.

Significant variation appears in the outside hiring rates among the different jobs. More than 10% of the jobs hire exclusively from the outside. Even the median job selects only 13% of its employees from among other insiders. This imbalance gives the impression that ports of entry may be relatively unimportant. Indeed, 6,789 of 8,147 workers in 1989 worked in jobs with high outside hiring rates (ex-

Exhibit 7-12   Port-of-Entry Analysis, Summary Statistics

Highest outside hiring rate	1
Lowest outside hiring rate	0
Mean	.78
Median	.87
90th percentile	1
10th percentile	.35
Number of jobs in analysis	38

ceeding .87). Of course, this proportion may merely reflect the fact that low-level jobs account for most of the workforce.

This issue can be investigated more fully. Again, it is possible to describe the characteristics of the jobs with the highest outside hiring rates by regressing the job-hiring rate on the mean level of various characteristics. The job is the unit of analysis. The results are reported in Exhibit 7-13.

Although variation in hiring rates occurs across jobs, the variation is not adequately explained by the job's measurable characteristics. The only important variable in explaining differences in hiring rates is a dummy for whether the job is a production job. Production jobs are somewhat more likely to hire from the outside than other

Exhibit 7-13   Regression of Outside Hiring Rates on Job Characteristics (Dependent variable: job outside hiring rate)

Independent Variable	1	2
Intercept	1.40	.963
	(.70)	(.108)
Average salary	.000028	−.000102
	(.000076)	(.000056)
Average education	−.0449	
	(.0512)	
Average tenure	−.0222	
	(.0123)	
Production	.165	
	(.089)	
R^2	.23	.08
Number of jobs in sample	38	38

Note: The number of jobs falls short of 45 because jobs were deleted if they were not held in 1989 by workers who had been with the firm since 1977.

jobs. An almost automatic relation also appears between average tenure and the likelihood that the job is a port of entry. Jobs that have many entrants from the outside are likely to have many individuals with less tenure, for they did not come from other jobs within the firm. Similarly, some weak evidence shows that lower-salary jobs have a higher outside hiring rate when other variables are not included in the regression. But the type of job, rather than its compensation level, is more important in explaining the outside hiring rate.

These findings seem consistent with the notion that the ports of entry concentrate among low-paying production jobs. But we must remember that even high-paying nonproduction jobs hire a substantial proportion of workers from outside. Exhibit 7-12 reveals that 90% of the jobs hire more than 35% of their workers from outside, which means plenty of chance for entry at high levels in this firm.

Equalizing Differences

Differences in salary among jobs reflect workers' characteristics such as education and experience. They also reflect nonpecuniary attributes of the job itself. Although no data on the nonpecuniary attributes are available, one implication can be tested. If residual variance reflects nonpecuniary differences, then the path taken in getting to the job should be irrelevant in determining its compensation level. If, on the other hand, most of that residual variance reflects either differences in ability or internal labor market considerations of the tournament variety, for instance—then the path to the job might well be important. The proposition is testable.

One easy test is to determine whether the number of jobs that each worker has held within the firm prior to his or her current job affects compensation. The test requires us to hold the job constant and then ask whether or not past history matters. Exhibit 7-14 reports the results of including job dummies in the earnings regression along with education, company tenure, job tenure, and number of previous changes.

Two results are of particular interest. First, the longer an individual remains in the job, given company tenure, the lower the salary. This relation suggests that the best workers are promoted out of the job and that stayers are likely to be of lower quality.

Second, the number of previous job changes affects salary on the present job. This relation implies that nonpecuniary characteristics

Exhibit 7-14 Effect of Job Path on Earnings; Job Dummies Included in the Regression (Regression dependent variable: ℓn [real monthly salary])

Independent Variables	
Constant	7.3
	(0.09)
Education	.0031
	(.0002)
Tenure	.00736
	(.00006)
Number of job changes	−.0252
	(.0007)
Job tenure	−.00372
	(.00006)
R^2	.66
N	219,674

do not solely determine the definition of a job, because there would be no reason for these characteristics to vary with the number of prior job changes. An individual who gets to a level without many intervening jobs makes more money than an individual who moves through many jobs to get to the current job.[24]

Matching

By providing evidence on the importance of matching, we can further illuminate the subject of job paths. Matching models were designed primarily to explain mobility and wages among firms.[25] But the concept of matching can also be applied to movement within firms.[26] It can be argued that people who are good matches to jobs are more likely to remain in those jobs, in the same way as people who are good matches to firms are more likely to remain in the firm. The problem is that one expects individuals with high ability to be promoted out of low-level jobs and into higher-level jobs. But the same could be true among firms, for high-ability workers might tend to move from low-ability to high-ability firms. The question is how much of performance is based on firm-specific capital and how much on general ability. The same question can be asked of internal job switches. If most ability is job-specific, rather than general to the firm, then individuals who are good matches should tend to stay in their jobs.[27]

If, instead, the most important variation among individuals is in their ability to do all jobs well, then the higher-ability workers should be in the more important jobs. An ability-learning model would then better describe the dynamics of internal mobility and wage determination than would a model that emphasizes job-specific components.

One implication of internal matching is that individuals who have been in the job for a long time are better at their work. As a result, they should receive higher wages. In other words, the implication is that job tenure should be positively related to wages.

In addition to matching, institutional features would lead one to expect a positive relation of wages to job tenure. Some jobs in this firm are unionized, and unions usually codify a wage-seniority relation within jobs. Thus, any finding to the contrary is even more surprising.

The regression in Exhibit 7-14 illustrates this issue: the effect of job tenure on earnings is significantly negative. Other factors being equal, individuals who have been in the job longer have lower earnings, suggesting that job matching is not important within the firm, unless the concept of matching is broadened to include general ability sorting.

Once again, heterogeneous ability is probably the dominant factor. Within a job, the best people are promoted out more rapidly. Those who are left for a longer time are likely to be of lower quality. The evidence suggests that this firm follows the practice of promoting out the best people.

Shape of the Pyramid

We can estimate the shape of the hierarchic pyramid from these data. Exhibit 7-15 plots the number of workers in each job by salary.

This is not a smooth pyramid. The numerically largest jobs seem to be in the midrange of salary, although we find some very low-salary jobs as well. The highest-paid jobs are the smallest ones in the firm.

Shortcomings

Before concluding, let us consider a few limitations in the preceding analysis. First, and most important, that jobs help explain the data cannot be taken to refute human capital analysis. Obviously, job title

Exhibit 7-15   Job Pyramid by Salary

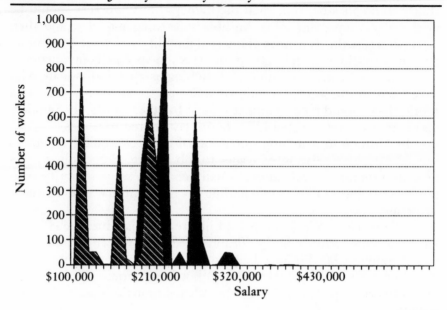

may be a proxy for human capital levels. Further, the measures of human capital used in this analysis—education and experience—are hardly comprehensive. But probably more compelling is that the firm is able to set standards and exercise discretion when individuals are hired. Individuals with low levels of measured human capital must make up for the lack by having higher levels of unmeasured characteristics.

The most reasonable interpretation for this analysis is that it focuses on internal rather than external mobility and determination of wages. It can thus use the notion of the job to help classify the information in the data. The questions asked in this analysis differ from those generally asked when human capital analyses are performed because answers can be obtained only with a firm-based data set, and because focusing on jobs rather than supply characteristics allows us to draw fresh conclusions.

Further, even though we pay attention to the job, jobs are taken to be exogenous. We make no attempt, for example, to explain the tasks that are assigned to each job, nor do we try to explain how jobs evolved.[28] To get inside the job definition requires detail that goes beyond intrafirm data. The current data set permits no investigation of these issues, but the data can be augmented with specific job descriptions, which change with time, in the future.

Conclusion

The notion of the job has been given too little attention in recent years in the literature on labor. In part, this omission has resulted from the failure to clearly define job. Jobs can be defined in a number of ways.

In tournament models, which emphasize incentives, and in insurance models, which emphasize risk sharing, a job is a name for a wage level or profile. A job has no technological attributes. The holder of the job is entitled to a specified compensation scheme.

In hierarchic theories, the job describes a control relationship: the boss makes the decisions and allocates work assignments.

Hedonic wage analysis defines a job as a series of attributes about which workers care; cleanliness, status, and security are all part of the definition.

Even human capital theory has a role for a job, which can be thought of as an investment opportunity.

Finally, a job can be described as a collection of tasks, thus emphasizing its technological features.

The importance of the job as a concept depends on its empirical relevance. The major reason jobs have been ignored in the past is that available data—primarily large individual-based micro data sets—do not permit analysis by the job. To examine the job, firm-based data are necessary.

Using panel data from a major American corporation, I have been able to answer a number of job-related questions. These are among the more interesting findings:

1. Changing jobs is the key to increasing wages. Changes occur relatively often and result in significant raises.

2. Internal turnover patterns are similar to external patterns previously examined in labor literature. Turnover is most frequent during the first few years on the job. By the time the worker has been with the firm several years, job switches within the firm are very unlikely.

3. Some jobs in the firm are much more likely than others to lead to promotions. This firm has feeder jobs and dead-end jobs. The low-wage jobs are the ones most likely to produce a promotion.

4. For most jobs a significant amount of hiring is done from outside. Although internal promotion is a common way to fill jobs, hiring from outside is frequent enough to suggest that this firm gives plenty of chance for entry at high levels. The firm seems to have no ports of entry throughout, but it is true that production jobs have somewhat higher outside hiring rates than other jobs.

5. Within-firm job matching does not seem an important phenomenon in this firm. Heterogeneous ability appears to matter more, for individuals who remain in the job for a long time do worse than those who are transferred out.

NOTES

1. These factors may include race, sex, ethnic background, and family ties.
2. See, for example, Doeringer and Piore (1971), Thurow (1972), and Reder (1955).
3. The major references here are Becker (1962, 1975) and Mincer (1962).
4. See Murphy (1984).
5. See Lazear and Rosen (1981), Nalebuff and Stiglitz (1983), and Green and Stokey (1983) for examples.
6. See Carmichael (1981).
7. See Baily (1974), Gordon (1974), and Azariadis (1975) for early studies and Grossman and Hart (1981) and Rosen (1986) for more recent surveys.
8. See Miller (1982) and Rosen (1982) for recent examples on hierarchies; see Sah and Stiglitz (1986) on organizations.
9. See Abowd and Ashenfelter (1981).
10. See Antos and Rosen (1975).
11. This is the approach used in Lazear and Rosen (1990) to examine male-female wage differences. There, the investment profiles of jobs are determined ex ante, although the number of individuals assigned to each type is endogenous.
12. See Groshen (1987) and Blau (1984).
13. See Lazear (1979, 1981).
14. See Mincer and Jovanovic (1981), Gronau (1988), and Hall (1982).
15. The literature on heterogeneity in the labor market is large. One of the early studies in this field is Heckman and Willis (1977).
16. Leonard (1989) has found elsewhere that entry into high-level positions in some major U.S. corporations is quite common. Although related, this observation is somewhat different from the question posed here. Entry may be high, but still much lower at top jobs than at lower-level jobs. Leonard also states that, in his data, entry from outside is commoner at higher levels in the hierarchy. His evidence, however, applies more to turnover rates and tenure than to career paths. He states, "Nine or ten levels down, less than 5% of all managers were hired from 1981 to 1985. But between two and seven levels down, more than 17% of all managers joined the firm in the past five years." This comparison may reflect higher turnover rates at levels two through seven or more new jobs at those levels. The evidence is suggestive but it does not directly apply to the importance of internal labor markets.
17. This formula is derived thus: A year consists of 365.25 days or 365.25/7 = 52.1786 weeks. Each week has 40 work hours, and so the work year = 2,087.14 hours, meaning that an average month has 2,087.14/12 = 173.93 hours.
18. See McCue (1990). She uses these data to examine the determinants of promotion

and the general effects of promotion on wage growth. Hers is among the few studies that even considers the job as an important unit of analysis.

19. Of course, using the wrong cut could actually obscure relevant mobility. For example, if the fifth digit referred to level within a job track, much of the movement might be from one fifth-level job to another fifth-level job within the same fourth-level job. As you will see, this firm has significant job mobility even when jobs are defined at the two-digit level. Furthermore, the mobility has the right properties. Most movement is to higher-wage jobs that appear to be promotions, but some lateral movement occurs as well.

20. For workers who worked with the firm before the sample period began, company tenure is recorded correctly, but the dependent variable refers only to the period of the data. The variable Z refers to the number of years worked during the sample period for all workers. They are highly collinear, differing only because of integer effects and because some individuals began work with the firm before our analysis. I am unaware of any potential biases introduced by this method. Furthermore, deleting individuals who started before the period had very little effect on the results.

21. See Lazear (1984).

22. Individuals who leave the firm are dropped from the sample during the year in which they leave, but are valid data points for all years up to that one.

23. It is possible to perform this analysis as a cross-section or as a time series. In a cross-section, the work histories of the current level-2 incumbents would be examined to determine the feeder jobs. In a time series, only individuals in the top 2% would be used. Their entire work histories would be constructed to get the actual paths of these workers. The cross-section approach was followed to prevent idiosyncrasies in a few individuals' careers from dictating the entire path. The disadvantage is that moves from level 3 to level 2 for level-2 incumbents may differ from moves from level 3 to level 2 for present level-1 incumbents. Thus, the path traced is not necessarily representative of any actual individuals. But the time series approach means that very few individuals are examined as we move down to the firm's bottom layers.

24. The worker with fewer job changes also has longer tenure in each job, which means lower wages. But the job tenure variable measures tenure on the current job, not on previous jobs. Job change is really a proxy for average tenure on previous jobs, for company tenure is constant as well.

25. See Jovanovic (1979).

26. In Lazear (1984), the matching story is questioned because of some empirical evidence that contradicts implications of the matching model.

27. See Lazear (1984) for a theoretical argument on this proposition.

28. See the span of control literature, such as Mayer (1960), F. M. Miller (1982), and Rosen (1982). More recently, Holmstrom and Milgrom (1989) have examined the specific tasks that are assigned to the worker.

REFERENCES

Abowd, John, and Orley Ashenfelter. "Anticipated Unemployment, Temporary Layoffs, and Compensating Wage Differentials." In *Studies in Labor Markets*, Sherwin Rosen, ed. Chicago: University of Chicago Press for National Bureau of Economic Research, 1981, pp. 141–170.

Antos, Joseph R., and Sherwin Rosen. "Discrimination in the Market for Public School Teachers." *Journal of Econometrics*, vol. 3 (May 1975), pp. 123–150.

Azariadis, Costas. "Implicit Contracts and Underemployment Equilibria." *Journal of Political Economy*, vol. 83 (December 1975), pp. 1183–1202.

Baily, Martin Neil. "Wages and Employment Under Uncertain Demand." *Review of Economic Studies*, vol. 41 (January 1974), pp. 37–50.

Becker, Gary S. "Investment in Human Capital: A Theoretical Analysis." *Journal of Political Economy*, vol. 70 (October 1962), pp. 9–49.

———. *Human Capital: A Theoretical and Empirical Analysis, with Special Reference to Education*, 2d ed. New York: Columbia University Press for National Bureau of Economic Research, 1975.

Blau, Francine D. "Occupational Segregation and Labor Market Discrimination." In *Sex Segregation in the Workplace: Trends, Explanations, Remedies*, Barbara F. Reskin, ed. Washington, DC: National Academy Press, 1984, pp. 117–143.

Carmichael, H. Lorne. "Firm-Specific Human Capital and Promotion Ladders." Working paper, Queen's University, 1981.

Doeringer, P., and M. Piore. *Internal Labor Markets and Manpower Analysis*. Lexington, MA: D. C. Heath, 1971.

Gordon, Donald F. "A Neoclassical Theory of Keynesian Unemployment." *Economic Inquiry*, vol. 12 (1974), pp. 431–459.

Green, Jerry R., and Nancy L. Stokey. "A Comparison of Tournaments and Contracts." *Journal of Political Economy*, vol. 91 (June 1983), pp. 349–364.

Gronau, Reuben. "Sex-Related Wage Differentials and Women's Interrupted Labor Careers— The Chicken or the Egg." *Journal of Labor Economics*, vol. 6 (July 1988), pp. 277–301.

Groshen, Erica. "The Structure of the Female/Male Wage Differential: Is It Who You Are, What You Do, or Where You Work?" Working paper No. 8708, Federal Reserve Bank of Cleveland, September 1987.

Grossman, Sanford, and Oliver Hart. "Implicit Contracts, Moral Hazard and Unemployment." *American Economic Review Papers and Proceedings*, vol. 71 (May 1981), pp. 301–307.

Hall, Robert E. "The Importance of Lifetime Jobs in the U.S. Economy." *American Economic Review*, vol. 72 (1982), pp. 716–724.

Heckman, James J., and Robert Willis. "A Beta-Logistic Model for the Analysis of Sequential Labor Force Participation by Married Women." *Journal of Political Economy*, vol. 85 (February 1977), pp. 27–58.

Holmstrom, Bengt, and Paul Milgrom. "Multi-Task Principal-Agent Problems." Mimeographed, Yale University, 1989.

Jovanovic, Boyan. "Job Matching and the Theory of Turnover." *Journal of Political Economy*, vol. 87 (October 1979), pp. 972–990.

Lazear, Edward P. "Why Is There Mandatory Retirement?" *Journal of Political Economy*, vol. 87 (December 1979), pp. 1261–1264.

———. "Agency, Earnings Profiles, Productivity, and Hours Restrictions." *American Economic Review*, vol. 71 (September 1981), pp. 606–620.

———. "Raids and Offer-Matching." In *Research in Labor Economics*, vol. 8, Ron Ehrenberg, ed. Greenwich, CT: JAI Press, 1986, pp. 141–165.

Lazear, Edward P., and Sherwin Rosen. "Rank-Order Tournaments as Optimum Labor Contracts." *Journal of Political Economy*, vol. 89 (October 1981), pp. 841–864.

———. "Male-Female Wage Differentials in Job Ladders." *Journal of Labor Economics*, vol. 8 (January 1990, part 2), S106–S123.

Leonard, Jonathan. "Career Paths of Executives and Managers." Unpublished manuscript, University of California, Berkeley, 1989.

Mayer, Thomas. "The Distribution of Ability and Earnings." *Review of Economics and Statistics*, vol. 62 (2, 1960), pp. 189–195.

McCue, Kristin. "Intrafirm Mobility and Wage Growth." Ph.D. diss., University of Chicago, 1990.

Miller, Frederick H. "Wages and Establishment Sizes." Ph.D. diss., University of Chicago, 1982.

Mincer, Jacob. "On-the-Job Training: Costs, Returns, and Some Implications." *Journal of Political Economy*, vol. 70 (October 1962), pp. S50–S79.

Mincer, Jacob, and Boyan Jovanovic. "Labor Mobility and Wages." In *Studies in Labor Markets*, Sherwin Rosen, ed. Chicago: University of Chicago Press for National Bureau of Economic Research, 1981, pp. 21–64.

Murphy, Kevin J. "Ability, Performance, and Compensation: A Theoretical and Empirical Investigation of Managerial Labor Contracts." Ph.D. diss., University of Chicago, 1984.

Nalebuff, Barry J., and Joseph E. Stiglitz. "Prizes and Incentives: Toward a General Theory of Compensation and Competition." *Bell Journal of Economics*, vol. 14 (Spring 1983), pp. 21–43.

Reder, Melvin W. "Theory of Occupational Wage Differentials." *American Economic Review*, vol. 45 (December 1955), pp. 833–852.

Rosen, Sherwin. "Authority, Control, and the Distribution of Earnings." *Rand Journal of Economics*, vol. 13 (October 1982), pp. 311–323.

———. "Implicit Contracts: A Survey." *Journal of Economic Literature*, vol. 23 (September 1985), pp. 1144–1175.

Sah, Raaj Kumar, and Joseph E. Stiglitz. "The Architecture of Economic Systems: Hierarchies and Polyarchies." *American Economic Review*, vol. 76 (September 1986), pp. 716–727.

Thurow, Lester. "Education and Economic Equality." *Public Interest*, vol. 28 (Summer 1972), pp. 66–81.

CHAPTER 8

The Performance Management
of Teams

Allan M. Mohrman, Jr., Susan Albers Mohrman,

and Edward E. Lawler III

Introduction

THE pressures of global competition in the 1980s generated many studies examining organizational factors contributing to aspects of competitiveness. The need for organizations to coordinate laterally across individuals, groups, and units more effectively appears repeatedly in this literature. Study after study illustrates the importance of lateral integration in such areas as innovation (Kanter, 1983), quality (Hauser and Clausing, 1988), new product development (Souder, 1988), time to market (Stalk, 1988), and sales and customer service (Cespedes, Doyle, and Freedman, 1989). Many organizations have found that proclaiming the need for teamwork is easy and comfortable. Many kinds of teamwork mechanisms have been advocated and implemented with varying degrees of success. Judging from the proliferation of teams in organizations, the formal designation of teams also appears to be easily done. Actually achieving teamwork is difficult. In our work with many organizations, we found that techniques for managing performance by teams are not well developed. Furthermore, management of team performance is at odds not only with the predominant, individually oriented performance-management mechanisms in most organizations, but also with the assump-

217

tions these organizations make about design, measurement, and control of work (Dertouzos, Lester, and Solow 1989).

In this chapter we describe some of the forces that are heightening the importance of teamwork in organizations today and the challenges they pose for managing performance. We then report findings from a number of studies investigating the relative individual and group contributions to the management of performance in settings that involve high degrees of task interdependence. Finally, we raise some of the complex issues in organization and measurement that must be resolved to manage and reward team performance successfully.

Importance of Lateral Integration

Many, perhaps most, organizations today exist in highly complex and turbulent environments with a great deal of uncertainty (Mohrman, Mohrman, and Worley, 1990). These conditions are particularly prevalent in companies that need to achieve breakthroughs in a rapidly developing technological arena, and to quickly introduce new high-quality products and processes (Von Glinow and Mohrman, 1990). Such environments have been found to require both enhanced differentiation and increased integrative mechanisms to ensure collaboration by interdependent subunits and individuals (Lawrence and Lorsch, 1967).

Galbraith's (1973) framework for understanding organizational design is based on the information-processing needs of the organization. He argues that in an organization where the work is complex, interdependent, and uncertain, the standard, vertically oriented coordinative mechanisms—goal-setting, hierarchy, and rules and programs—must be supplemented by other approaches. A complex organization therefore may have to rely heavily on lateral coordination procedures to supplement vertical integrative approaches.

Support for the argument that organizations need to change is provided by the performance demanded of organizations today. The demands include these:

1. Quality
   The need for quality has led to widespread implementation of quality improvement frameworks (Deming, 1986; Juran, 1964). These systems emphasize breaking down both vertical and horizontal organizational boundaries to facilitate the lateral,

cross-functional collaboration necessary to improve processes and enhance quality. They define quality as responsiveness to customer requirements rather than to hierarchically determined standards. This orientation emphasizes close working relationships among design, manufacturing, and marketing to keep the organization in touch with its external market.

Quality improvement frameworks identify "continuous improvement" of processes as the appropriate goal for the organization. The people actually carrying out the processes systematically measure and study them and introduce changes to improve them. Consequently, substantial information-processing requirements are introduced into the organization's technical core. Individuals at the lowest levels in the organization need good data about their work processes in order to track trends, identify patterns, and seek out and correct problems.

The emphases on processes that cut across units of the organization and on customer orientation lead to a lateral view of the organization and an understanding of its integrative needs. To accomplish this integration, quality improvement approaches often create improvement structures (teams, steering groups, and so on) parallel to the organization (Lawler and Mohrman, 1985; Scholtes, 1988) and may cut across multiple units. Organizational units also orient their activities to the internal customers' needs.

2. Time

Demands for more rapid new-product development and time-to-market cycles, and for on-time delivery, create pressure for speedy execution (Stalk, 1988). Cross-functional teamwork is generally mentioned as key in achieving fast cycle time in new product development (e.g., Takeuchi and Nonaka, 1986; Bower and Hout, 1988; Souder, 1988). That cooperation permits parallel processing and real-time resolution of coordinative needs, and fosters the learning that organizations require to introduce new products quickly.

3. Cost

Cost pressures require that organizations implement "breakthrough" manufacturing and design techniques (Haas, 1987), most of which require interfunctional collaboration and teamwork. These include concurrent engineering, workcell designs, and just-in-time procurement (Dertouzos, Lester, and

Solow, 1989). Effectively utilizing these approaches requires that lateral entities make decisions without waiting for an issue to make its way through the hierarchy.

Management and employees in general have not always been preoccupied with cost. Traditionally, the major pressure has been to get the work out on schedule. Cost breakthroughs require employee ownership of cost numbers. For this reason productivity-based group incentives such as gainsharing have been used to foster a sense of ownership. Group incentive plans have been shown to be effective if they use extensive employee involvement and teamwork (Blinder, 1990; Lawler, 1990).

4. Process Technology

Rapid technological advances in information-processing tools make possible heretofore unthinkable levels of real-time lateral integration. They permit parallel processing and inter-functional problem-solving. Distributed information capability, real-time networks, shared data bases, and powerful common languages enable lateral real-time processing of uncertainty once left for hierarchic and sequential resolution. For example, CAD/CAM promotes information processing across the units involved in the design-to-production process. Collaboration among these units is required in developing and implementing the CAD/CAM system itself and in its day-to-day utilization (Adler, 1990).

5. Innovation and Learning

Innovation, solving complex problems, and organizational learning are becoming increasingly important to competitiveness. Simply making processes more efficient is an insufficient organizational response to today's challenges. Organizations need to learn new ways of operating—innovative breakthroughs that go beyond incremental improvements.

Innovation, complex problem-solving, and learning processes often are produced by teamwork (Kanter, 1983; Pinchot, 1985; Mohrman and Mohrman, 1989). Novel combinations of perspectives and knowledge bases must be applied to issues, problems, and needs that cannot be resolved within one frame of reference. Addressing today's performance challenges requires simultaneous juggling and resolution of the logics that have dominated the organization's way of thinking about cost, schedule, and quality. This goal generally requires collaboration among functions that have historically borne the responsibility for one of these aims. Lateral integration helps conceptualize these breakthroughs and implement change.

Organizing for Lateral Integration

In response to these competitive issues, organizations rely increasingly on cross-functional teams (such as product development, project, program, and customer service teams) and other lateral integrating approaches (such as meetings, technologically mediated networks, special integrating roles, task forces, temporary teams, and matrix structures).

In our experience, members of organizations generally appreciate the importance of these lateral processes. But they are often frustrated that so little lateral integration is achieved and that the organization erects impediments to it.

Two fundamental organizing principles work against lateral integration in most organizations: functional specialization and hierarchic control. To reduce the amount of information processing required of any one person or unit, organizations are typically structured analytically. Different types of expertise are separated into specialties, and these are organized into units. Specialized units are further broken down into jobs, which specify the tasks for which an individual is responsible.

The emphasis on hierarchic control is embodied in the distinctions between three conceptual layers of the organization: (1) the technical core that performs the work; (2) the top-management group that addresses strategic directions and sets targets, objectives, and policy; and (3) the often sizable group in the middle responsible for controlling the work of the technical core and translating the strategic direction developed at the top into goals and processes for the technical core (Thompson, 1967). In large firms, these three conceptual layers have burgeoned into many more, as levels have been added to reduce spans of control and achieve coordination.

Analytical organizing principles and hierarchic control mechanisms reduce the need for lateral organization, but also work against its successful operation. When work is packaged for highly differentiated units, it is difficult to achieve integration and simultaneously to bring multiple perspectives to bear in problem-solving and coordination. Control functions that are vested in special hierarchic positions make it difficult for those performing the work to make on-line adjustments and to perform the necessary coordination.

The human resource practices in most organizations today were developed to support analytical and hierarchic approaches. For instance, superiors review individual subordinates' performance, employees are rewarded for individual performance, performance is measured against specific job standards, and people are trained for specialized work. Less attention has been paid to performance management approaches that support the synthesis of various parts of the organizational system and the building of lateral processes.[1]

The lateral integration necessary for addressing stringent performance challenges, effectively integrating myriad types of technical expertise, and solving complex problems, requires new ways of organizing. These new approaches need to emphasize systemic (as opposed to specialization) approaches, and to foster continual self-design (as opposed to hierarchic control) (Mohrman and Cummings, 1989). Organizations need to be flatter, rely more heavily on teams, and be less segmented (Mohrman, Mohrman, and Cohen, 1991). New performance-management systems are required to support these systemic and self-designing approaches to organizing.

Managing Team Performance:
Research Findings

We have done research to determine how performance management practices (including performance measurement and incentive compensation) contribute to successful performance. In this section we describe the first stage in this research in three organizations that were redesigning their performance appraisal or pay-for-performance practices or both.

Sample and Approach

The three organizations are (with pseudonyms): Avionics, Inc., a defense contractor—a division of a larger corporation that manufactures products for both commercial and defense markets; Aerocorp, a large aerospace contractor with several divisions manufacturing products for both defense and commercial use; and Oilco, a large energy company with a chemicals division as well as upstream and downstream oil and gas divisions. All are *Fortune* 500 organizations.

Exhibit 8-1 Model of Performance Management Impacts

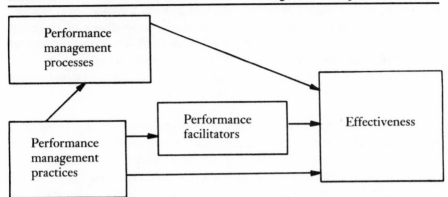

Diagnostic studies were conducted in each company. They consisted of interviews with representative professional and management individuals across all levels and parts of the companies and surveys of samples of these same employee groups. In Avionics, the survey sample was 100% of the exempt employees in the division. In Aerocorp and Oilco, the samples were 20% of the corporate populations. Survey response rates were about 60% (Avionics, $N = 400$; Aerospace, $N = 4,900$; and Oilco, $N = 2,500$).

Diagnostic Model

Exhibit 8-1 presents our basic model for diagnosing the effects of performance management practices in these organizations. The model portrays the causal paths that are implicit in much of the literature about the management of performance (see, e.g., Mohrman, Resnick-West, and Lawler, 1989). Performance management practices include reward and appraisal practices ensuring that performance is reviewed and rewarded. Performance management processes are the interpersonal procedures that people use to manage performance in a continuous way. They can be performed by supervisors or by workgroup peers. Performance facilitators are conditions in the workplace that enable people to know what is expected of them in their job and how to do it. Effectiveness is the degree to which valued results occur, including performance and human outcomes such as specialization.

According to the model, performance management practices can influence effectiveness directly. Pay-for-performance might achieve this result by motivating people. Practices can also encourage interpersonal processes and performance facilitators. For instance, performance appraisal is often expected to encourage feedback or to result in establishing goals that may in turn promote effectiveness. Interpersonal processes such as supervisors' structuring of work may directly contribute to effectiveness, or may operate by setting up performance standards that then contribute to effectiveness.

Performance management practices. Questionnaire scales measured three practices that were the significant performance-management activities in these organizations. Pay for Individual Performance measured the degree to which respondents perceived their pay to be based on their performance. This link was intended to be made formally by basing pay increases on the individual performance-appraisal system. Each company also had a special program giving one-time awards to both individuals and groups. These programs were the only avenue available for rewarding teams with cash bonuses. Special Awards measured the extent to which employees perceived that an effective special-awards program was in operation. Workgroup Self-Appraisal measured the extent to which workgroups and project teams regularly discussed the effectiveness of their work.

Performance management processes. Three questionnaire scales measured the extent to which supervisors: (1) gave feedback to group members (Supervisor Feedback); (2) structured tasks and set goals (Supervisor Structuring); and (3) stressed and exhibited a high-performance orientation (Supervisor Performance Norms). Three parallel scales measured the degree to which the workgroup engaged in the same three processes (Workgroup Feedback, Workgroup Structuring, and Workgroup Performance Norms).

Performance facilitators. Five facilitators were measured. Skill Level measured the degree to which the employee felt adequately trained and sufficiently skilled for the job. Job Specifications measured the degree to which employees reported that they had clearly specified jobs and clearly prioritized job responsibilities. Performance Standards measured the extent to which employees have jobs for which goals and performance standards could be and were defined. Understanding Role in Group measured the extent to which employees knew how their work fitted into that of the workgroup. Teamwork measured the active assistance that workgroup members gave one another.

Effectiveness. We measured four types of effectiveness. Individual Performance was measured in two ways: employees rated several aspects of their own performance and reported their perceptions of their supervisors' ratings of their performance on the same aspects. Previous research utilizing the same measures indicated that subordinates usually have an accurate sense of their supervisors' ratings (Lawler, Mohrman, and Resnick, 1984). Workgroup and Project Effectiveness measured the respondent's perception of the quantity and quality of workgroup or project performance or both. We also measured some attitudinal aspects of effectiveness: Trust (in the organization and its management) and perceptions of Pay Equity.

Analyses

Multiple regressions were based on the causal path assumptions in the model. First, we regressed each of the processes on the practices, giving us a picture of how the practices contribute to the processes. Second, we regressed each facilitator on both the practices and processes, giving a pattern showing how each of the latter variables contributes to establishing the facilitators. Finally, we regressed each measure of effectiveness on the practices, processes, and facilitators, which indicated how each of these contributed directly to effectiveness. This approach allowed us to discover paths that began with practices and ended with effectiveness, enabling us to see both direct and indirect relationships. The structure of the model and the path analyses imply a causal direction. Because the data are from surveys collected individually and the paths are based on correlations, causal relationship cannot be proven. It does allow us to examine the existence of relationships germane to the development of performance management systems in organizations. Nevertheless we will describe the results as though they were causal because of the logical causal model that guided our collection of data.

Findings

Our main interest was the pattern of results showing the relative contributions to effective organizational performance of individual and group-oriented performance management. The regressions described above were calculated separately for each organization's data. Exhibit 8-2 presents only the paths that consistently and significantly show up throughout the three separate studies of organizations. We

Exhibit 8-2   Stable Paths Across Organizations

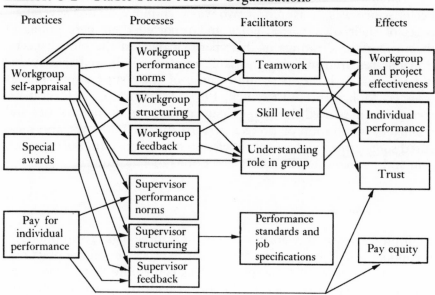

describe the results as they show the patterns of variables that contribute to effectiveness.[2]

Workgroup and Project Effectiveness show similar relationships to the performance management variables, and so we combine them and their explanatory paths in the exhibit to simplify the chart. Similarly, Performance Standards and Job Specifications are combined because their relations with the other variables are similar.

We will discuss Exhibit 8-2, starting with performance management practices.

As mentioned above, Pay for Individual Performance in these organizations is handled by individual merit pay systems. It consistently supports the three supervisor process variables: feedback, structuring, and performance orientation. This link is understandable, for in all the organizations the supervisor had sole or primary input into decisions about an employee's pay. When respondents see their pay connected to their individual performance (as appraised by their supervisor) it heightens their awareness of their supervisor's role in managing their performance. Most appraisals in these organizations have been mechanisms for ensuring supervisory feedback, goal-setting, and performance norms.

The only direct or indirect way in which Pay for Individual

Performance influences the effectiveness variables is on the attitudinal outcomes, Pay Equity and Trust. The functionality of pay-for-performance in these organizations then is twofold: when done well, it strengthens and supports the supervisor's role in engaging in performance management behaviors, and it provides a way of distributing pay which is perceived to be equitable and which leads to trust. We found no consistent effect of Pay for Individual Performance on group or individual performance measures. In one of the organizations, Oilco, Pay for Individual Performance did show significant positive influence on the workgroup processes, and therefore indirectly affected group performance. At Avionics, Pay for Individual Performance actually shows an indirect negative relation to Project Effectiveness because the supervisor process variables that it positively affected were negatively associated with project-effectiveness measures. This finding is no surprise because Avionics used a heavily matrixed structure for its organization. Individuals tended to be matrixed into projects, but their supervisors remained in their functional bases. In such a situation any practice that strengthens the supervisor's influence is liable to do so at the expense of the project because supervisors will stress measures of performance based on function.

Workgroup Self-Appraisal is the primary embodiment of team-based performance management in these companies. It shows a universal effect on all the process variables, both workgroup and supervisor. It also directly affects two of the facilitators, Teamwork and Understanding Role in Group, as well as Workgroup and Project Effectiveness. Workgroup Self-Appraisal apparently fosters workgroup performance-management processes, but not at the expense of supervisors' performance-management processes. It allows supervisors' processes to be carried out as a group rather than in the traditional one-on-one arrangement associated with performance appraisals and pay-for-performance practices. Although Workgroup Self-Appraisal relates to both supervisor and workgroup processes, only the workgroup practices and processes consistently influence both Workgroup and Project Effectiveness and Individual Performance. Much of this influence comes from the facilitators that these workgroups enable. They influence Teamwork, which in turn facilitates Workgroup and Project Effectiveness, creating a context in which individuals come to understand their role in the group, which then facilitates individual performance. These workgroup processes even help heighten the group members' skills, which facilitates performance for both individual and group.

Special Awards programs consistently influenced two forms of performance management: Workgroup Structuring and Supervisor Feedback. Special Awards also exhibited sporadic relations to other process variables in single regressions (not shown) but with little strength or consistency. This pattern of Special Awards effects mirrors the incompleteness with which Special Awards programs had been implemented in the three organizations. These programs were new in all three. That they are at all related to processes hints at their potential power in managing performance.

Performance Standards and Job Specifications are two facilitators that have no connection to any of the effectiveness variables. These facilitators are set up by supervisory structuring and goal-setting, mainstay components of most performance appraisal practices and supervisory roles. Under the stress that management usually puts on individual goals and job duties, it is striking to see no connection to performance or effectiveness of any kind. On the other hand, when workgroups use structuring and goal-setting, the results are not standards and specifications but teamwork, and increased skills and role understanding, all leading to better performance. One reason individual performance standards and job specifications do not lead to performance may be that they are static and poorly adapted to dynamic interdependent settings.

The pattern of relationships in these three companies opens to question practices in performance management that have become common in organizations. Pay for Individual Performance does not directly influence individual or group performance. The pay-for-performance practices in these organizations were based on the assumption that the way to manage performance was by hierarchic means and by focusing on individual performance. These assumptions are challenged by the importance of workgroup compared to supervisor processes and the lack of relation between standards and specifications to effectiveness.

Our findings did not explain compensation based on team performance. None of the organizations we studied had team-based incentive compensation. The closest they came were the Special Awards programs. In all these programs, performance that merited awards was defined after the fact so that the programs could not function as incentives toward specific performances. At best, they might be global incentives to do well (particularly on special projects) because of the possibility that one might be recognized. They might also create an environment in which project teams felt appreciated and rewarded for good performance. Special award practices do relate to workgroup procedures, giving us weak evidence that instituting group and team rewards may influence performance.

As mentioned, Oilco's Pay for Individual Performance practice contributes slightly to group processes, perhaps because the organization stresses group objectives and jointly accountable goals in its MBO-like management practices. This was the only example of teamwork-related practices found in these three organizations.

In summary, the performance management paths to effectiveness shown in Exhibit 8-2 illustrate how inadequate traditional performance-management practices are. First, none of the effective practices relies primarily on the supervisor. Second, the workgroup's dominance is clear from its great influence on performance. Even an individual practice focused directly on performance, like Pay for Individual Performance, contributes little to performance, although it is important to the equity and trust that employees feel. Pay for Individual Performance appears to be a tool less for motivating performance than for satisfying individual needs for equitable treatment.

In all three organizations the respondents reported much dependence upon others with whom they needed to coordinate to do their work. The findings therefore should be thus interpreted. They do not necessarily apply to settings that have little task interdependence.

Organization and Measurement: Issues and Responses

So far we have advocated organizing and managing with a team-oriented, lateral approach. The research illustrates the potential of team approaches and the limitations in the dominant individual approach to performance management. One important implication of our findings is that organizations need to develop practices for managing the performance of teams just as they have for individuals. We now describe some of the challenges in designing such approaches.

Identifying and Measuring Performance Units

The need for teams and lateral organizational mechanisms arises out of interdependence, especially when it is complex and reciprocal. Traditional organization logic frequently divides the organization at points of high interdependence. Quality assurance departments have historically been separated from production units, sales from service, manufacturing from design, and so on, making it difficult to find acceptable measures of performance at the group level. Measures with which departments and organizational units judge their own performance are often strongly influenced by other units' performance. It is hard therefore to use these measures to properly judge the group's performance. Furthermore, improvements on measures of each sub-unit of an organization often don't translate into improved measures of organizational performance (Adler, 1990), because they fail to capture systemic aspects of performance. Sometimes the measures tell only how the group has performed its part and not how well it supports others.

An attempt at solving the measurement problem is to search for better measures such as those which factor out contributions by other groups. This solution fits the paradigm for breaking down specialization of the work of organizing, but results in suboptimizing the organization's performance. A better solution may lie in creating performance units that incorporate the interdependencies into the same group. Then, measurement is not such a problem, because the team is responsible for a whole task, including the major interdependencies, and can be meaningfully measured.

This approach can include organizing teams around products, customers, processes, programs, and mini-enterprises. New product development, for instance, has usually been handled as a sequential exercise starting with defining the product and moving through designing, prototyping, manufacturing, and introducing the product into the market. Different stages have traditionally been handled by different units in the organization that are measured by their primary responsibility. Research and development is often measured according to its own budget and schedule as well as the technical quality of the work done. Important interdependencies are ignored by this approach, however. Manufacturability of the product can greatly influence budget and schedule at the manufacturing stage but needs to be incorporated into the product during the design phase. Simply making manufacturability a criterion for measurement for engineers during the design phase is not sufficient because design for manufacturability is a highly interdependent task that can be worked out only interactively during design. The project's overall effectiveness may be enhanced by relaxing schedule requirements for design and building in more time for planning manufacturing at the front end. Similar reciprocal interdependencies apply to marketing and design and marketing and manufacturing.

In a highly competitive world, time to market, development costs, and market acceptance are all critical strategic factors. They can be simultaneously pursued if the organization addresses the interdependencies they drive by concurrently teaming the various functions around the entire new-product development cycle (Larson, 1988; Wolff, 1988). Once such a cross-functional team is created, it is possible to utilize metrics that incorporate the strategic business issues. Hewlett-Packard is actively refining the systemic notion of "break-even time" (BET) to drive the necessary integration and teaming behavior in its efforts at new product development. Essentially, BET is the time it takes from the beginning until sales revenues from the new product exactly cover all its development costs. It is influenced by the product's technical excellence, market acceptance, manufacturing cost, and time to market. Once the cross-functional team is formed, BET is a sensible metric by which to manage its performance. Without such a team there is no organizational entity to which BET can be applied.

Other bases for organizing help solve the team measurement problem. Teams are increasingly being established to focus on both internal and external customers. Oilco is establishing teams around customers such as service stations and credit card users. Teams consist of representatives of different functions that the customer used to deal with separately, depending on the problem at the time. Customers were bounced around and often fell through the cracks between functions. Now each team is assigned a customer base and offers it an integrated multifunctional service. Pacific Bell and other phone companies have similarly organized around groups of customers, and base incentive rewards on the measured quality of service for that customer group. Security Pacific Bank offers full financial services by customer-based teams. Global measurement of how the customer-based team is doing is now possible by tracking how well customer needs are met. The best source of this information is the customer. It can be gathered in various ways, including periodic surveys of the customer groups. The results can be used to manage teams' performance and to determine group rewards.

Teams can also be organized around processes that cut through the organization. Oilco is organizing teams around the physical management of all its pipelines and the transferring of the material they carry. This control is possible because of automation and information technology. Geographic teams are responsible for pipelines in relatively independent regions. Teams are co-located in a nerve center from which all pipelines are operated via satellite. They can now manage their performance around overall measures of transportation efficiency and timeliness. These teams also strongly identify with customers, which are mostly other parts of Oilco (such as refineries).

The most thorough approach to organizing around teams is to create mini-enterprises within the organization. In these the team sees and manages itself as a business. The organization's traditional financial measures can then be applied, but to a smaller unit that is better able to work out interdependencies. These mini-enterprises can be organized around any of the bases we have discussed. New products can be spun off as their own businesses. Mead has done just that in starting up its new color-copier business. Xerox has organized its regional sales and service organizations as enterprises. An organization's support function, such as organizational consulting or word processing, can sell its services to the rest of the organization (and even to outside entities) and therefore compete with external groups providing similar services. Mini-enterprise teams can use such group incentives as profit-sharing and gainsharing, as Xerox has done with its sales and service organization.

In conclusion, moving to team-level performance management is not simply a matter of finding the measures. Finding the right measures is inseparable from the task of designing the right structures for team and organization. Shifting to a team-based organization demands extensive change. Our experience was that measurement and incentive issues lag behind the actual formation of teams. We also found that the specter of difficulties in measurement sometimes prevents organizations from attempting to manage teamwork.

Creating Fit among Organizational, Team, and Individual Performance

Our studies showed that trying to affect the team's performance (and, by extension, that of the organization) by focusing on the individuals' performance, is ineffectual. Appraising the performance of individuals and rewarding them for that performance no doubt affects what they do; however, these practices did not appear to influence effectiveness in our sample organizations. The data show that individual performances are facilitated by the employees' understanding of their roles within the group performance-management processes. These processes also relate positively to group performance.

If interdependencies appear among team members, then individual performance measures and rewards based on direct comparisons among performances by team members are likely to instill competition that works against achievement of group performance (Deming, 1986). We can apply a similar argument to the team's performance compared with that of the organization. The team's performance should be defined and understood in the context of the larger organization. To pursue team performance on its own terms is to risk pursuing performance that has no relation to the organization's desired performance.

The general principle here is that performance at any level must be defined and measured in the context of the next-higher level of analysis. The common tendency is to segment higher-level definitions of performance into components and then assign those segmented definitions to different performance units. The problem with this approach is that it often quickly reaches the point of diminishing returns—it is difficult to define and measure what is wanted among smaller and smaller performance units. Such definitions of performance are increasingly buffered from organizational performance needs. Further, with extensive division of labor, costs for coordination and overhead usually expand.

At Aerocorp, one of the elements in a new performance-management system that was most positively received (subsequent to the study) set off a cascade of goal-setting throughout the organization. Individuals could now see the goals of higher-level units in the organization. They were involved too in converting those higher-level goals into a definition of their own performance. This sense of how one's performance fits into the bigger picture definitely met a need that Aerocorp recognized.

To address the need for fit at all levels, members of a group, not simply the individual and supervisor, should discuss goals. Because performance environments are dynamic, influence must flow both laterally and hierarchically in the organization. Interdependent units and individuals should agree to objectives requiring one another's support, and renegotiate as conditions change.

Performances among individuals, teams, and organizations need to fit, but individual needs must be met at the same time. The diagnostic data show that pay for individual performance positively influences employees' affective reactions, such as equitable pay and trust.

Unfortunately, the data do not indicate that the companies received better performance as a result of their pay-for-performance systems. In our studies, performance is influenced by a very different performance-management dynamic: group-level sharing (of feedback, structuring behaviors, and performance norms).

How can a system for rewarding groups be structured to meet individual needs and encourage the sharing required at the group level? The solution is dual. First, teams have to be managed in a way that enables individuals to feel they can influence group performance. They must provide opportunities for involvement and for team self-management. Second, the team must be managed so that the individual's need to have excellent performance recognized are met. Because the supervisor's individual rewards may be perceived as arbitrary and can undermine team cohesiveness, however, input from the team should be a big component of individual performance management.

Interdependence among Teams

Although ideally teams should have the greatest and most complex interdependence, in most organizations interdependence will also appear among teams. Rewards for team performance can make teams focus on their own performance at the expense of other teams' performance, and especially that of the organization. The same can happen to individuals who are interdependent but rewarded for individual performance.

One way to address this issue is to manage teams as performance units, and to use a higher-level incentive based on the performance of a larger unit in the organization. Thus team members could conceivably be affected by multiple incentive plans based on performance at several levels of organization (Lawler, 1990). All members could be rewarded for their own individual performance, for that of their team, and for that of the organization in which the team performs. Lately we have seen more organizations pursue just this type of nested reward and incentive plan. Separate but interdependent manufacturing plants in one corporate division created their own gainsharing plans, and the division itself created a division-level profit-sharing plan.

Overlapping Membership

Because teams are used to perform multiple activities, individuals may be members of several teams. Factory workers might be part of both an autonomous workgroup and a quality improvement team. An engineer might be a key member in more than one product development team. A manager might be in a customer service team, an executive team, and a special task force.

Each team's performance has to be managed; otherwise, the benefit derived from integrating different types of expertise will not be achieved. When team membership overlaps, several approaches to measurement are possible. The first is to reward at the performance level to which all the endeavors are contributing. If every team is a member of a unit such as a division or a product line enterprise, then the performance bonus can be based on performance by that unit as a whole. The second approach is to cumulate performance by the individual across teams. Input from each of the teams can be combined to determine an appropriate individual bonus or pay raise. Third, each team can operate with its own way of managing performance including team-level rewards. Then employees can be eligible for performance incentives for each of the teams of which they are party perhaps weighted by their relative involvement with each.

Continual Change

Processes, products, structures, technologies, knowledge, and strategic sources of competitive advantage are dynamic. Change may demand forming and reforming teams and other lateral alliances. Performance management must be flexible. Often, its cycles must be relatively frequent, the performance unit changes constantly, and measures must be continually reassessed and redeveloped and may be idiosyncratic. Incentives need to be timed. Systems based on a calendar year often are inappropriate. Rewards need to be administered when projects and activities are complete and when teams have reached milestones.

Measurement Factors

Organizations must become comfortable with varied approaches to measurement that are applicable at different levels and in different situations. Traditional economic measures will be useful at the organizational level, and for self-contained, independent units that can be cleanly related to corporate performance. These include freestanding business units of various kinds. Basing incentives on economic performance at the organizational level has the advantage of aligning individual outcomes directly with organizational performance, and the disadvantage that motivation is diluted by the distant line of sight (Lawler, 1990).

Economic measures have less utility for smaller units or units that are heavily interdependent with other parts of the organization. Here, measures of controllable performance elements such as labor cost, waste, and other factors that are under the unit's control and clearly related to its performance are suitable. Productivity gainsharing is an incentive system that has been shown to contribute to a sense of shared fate and teamwork as well as performance (Mitchell, Lewin, and Lawler, 1990). Its philosophical underpinning is different from the exchange logic associated with most incentive approaches—that is, a specified dollar amount is exchanged for a prespecified degree of performance. Gainsharing may thus be the key to ensuring that performance and incentive coincide, because the definition of performance is identical with the source of the incentive bonus pool.

Special-purpose teams have to be measured utilizing project goals that may be qualitative but capture the intended relation between the team's performance and the larger organization's short- and long-term performance outcomes. Because quantifying such measures is so difficult, special awards may be a more suitable form of reward than an incentive scheme.

Measurement issues arise because organizations must simultaneously manage organization, business unit, team, and individual performance. At each level, the performance management practices must be nested within and compatible with those of the broader unit, but each level may require different practices, measures, and rewards. The key is to base rewards on measures which are complementary and which foster the same performance values (Schuster, 1984).

An organization may base its organizationwide payouts on measures of its strategic objectives in market share, customer satisfaction, and rate of new product introduction. It is a mistake to base an individual team's rewards only on the technical quality of its work because it might be achieved at the expense of time or customer requirements. In another example, tension occurred in a plant that had a gainsharing plan because the plant manager's corporate bonus was partly based on being able to keep labor costs low. A bonus paid to the workforce raised labor costs and counted against the bonus paid to the plant manager. Multiple simultaneous rewards that pit self-interests against each other leave people and groups working at cross-purposes. The measurement challenge is to find measures of the part that complement the larger unit measures.

Future Directions: Research and Practice

Incentive systems at any level run the risk of focusing performance on the limited quantitative measures used in the system. A critic of American management practices (Deming, 1986) remarks that numerical standards have led to mediocrity at the organizational level. He also claims that the use of standards-based performance appraisal and pay-for-performance also leads to mediocrity in the individual's performance. For this reason Deming recommends using measures as information to improve the processes being measured and not as evaluations of the processes' outputs. Some consultants working with new greenfield plants using team concepts and sociotechnical systems methodologies also have vehemently opposed gainsharing and other incentive approaches on similar grounds. They argue that such systems destroy the intrinsic motivation set up by the high-involvement structures and thus destroy the high-involvement character of the organization itself.

The validity of these claims is unclear, although some evidence shows that extrinsic rewards can reduce intrinsic motivation (Deci, 1971). On the other hand, gainsharing research points in the opposite direction. Evidence says that gainsharing can motivate more effective team coordination and improvement (Mitchell et al., 1990). Perhaps it works better because the payout depends on improvement in performance, not on attaining an artificially determined target. Nevertheless the issue is a troubling one. What attributes in the design of reward and performance management systems encourage continued improvement and organizational learning? Answering this question may be the most important task in future research and practice in this field.

An equally important question is whether group-level rewards and other performance management techniques will make any more difference in performance than individual-level approaches. Our data show no indication that, where interdependencies are high, individual pay-for-performance has any effect on individual performance. Pay-for-performance seems primarily to foster supervisory processes, to meet individual needs for equity, and to establish trust. It does so because pay-for-performance is structured under the assumption that supervisors should take primary responsibility for managing performance and that getting paid for individual performance is a fair way of paying.

Do group-level rewards function similarly? Such rewards might foster group processes, our data begin to suggest by the connection between Special Awards and Workgroup Structuring—but do group processes lead to performance? Although our data show a positive relation between group processes and the organization's effectiveness, general evidence from research is conflicting.

Gladstein (1984), for example, provides evidence suggesting that fostering effective group process is not sufficient to stimulate performance. She studied more than one hundred sales teams and found that members see team performance as a function of internal team processes very similar to the group performance-management processes in our studies. Her data indicate, however, that team performance in actual sales was a result of an external factor, market growth. The internal group factor that contributed to performance was the degree of market orientation the team members had, not group-functioning variables. When teams were rewarded for actual sales above objectives, the rewards did not strengthen the team's market orientation; rather, they strengthened its internal performance-management systems (leadership, structuring activities, and interpersonal processes). This reaction evidently occurred because team members believed such systems to be the source of their performance. This study at least makes clear that we must define the team's performance in relation to its customers and its larger organizational context.

In our study, finding that workgroup self-appraisal is so strongly related to performance with no sign of group incentives raises other questions. What additional influence on performance would group rewards provide? Also, can group rewards lead to better performance without performance management by the group? On the largest scale we find consistently that such organization-level incentive programs as profit-sharing, gainsharing, and ESOPs show no connection with improved productivity until they are accompanied by some ways of involving employees (Blinder, 1990). These techniques for involvement are comparable to the workgroup self-appraisal practices in our study; groups of people need them to perform together as a team.

Pritchard et al. (1988) performed a controlled experiment to investigate the other side of this issue. Does adding an incentive to workgroup procedures improve performance? They found that performance feedback to the group was, by itself, capable of boosting performance 50% over a productivity baseline. When involvement in goal-setting was added, productivity was boosted another 25% over the original baseline. Adding group incentives brought the gain up a mere 1%.

It seems clear therefore that group incentive pay does not work without ways of involving the group. And it may be that group incentives add no performance increment to those created by the involvement methods. What then is the role, if any, of group incentives, and in general of group rewards? Perhaps at the group level lies a phenomenon similar to the relation between individual pay-for-performance and individual perceptions of equity. As organizations move more to group and teamwork designs, group-level pay-for-performance may become part of the subjective equity formula for employees. In fact, Mohrman, Ledford, and Demming (1987) showed that implementing a gainsharing plan in a team-based organization increased perceptions of equity.

We have raised a number of important unanswered questions about group performance-management approaches. Our data suggest that where interdependence is high, the old individually oriented approaches offer little leverage on performance. We expect to see team and organization-level approaches proliferate. But this is relatively unploughed ground, and much research must be done. Such approaches too are inextricably related to work and design of organizations. Consequently, we offer a word of caution. New team-level performance-management approaches should be developed carefully and implemented in a manner that enables the organization to learn and to refine the design iteratively. We hope the published literature on such approaches will grow and offer useful design frameworks.

NOTES

1. "Performance management" is used throughout to refer to the broad array of management practices that are aimed at managing people's performance, including appraisals, goal-setting, rewards, and developmental planning.

2. More extensive reporting of regression analyses is available elsewhere (Mohrman, Mohrman, and Worley, 1988).

REFERENCES

Adler, Paul S. "Managing High Tech Processes: The Challenge of CAD/CAM." In *Managing Complexity in High Technology Organizations*, Mary Ann Von Glinow and Susan Albers Mohrman, eds. New York: Oxford University Press, 1990, pp. 188–215.

Blinder, Alan S., ed. *Paying for Productivity: A Look at the Evidence*. Washington, DC: The Brookings Institution, 1990.

Bower, Joseph L., and Thomas M. Hout. "Fast-Cycle Capability for Competitive Power." *Harvard Business Review* (January–February 1988), pp. 110–118.

Cespedes, Frank V., Stephen X. Doyle, and Robert J. Freedman. "Teamwork for Today's Selling." *Harvard Business Review* (March–April 1989), pp. 44–58.

Deci, E. L. "Effects of Externally Mediated Rewards on Intrinsic Motivation." *Journal of Personality and Social Psychology*, vol. 18 (1971), pp. 105–115.

Deming, J. Edwards. *Out of the Crisis*. Cambridge, MA: Massachusetts Institute of Technology, 1986.

Dertouzos, Michael L., Richard K. Lester, and Robert M. Solow. *Made in America*. Cambridge, MA: MIT Press, 1989.

Galbraith, Jay R. *Designing Complex Organizations*. Reading, MA: Addison-Wesley, 1973.

Gladstein, Deborah L. "Groups in Context: A Model of Task Group Effectiveness." *Administrative Science Quarterly*, vol. 29 (1984), pp. 499–517.

Haas, Elizabeth. "Breakthrough Manufacturing." *Harvard Business Review* (January–February 1987), pp. 75–82.

Hauser, John R., and Don Clausing. "The House of Quality." *Harvard Business Review* (May–June 1988), pp. 63–73.

Juran, Joseph M. *Managerial Breakthrough*. New York: McGraw-Hill, 1964.

Kanter, Rosabeth Moss. *The Change Masters*. New York: Simon & Schuster, 1983.

Larson, Clint. "Team Tactics Can Cut Product Development Costs." *Journal of Business Strategy* (September–October, 1988), pp. 22–25.

Lawler, Edward E., III. *Strategic Pay*. San Francisco: Jossey-Bass, 1990.

Lawler, Edward E., III, Allan M. Mohrman, Jr., and Susan Resnick. "Performance Appraisal Revisited." *Organizational Dynamics* (Summer 1984), pp. 25–35.

Lawler, Edward E., III, and Susan Albers Mohrman. "Quality Circles after the Fad." *Harvard Business Review* (January–February 1985), pp. 64–71.

Lawrence, Paul R., and Jay W. Lorsch. *Organization and Environment*. Boston: Harvard University, Graduate School of Business Administration, 1967.

Mitchell, Daniel J. B., David Lewin, and Edward E. Lawler III. "Alternative Pay Systems, Firm Performance, and Productivity." In *Paying for Productivity: A Look at the Evidence*, A. S. Blinder, ed. Washington, DC: The Brookings Institution, 1990, pp. 15–88.

Mohrman, Allan M., Jr., Gerald E. Ledford, Jr., and Sheree Demming. "Gainsharing Congruence with High-Involvement Organization Design." Working paper, Los Angeles: Center for Effective Organizations, University of Southern California, 1987.

Mohrman, Allan M., Jr., Susan A. Mohrman, and Christopher Worley. "High Technology Performance Management." In *Managing Complexity in High Technology Organizations*, Mary Ann Von Glinow and Susan Albers Mohrman, eds. New York: Oxford University Press, 1990, pp. 216–236.

Mohrman, Susan Albers, and Allan M. Mohrman, Jr. "Organizational Change and Learning." In *Effective Organizations: The Next Ten Years*. Los Angeles: Center for Effective Organizations, University of Southern California, 1989.

Mohrman, Susan Albers, Allan M. Mohrman, Jr., and Susan G. Cohen. "Human Resource Strategies for Lateral Integration in High Technology Settings. In *Human Resource Management Strategy in Higher Technology*, Luis R. Gomez-Mejia and Michael W. Lawless, eds. Greenwich, CT: JAI Press, in press.

Mohrman, Susan Albers, Allan M. Mohrman, Jr., and Christopher Worley. "Performance Management in the Highly Interdependent World of High Technology." Los Angeles: Center for Effective Organizations, University of Southern California. Working paper 88-4(117), 1988.

Pinchot, Gifford, III. *Intrapreneuring*. New York: Harper & Row, 1985.

Pritchard, Robert D., et al. "Effects of Group Feedback, Goal Setting, and Incentives on Organizational Productivity." *Journal of Applied Psychology*, vol. 73, no. 2 (1988): pp. 337–358.

Scholtes, Peter R. *The Team Handbook*. Madison, WI. Joiner Associates, 1988.

Schuster, Jay. *Management Compensation in High Technology Companies*. Lexington, MA: Lexington Books, 1984.

Souder, William E. "Managing Relations Between R&D and Marketing in New Product Development Projects." *Journal of Product Innovation and Management*, vol. 5, no. 1 (1988), pp. 6–19.

Stalk, George, Jr. "Time—The Next Source of Competitive Advantage." *Harvard Business Review* (July–August 1988), pp. 41–51.

Takeuchi, Hirotaka, and Ikujiro Nonaka. "The New-Product Development Game." *Harvard Business Review* (January–February 1986), pp. 137–146.

Thompson, James D. *Organizations in Action*. New York: McGraw-Hill, 1967.

Von Glinow, Mary Ann, and Susan Albers Mohrman, eds. *Managing Complexity in High Technology Organizations*. New York: Oxford University Press, 1990.

Wolff, Michael F. "Teams Speed Commercialization of R&D Projects." *Research Technology Management* (August 1988), pp. 8–10.

PART **III**

Performance Measurement and Productivity

CHAPTER 9

An Examination of Control Mechanisms in Organizations with Ill-Defined Technology and Output

K. J. Euske

Introduction

AN implicit assumption underlying incentive compensation systems is that the systems' performance measures should relate to desired or successful outcomes for the organization. The predominant view is that efficiency is, or at least should be, the underlying metric for decisions on resource allocation and that control systems should be designed to promote efficiency. It is not clear, however, that all organizations use the efficiency criterion or that it explains behavior within all organizations. At least some organizations adopt control systems for reasons other than efficiency (Tolbert and Zucker, 1983). Some control systems may have a symbolic role (Meyer and Rowan, 1977).

A number of researchers have investigated symbolic and other

I thank Robert Hayden, Michael Query, Graham Shipley, and Alex Snead for their assistance on this project. Helpful comments were provided by Steven Funk, Mark Haskins, John Norton, William Rotch, and participants in the Performance Measurement and Incentive Compensation Colloquium at Harvard University, Darden School Research Workshop, and the University of Maryland and VPI Accounting Workshops.

uses for control systems (e.g., Ansari and Euske, 1987; Boland and Pondy, 1983; Burchell et al., 1980; Covaleski and Dirsmith, 1983; Covaleski and Dirsmith, 1988), but the influence of a role other than efficiency for the control system is not always well understood or described. Yet an organization's performance depends on its ability to control the use of resources available to it; understanding how the resource control system relates to organizational performance is an important element in creating incentive systems. Assuming that the relationship promotes efficiency even though it does not could lead us to reward efficiency, which here could be detrimental to the organization. The work described in this chapter is meant to help us understand how the control system performs.

In organizations whose technology and output are ill-defined, the control of resources is understood, with few exceptions, less well than organizations with well-defined technology and output (Anthony, Dearden, and Bedford, 1989). For this discussion, the distinction between well- and ill-defined technology is defined by the degree to which the means to achieve a specific end or output can be specified. Levitt and Nass (1989) define the concept as "ambiguous technology." The ambiguity derives from "unclear connections between means and ends" (Levitt and Nass, 1989, p. 193). Not only can clarity be lacking in the connections between means and ends, but identifying, measuring, or evaluating the entity's output can also be difficult; that is, we may consider the output ill-defined.

The output distinction is similar to that made by Ackroyd, Hughes, and Soothill (1989) between services and manufactured goods. They argue that the difference "might be expressed by saying that the utility of a service is intrinsic to the relationship of provision, whilst the utility of a good is intrinsic to the object sold" (p. 607). So too with ill-defined output: the utility of the output is intrinsic to, or at least highly dependent on, how the receiver perceives the service. Such technology and output are so strongly stressed in our society (see Heskett, 1986) that we need to systematically understand how resources are controlled in organizations that subsist in environments with ill-defined technology and output.

We focus this study on organizations with ill-defined technology and output, analyzing three aspects of the organizations.

- the organization's profit orientation (is it organized for profit or not?)[1]
- source of funding (single or multiple)

- proximity of activities to the organization's core transformation process

We discuss the reasons for including these variables below.

The institutional model (e.g., Meyer and Rowan, 1977) and the technical-rational model (e.g., Thompson, 1967) of organizations suggest that resources in environments with ill-defined technology are differently controlled in the profit and nonprofit sectors. Furthermore, the control of resources may also be influenced by their source—that is, whether those resources are from one relatively significant source or from a broad base of clients or customers (Euske and Euske, 1991). The models indicate that control systems in a client-funded profit organization should be designed for efficiency; the control systems in the nonprofit organization with one source of funding (sometimes referred to as block funding) should be configured to maintain the organization's legitimacy. The control systems differ because success in the respective environments is evaluated from fundamentally different perspectives (Meyer, Scott, and Deal, 1983). Another way of looking at the distinction is that in the two types of organizations rationality serves different purposes. In the nonprofit organization, rationality is called upon primarily to project an image of legitimacy to the organization's publics (Meyer and Rowan, 1977). In the profit organization, rationality is used primarily to discover ways of becoming more efficient (Thompson, 1967). Although the theory suggests that both profit and nonprofit organizations with client or block funding, employing the same technology (such as child care organizations), should control their resources differently, whether they do so is not clear. For instance, Macintosh, Moore, and Williams (undated) found that lower-level managers in nonprofit public sector organizations use budget information for technical and rational decision making. A cover story in *Business Week* ("Learning," 1990) indicated that nonprofit organizations combine efficiency and legitimizing techniques.

The apparent inconsistencies may in part be explicable by the focus chosen for previous research. Demonstrating that control systems are used for various purposes and that organizations adopt control systems for reasons other than efficiency, such research has been focused on the institutional level (Macintosh, Moore, and Williams, undated). Hofstede (1981), examining systems within the organization, argued that the range of processes in nonprofit organizations requires a variety of control methods. The need for such variety can be viewed in terms of the internally rational efficiency focus of the technical-rational model and the externally rational legitimizing focus of the institutional model. The more proximate the control activity or process is to the organization's core transformation process (i.e., core technology), the more likely it is to be directed toward internal efficiency. Control processes peripheral to the core transformation function are more likely to have an external legitimizing focus (Meyer and Rowan, 1977). The questions here are: What occurs at the organizational level? Do profit and nonprofit organizations adopt different control systems? Are the control systems used for different purposes at different levels in the organization? Are the control mechanisms in these two types of organizations essentially the same or different?

Research Method

Designing the Research and Selecting the Sample

To investigate the variables for this study, we adopted a multiorganization and multisector design. The sample was selected with two major objectives. First, the variables had to be readily available for investigation (Glaser and Strauss, 1970) because our goal was to identify properties of the control systems and suggest possible relationships within organizations, which are not well understood.[2] Second, the results, taken collectively, would provide information on the variables.

The sample was drawn from two service industries. One industry provides information on the distinction between profit and nonprofit and funding. The other industry provides information on the distinction between profit and nonprofit and effects of the core processes of the organization's transformation function. The profit-nonprofit distinction is relatively clear in the United States. The funding distinction, though conceptually simple, tends in practice to be a continuum from one source of funding to a large number of sources.

To clarify the profit-nonprofit distinction and the extent of funding, we sought an industry that included (1) ill-defined technology and output, (2) profit and nonprofit organizations, and (3) client-funded organizations and organizations with one or relatively few sources of funding. The child care industry met these criteria. "Good care" and the means for achieving such care are poorly defined and hard to measure. Relatively clear indicators of care are expected by parents—clean facilities, accepted staff-to-child ratios, children who do not appear to be mistreated—but beyond such obvious measures, good and appropriate care is difficult to define and measure (Kamerman, 1986; Patten, 1986). Also, the child care industry has both profit and nonprofit organizations. (Adams, 1986; "America's Child," 1989; "Early," 1990). Thus the industry can provide information about the effects of funding and profit orientation on the control of resources.

To capture the profit-nonprofit distinction and the effects of the core processes in the transformation function, we sought a second industry that would include (1) ill-defined technology and output, as with child care, (2) profit and nonprofit organizations, (3) single-source funding, and (4) departments or parts of the organization that would specialize in various aspects of the core processes. The specialization was seen as a way to help ensure that proximity to the core processes of the organization would be identifiable and variable. The fire protection industry met these criteria. "Good fire protection" indicates neither specific means nor outputs. Elements of it, however, have well-specified means-ends relationships such as using specific compounds for extinguishing particular types of fires. Fire departments have staff and departments specializing in various elements of fire protection. These organizations, along with the child care centers, should provide information on the relation between the core transformation processes and the control system.

Although both industries had ill-defined technology and output, fire protection would probably be considered to have the better-defined technology and output. Fire departments' success in saving structures can be evaluated routinely, albeit informally, by passersby. Evaluations of child care services are more difficult because the output takes longer and is influenced by confounding factors such as family life. Thus the degree to which technology can be considered ill-defined does vary with the industries. Exhibit 9-1 presents the variables for which the sample could provide data.

Research Sites

Ten organizations were included in the study: eight child-care centers and two fire departments.[3] Exhibit 9-2 gives the characteristics of the child care centers. Two centers (A and B) were profit oriented and totally funded by clients; two (C and D) were nonprofit and client-funded with rent-free facilities provided by the sponsoring (or host)

Exhibit 9-1   Variables Included in the Study

Ill-Defined Technology and Output

Profit	Client Funding	Proximate to Core
	Block Funding	Peripheral to Core
Nonprofit	Client Funding	Proximate to Core
	Block Funding	Peripheral to Core

Exhibit 9-2   Characteristics of Child Care Centers

Center	Orientation	Funding Source	Sponsor-Funded Facilities	Potential and Actual Enrollment
A	Profit	Client	No	20/20
B	Profit	Client	No	36/36
C	Nonprofit	Client	Yes[a]	36/25
D	Nonprofit	Client	Yes	54/45
E	Nonprofit	Client 85% Block 15%	Yes	48/48
F	Nonprofit	Client 80% Block 20%	Yes[b]	37/37
G	Nonprofit	Client 50% Block 50%	Yes	75/75
H	Nonprofit	Client 15%[c] Block 85%	No	156/156

[a]Cost of facilities was approximately 15% to 30% of a child care center's operating budget.
[b]Part of block funding.
[c]Clients = 10%; fund raisers and charities = 5%.

organization; two (E and F) were nonprofit, client-funded, and received less than 20% of their funding and subsidized rent from a sponsoring organization; two (G and H) were nonprofit and received at least one-half of their funding from the state. Child care center G received 50% of its funding from a state "latchkey" grant. Child care center H received 85% of its funding from the state.

Exhibit 9-3 presents characteristics of the two fire departments. Fire department A was part of an employee-owned company, corporation A, which employed about 1,800 people and provided fire, ambulance, health care, and related services in six states. It supplied contract fire service to the city of Glencoe,[4] with a population of approximately 125,000 people in a 182-square-mile area. The city was a bedroom community for a larger, growing community. Fire department A provided this service with 84 staff and firefighting personnel. Glencoe provided 40 paid reserves. The city's 1989–1990 fire department budget was $4.9 million, $4.4 million of which went to corporation A. The other $0.5 million supported the city staff who monitored the contract and the 40 paid reserve staff who were employed by the city.

Fire department A was located in the same community as the corporate headquarters and was in many ways an extension of the headquarters. This connection provided a benefit for gathering data:

Exhibit 9-3　Characteristics of Fire Department

	Fire Department A	Fire Department B
Orientation	Profit	Nonprofit
Community served		
Population	126,000	102,000
Area	182.5 square miles	52.7 square miles
Staff	84 full-time	98 full-time
	40 paid reserves	
	124 total	
Budget	$4.4 million direct	$5.6 million
	$0.5 million indirect	
	$4.9 million total	
Cost per capita	$38.70	$54.66
Cost per square mile	$26,760	$105,722
Fire loss per capita	$13.32	$20.26
Average response time (minutes)	4:08	3:00

the proximity of headquarters provided direct access to information on how the company handled the profit motive. The relationship did, however, make it difficult to identify if fire department programs and procedures had originated at corporate headquarters rather than fire department A.

Fire department B was a public fire department serving Joplin, a farming community with a population of about 102,000 in a 52.7-square-mile area. It provided this service with 98 staff and firefighting personnel. The 1988–1989 fire department budget was $5.6 million.

Data

This study used two main sources of data. Interviews were conducted with members of each of the organizations included in the study. The purpose was to obtain a description of how resources were controlled and of the core transformation processes. The interviews were semi-structured; the protocol that served as a general guide is given in Appendix A. With one exception, at least two individuals were interviewed in each organization. In the one organization with a staff of three, only one individual was interviewed. Appendix B lists the titles of the individuals interviewed. The interviews lasted from two to four hours and were conducted on-site at the organizations. In addition to the formal interviews, informal conversations were held with other members or clients of most of the organizations.

The second source of data was archival information obtained from the organizations and other sources. Whenever possible, archival data were gathered to corroborate the interview data. Appendix C provides examples of the types of documents reviewed. To help ensure accurate findings, drafts of this paper were sent to the participating organizations for critiques.

In the following section we present our results from analyzing the interviews and inspecting the archival data for the child care centers and the fire departments in the study. In the last section we list our conclusions from the study.

Analysis and Results

Child Care

Findings. First, we discuss the technology and output of the organizations, followed by two components of the resource control system—budget and capacity utilization.

State regulations influence the degree of standardization (such as staff-to-child ratios) among child care organizations. Except for child care center F, all the centers in this study had to pass regular state inspections to maintain their legal status to operate. Center F was federally operated and subsidized; thus it was not subject to state control, but had to adhere to federal guidelines. The federal government sent inspectors annually to monitor center F's compliance with those guidelines. Center F also followed state and National Association for the Education of Young People guidelines to help ensure that it was providing "quality" child care. Each of the directors indicated that meeting the official requirements was necessary to operate. They suggested that meeting these requirements was primarily a way of providing an indication to the marketplace that basic care was provided.

All the child care centers in this study attempted to present an image of professional caregivers with whom parents would feel comfortable leaving their children. "The image [center H] wants to present is that they care about children and the families, and they are accountable and credible." The director of center B said, "I want the public to think of [center B] as clean, quality day care." The image was projected by state licensing, parent's handbooks or newsletters, clean facilities with identifiable equipment for education and recreation, organized and scheduled activities, and organizational goals emphasizing quality care.

The directors emphasized that the organization's most important role was to provide quality care to the children. The director of center A, a "drop-in" center in a shopping mall, expressed the importance of providing "a safe and enjoyable experience for each child while they are at our center." Although the director of center B emphasized financial stability and stressed operating at capacity, she stated, "I don't cut corners on quality."

The emphasis on quality permeated the organizations. Although personnel had to meet credential requirements, all the directors saw this as a necessary but not the "real" measure for evaluating new employees. When asked to list the most important factors in hiring staff, each director stated the need to have a sense or a feeling that the potential employee cared about providing quality care. The director of center A said, "I'm looking for a nurturing person"—that is, someone who had "the ability to respond well to children and make them feel good about themselves." The director of center C stated that she wanted individuals who cared about "maintaining kids' self-esteem" and who had the "right personality and [would] react well to kids."

Even though quality care was generally discussed in terms of the children's well-being, the definition of the desired effect or output of the care varied. Quality care for the drop-in center meant "providing parents with a baby-sitting service that they could feel secure with." For centers C and D, quality care was defined as providing religious exposure. Center F defined quality care as "providing physical and mental stimulation, social contacts, and trustful relationships." Center H defined quality care as availability and affordability while meeting community needs. In some of the organizations, quality care was closely tied to the religious beliefs of the sponsoring organization; in others, it was focused more on maintaining the child's sense of value and self-worth.

Differences were observed in the control of resources, particularly budgets and utilization of capacity. Exhibit 9-4 identifies use of budgets at each of the child care centers. All the nonprofit centers (C through H) prepared budgets to meet legal or organizational requirements. The directors discussed the importance of the budget as a way of demonstrating to a higher-level body that the child care operation

Exhibit 9-4   Child Care Centers' Use of Budget

Center	Budget Used for	Budget Used by
A	Basic analysis of profitability to identify the organization's financial position.	Owner
B	No formal budget; the director-owner used the annual financial statements to determine tuition and salaries.	Director-owner
C	Required by the church child care committee to keep them advised of the center's financial health; to monitor the director's stewardship.[a]	Director; church child care committee
D	Required by the church board of directors to keep them advised of the center's financial health; to monitor the director's stewardship.	Director; church board of directors
E	Required by the board of directors to keep them advised of the organization's financial health.	Director; board of directors
F	To fulfill agency requirements; to identify the center's financial position.	Director; director's superior
G	To fulfill state requirement; center modified daily operations and expenditures based on financial position.	Director; assistant director; director's superior
H	To fulfill state requirement; to identify the organization's financial position to avoid funding shortfalls.	Director; board of directors

[a]Stewardship was defined as the responsibility the board of directors gave to the director to spend the organization's funds in an appropriate manner.

was using its resources appropriately. Little difference appeared between client-funded nonprofit centers (with facilities provided) and those with one source providing most of the funds. At centers G and H, the two larger nonprofit centers, the budget was actively used as a management tool. At center H, monthly variance reviews were conducted and the results were reported to the board. At center G, the budget was used for daily operating decisions. The specific use of the budget in these organizations appeared to be a function of the size of the organizations (that is, size is a confounding factor for these two organizations).

At the two profit centers, budgets were used to control the organization's internal functions, not to satisfy a legal or organizational requirement. Center A prepared a formal budget. Center B used the previous year's financial statements, matched with current revenues and expenses, as a budget "proxy." The owner prepared these budgets as internal management tools.

Except for center G, detailed knowledge of the budget or use of its contents did not extend below the level of the director at any of the child care centers in this study. Center G (nonprofit, block and client funding) was the only organization in which the assistant director was more than casually familiar with the budget. The director was teaching the assistant director to use the budget for planning operations. Although the assistant director said she "did not know a lot about the budget process," she did say she used the budget to help plan her daily activities. In discussing the budget she said, "For example, if funds are tight, I will substitute graham crackers for muffins as a snack in order to save money." Even those assistant directors who had major responsibility for daily operations were but vaguely familiar with the budget.

Control over budget information does not necessarily mean that the staff of the organizations were unaware of the organization's financial status. At center B, the assistant director participated in annual tuition and salary discussions. The owner of center A said she did not believe the director used the budget as a management tool; the owner said her directions to the director were to "buy whatever you need." The director said, however, "I know how the budget is doing—what's coming in. So I spend based upon that." The center E director said, "We consider the budget really important." The center E staff member interviewed said she did not know how the executive director decided "who gets what." From the staff member's point of view, however, the system provided needed items: "[The director] has never failed to get me something I needed. I've never had to ask more than once." The organizations' relatively small size appeared to allow the directors to allocate and control resources informally, rendering unimportant specific knowledge of the budget at lower levels.

Child care centers that received some form of block funding had more formal budget processes than the other centers. Formal procedures were identified as those having such characteristics as prescribed cost relationships, standardized forms, specified time schedules, and well-defined committee structures. The process in centers C and D (client funding and facilities provided) was more informal than in centers E through H (client and block funding). Because centers G and H were two to three times larger than centers C and D, the differences in formality could, in part, be a function of size. Centers E and F, however, were about the same size as centers C and D, and yet they had the more formal systems.

Utilization of capacity differed among the child care centers. The owners of the profit centers in the study viewed enrollment as a key to survival. The director-owner of center B (profit, client funding) stated that full-capacity enrollment (as determined by the state) was critical to the success of a child care center. According to this owner-director, "A lovely, quality day care center is nice, but if it is operating below capacity, it won't survive."

The directors of centers C and D (client funding with facilities provided by the sponsoring churches) cared less about full capacity than about ideology. Center C's policy statement read, "The objective of [center C] is to teach the children the concept of God." The director of center D stated that a goal of the center was to "provide a Christian ministry for preschool children." The *Parent's Handbook* for center D stated that the organization's objective was "to teach the concepts of God . . . and how these concepts relate to everyday living." The directors at both these centers indicated that they intentionally operated below the state-authorized capacities. The director of center D stated that this decision "provides better-quality service and a more relaxed atmosphere." That is not to say that the directors were unaware of the effects of varying enrollment. The director of center C said,

If we have 15 paying regularly, then we meet expenses for a director and a teacher's aide. If we get 20, we can pay for an additional teacher too. If we go more than 25, I'd have to buy more equipment and it would be too crowded. The state thinks we have adequate space for 36. With that many children, it gets too wild; 20 is perfect.

The remaining child care centers (E through H), which received some form of block funding, operated at full capacity, as did centers A and B. The staff at centers E through H, however, expressed different reasons for operating at capacity from the staff at centers A and B. Centers E through H existed (and received block funding) to provide services to the members of their supporting communities. For centers E and F, the communities consisted of "employees" of the sponsoring organization. For centers G and H, the community consisted of the taxpayers who ultimately provided the block funding for the centers. Both centers G and H were part of state-funded social programs to provide care for children. Attendance records for centers

G and H were reviewed by its funding source to validate remuneration.

The decision on how many children to enroll at a center varied with the type of center and its source of funds. The profit, client-funded centers used an efficiency metric to determine their enrollment. The nonprofit, client-funded centers that had a religious orientation operated at less than capacity, expecting that their clients preferred smaller child care centers for their children. The nonprofit, client- and block-funded centers appeared to base their enrollment decisions on the sponsors' expectation that the centers would provide as much service as possible for the block funding provided. Each of the eight directors indicated that it had a waiting list of clients for the center's services.

Discussion

The findings are generally consistent with the theoretical predictions. The profit organizations approached the budget from an internal-efficiency focus. The owners developed the budget primarily for their own use to help ensure survival for the organization. The directors of the profit centers described the budget as a major internal management tool. For each of the nonprofit organizations, the budget had an external focus. The nonprofit directors recognized that the budget had internal importance but emphasized the external reporting function. The budget was a vehicle by which the nonprofit organization could demonstrate to its sponsoring or funding organization that resources were being used appropriately. At the two larger child care centers (G and H), the budget's internal importance for management control was more visible than in the small centers.

Although the internal (efficiency) versus the external (legitimacy) focus is consistent with the technical-rational and institutional perspectives, notice that only the nonprofit centers had a superordinate organization to which reporting was required. The boards of directors for the profit organizations were described by the directors (that is, the managers) as legal requirements and not policy-making or controlling bodies. More active boards of directors for the profit-making organizations might create a more external focus for budgetary reporting, as in the nonprofit organizations.

The budget processes of the organizations receiving block funding were more formal than those of the other nonprofit organizations or of the profit-making organizations. The formalization could be a function of the budget's importance as a source of funding. That is, the budget not only served as an internal management tool and means for providing stewardship information to superordinate organizations, it was also a means for generating resources to operate the organization. This formalization can be seen as a way of becoming isomorphic with key elements in the environment to ensure survival (DiMaggio and Powell, 1983; Scott, 1987). In any case, each organization used the budget as an internal management tool, but the intensity of use varied.

Although all the organizations could be described as staffed by "caring individuals" and quality of care was highly important in all, utilization of capacity was driven by different needs. The profit-making organizations used an efficiency metric to evaluate how they utilized capacity. The church-affiliated centers used capacity utilization to demonstrate that quality care was being provided. From another point of view, maintenance of excess capacity by centers C and D could be considered a way of "paying the rent." That is, the excess capacity showed the sponsoring church that a unique quality of care was being offered.

Organizations receiving block funding all ran at maximum capacity. The directors said the reason was the community's great need for their services. The need justified the existence of these organizations to the funding sources. Also, running at less than capacity might suggest to the funding sources that the funds provided could be better used in other programs.

This use of capacity raises questions about performance measurement within the different organizations. If an efficiency metric were used in the two church-sponsored child care centers, they would be relatively inefficient in their utilization of capacity. If the managers were to run the organizations "efficiently," however, the rent subsidies might well be lost. Although the managers would then have been efficient in the short run, long-run efficacy probably would have been sacrificed. Incentive compensation plans tied to the "efficient" use of resources would probably be detrimental to the organizations.

Finally, although the centers were in general "doing the same thing" (that is, providing quality child care) and focused on similar characteristics of the child care process (such as hiring caring individuals), the centers identified the product or output differently (such as babysitting, Christian ministry, and physical and mental stimulation).

In summary, the findings from the child care centers indicate that, although the centers differed in size and funding, all focused internally on providing the highest quality of care they could with their resources. The degree of use of the budgets varied with the center's size and profit orientation; nevertheless, all the organizations used the budget. The internal and external budget orientation of the child care centers was congruent with predictions made by the technical-rational and institutional theories.

Fire Protection

Findings. We follow a brief introduction to the industry with a description of the organizations and key elements of the core technology.

Community fire protection service normally is provided by local governments. A community fire-protection organization can be all volunteer, it may be fully paid, or it may combine the two. The choice normally is a function of the community's resources.

Volunteer departments are normally located in sparsely populated areas with little industrial base; as wealth in the community increases, one would expect some full-time personnel to be employed. The addition of some full-time employees has a direct payoff to the community in terms of faster response to a fire, better training of the volunteers, and perhaps lower fire insurance premiums. (Ahlbrandt, 1973, p. 18)

The United States has only about a dozen private fire departments (Gilman, 1979, p. 23). Their use generally arises from a need not being served by local government. Private fire departments sell subscriptions for their services to individuals. As communities grow, the local governments often assume the responsibility of providing fire protection, which usually eliminates the private firms. In a few cases, contracting with a private firm to provide the service has become an alternative for local governments. A local government can negotiate a contract that allows it to purchase specific services that reflect the community's desires. The fire stations and capital equipment can be owned by the local government, later allowing it to change contractors or organize a public fire department more readily than if the contractor owned the assets (Ahlbrandt, 1973; Institute for Local Self-Government, 1977; Gilman, 1979).

The fire departments in this study were similar in many ways. Both were dedicated to providing professional fire protection to their communities. Both received funding from one source. Both had traditional hierarchic organizations, with similar chains of command (e.g., chief, assistant chief, district chiefs). Both used the minimum acceptable manning for the fire equipment as defined by the National Fire Protection Association. The managers in both organizations said technical training was essential to successfully accomplish the organizations' mission. Both had mid-level managers who tracked state-required training.

Differences were observed, however. Although both organizations had efficient and well-documented programs to ensure appropriate training, upper managements' views of the programs differed. Both organizations presented three reasons for the program:

1. To have appropriately trained firefighters for the community.

2. To demonstrate to the city government that the organization was qualified to do its job.

3. To make firefighters more efficient at their tasks.

The interviewees at fire department B (nonprofit) emphasized the first two reasons. The interviewees at fire department A (profit) emphasized the third. The interviewees at fire department A described training as a way of decreasing staff by "overtraining" individuals, thereby providing a specified level of coverage more efficiently. Fire department A was part of a profit-making organization. The view consistently expressed there was that the organization was in the business to make a profit. Profit would be generated by providing better service more inexpensively than public sector fire departments would. In its publications, fire department A presented assorted statistics, similar to those in Exhibit 9-3, documenting that it provided higher-quality fire protection at lower cost than other municipalities. In one publication, the fire chief was quoted as saying, "In order to succeed, we have to be *better* than public sector fire service, and [Glencoe] allows us to do that by exploring new, improved methods and technologies." [emphasis in the original]

Although Glencoe was proud of its relationship with fire department A, threats to the relationship were evident. A recent example involved an effort by the larger neighboring community to tie all the communities in the area together under a common 911 dispatcher. Fire department A chose not to join. Critics of fire department A argued that this move was an example of the isolation Glencoe experienced from common emergency services because of its private fire department. Fire department A's rebuttal was:

[Glencoe] *does* have mutual aid on the same basis as any other [local] city. In fact, under the existing mutual aid system, [fire department A] provides assistance more often outside its service area than it receives assistance from other fire departments. And [Glencoe] *isn't* part of the [larger community's]-controlled dispatch system for the same reason [another neighboring community] isn't. Having its own dedicated dispatch system gives [fire department A] more control and quicker response." [emphasis in the original]

Fire department B, on the other hand, was a part of the Joplin governmental structure. Replacing fire department B simply did not enter into the discussions. For the fire department to continue receiving a "fair share" of the city's annual budget, however, it had to demonstrate that resources were used appropriately. One means of doing so was to have trained fire department staff.

The relationships between the fire departments and their communities were fundamentally different. Fire department A negotiated the services that it would supply to Glencoe. Fire department A provided the manning within the framework described to meet its contractual responsibilities. Fire department B had to respond to any request for service by Joplin.

The departments' goals and objectives also differed. Those of fire department A were not as specific and technically oriented as those of fire department B. Fire department A's mission statement was to "provide the citizens of [Glencoe] a safe community to live and work in by providing education, information, code enforcement, and quality cost-effective emergency services." In support of the mission statement, fire department A had six strategic goals:

- To improve employee morale as much as possible by innovative management techniques.
- To evaluate and increase the skills of all personnel.
- To continue to improve and develop managerial skills.
- To improve and integrate reserve and support programs.
- To continue and improve strong city–fire department relations.
- To improve the community's awareness.

The mission statement and goals were posted in the corporation's offices and in the fire stations. They were also disseminated at employee orientations. Along with the company's goals and plans, the operations plan had six more detailed action plans and nine tactical plans.

The "Program of Services" portion of the City of Joplin budget plan detailed program goals for fire department B:

To provide 24-hour-a-day emergency medical service and protection against fire deaths, personal injury and damage to property by analyzing hazardous conditions, by determining the causes of incidents that have occurred, and by evaluating losses, so that patterns of threat are known and preplanned to allocate personnel and equipment quickly and powerfully.

The goals were listed for the five major activity areas—fire protection, emergency medical services, fire prevention, training, and hazardous-material control. Forty-seven major program objectives for the activity areas were also listed. Examples of program objectives are:

- To prevent obsolescence of fire apparatus and equipment fleet.
- To build in fire protection with automatic fire sprinklers in all fire stations.
- To monitor and modify the preventive-maintenance schedule.

The goals and objectives evolved from year to year. When a new service was required or a higher priority was determined, the list would be modified.

Differences between the departments in specific goals and objectives appear to relate to the different relationships they had with the cities. Fire department A's goals and objectives were structured to allow the flexibility not only to provide cost-effective fire protection but also to demonstrate to the community continually that the organization was doing so. Fire department B's goals and objectives were structured to provide specific indexes that the community's resources were being appropriately used.

Both organizations cared about efficiency. For fire department A, efficiency was a way of ensuring that the contract would continue and of generating a positive bottom line. Also, if fire department A did not operate efficiently, the parent corporation could decide to invest its money in another business. The corporate vice president said that profit was of prime importance. Efficiency was fostered in ways such as budget reviews, reward and incentive programs, extensive cross-training of personnel, and temporary fire stations. Probably the best example of fire department A's emphasis on efficiency is that it used a modified two-platoon system.[5] Fire department B used the more traditional three-platoon system. The modified two-platoon system allowed fire department A to operate with 20% fewer personnel than if it had used a three-platoon system. Fire department A's firefighters worked more hours per year, however, than fire department B's.

Efficiency was also important to fire department B, which faced both limited resources and the need to provide increasing services. Fire department B's manpower had not increased since 1973, but the community's population had increased by 50%, and the number of response calls by 550%. As additional responsibilities arose, they were added to current duties. In response to the need for more emergency medical service, the department had recently adjusted its program of services to include advanced lifesaving service. The department had also enlarged its hazardous-material efforts and its training in response to community demands. The station chief, commenting on the extra responsibilities, said, "There is not as much brass polishing going on any more," meaning that the resources were needed for operational requirements rather than cosmetic or nonessential activities.

Fire department B had been able to keep its level of service satisfactory by further training its personnel to improve productivity. The station chief said that the city was now in a quality-versus-quantity trade-off, but if it wanted an increase in service without an increase in personnel, the quality of service would suffer. He commented, "[Joplin] is resigned to the fact that their service will start to suffer, even though you won't hear a public official say it."

The two fire departments defined their customer bases differently. They also interacted with the communities differently. Customer satisfaction was an important element in fire department A's strategy. It defined its customer as the community resident and used customer satisfaction as a proxy to measure success, surveying customers regularly. The department's written policies were emphatic: "It is the responsibility of every employee to exploit opportunities to enhance good will and public relations." The station chief said, "We always remember: the customer pays the bills." Fire department A appeared to take actions that cost it money just to improve customer satisfaction, such as participating in local parades or posting idle emergency equipment at local sporting events.

Fire department A funded a public relations program (it had a full-time public relations person on staff), which it considered an important tool in promoting a positive image to the city, its residents, and the department's employees. If the city and its residents had a favorable opinion of fire department A, the interviewees said, they believed the department had a better chance of getting the contract renewed.

Fire department B defined its customer as the entire community and attempted to demonstrate to the community's elected representatives (the city council) that the department was providing professional fire protection.

Fire department B did not have a public relations program, and no funds in the budget for such activities. A manager said that the department did not try to improve its image in the community (to influence the funding level), because the city council disliked having departments bring external pressure on it. The only community activities supported were those in the course of business (fire-prevention activities, school presentations, station tours, and presentations to organizations). Fire department B had no formal means of determining how it was being perceived by the public or whether its performance conformed to public expectations. Feedback was not actively solicited, but it did make an attempt to correct situations brought to its attention.

Budgeting was done differently in the two organizations. Corporation A used top-down, zero-based budgeting; it had a formal budget process and issued written instructions to fire department A. Department A was required to give Glencoe its budget and cost data. After Glencoe and fire department staff informally agreed on a fire department budget, it was processed through the city's system like the city's other departmental budgets and presented to the city council for approval.

Corporation A held monthly budget reviews that started at a level above the stationhouse and went up through the corporate level. Year-to-date variances, by amount and percentage, were presented and discussed. Staff analyzed the variances and alerted management to problems. The corporate vice president explained that every line-item variance was studied in detail. He said, "This is how we learn where our losers are."

Fire department B's budget formulation was essentially done by the fire chief. Each division submitted a wish list to the chief, but according to the assistant fire chief, no written instructions were given to the divisions for the budget process. The chief made the final budget request based on goals and objectives he had identified. The chief then presented the budget to Joplin's city manager and budget director. The city council evaluated the budget along with those of the other city departments. Once given his budget figure by Joplin, the fire chief worked with his divisions to fit their wants within his priorities and the dollars available.

The assistant fire chief for fire department B indicated that no formal budget reviews or updates occurred. He said, "The process is computerized to allow for easy tracking of expenditures and variances, but no formal reports are produced." Fire department B staff did monitor the variances to ensure that it was staying within budgetary limits. All revenues came from the city's general fund, and only 2% was spent on capital outlays. The chief had discretion to move noncapital-project money within the department.

Discussion. Our purpose in studying these two fire departments was to investigate whether differences in the control of resources varied relative to elements in the transformation processes. The control of activities close to the organization's core transformation process (such as learning firefighting techniques) showed greater similarity between the two organizations than did peripheral elements (such as budgeting and public relations). This result is consistent with arguments presented previously.

State requirements specified the amount and frequency of training, and the two formal training programs for the firefighters were similar. The fire departments both emphasized technical training and managed the training similarly. Both sought an efficient way of achieving the specific training goals. Even though both organizations had efficient and well-documented programs to ensure appropriate training, however, the uses of the training programs in more peripheral activities differed: for fire department A, the program was an efficiency mechanism; for fire department B, it was a legitimizing mechanism. Notice that "efficiency," in turn, was a means for fire department A to legitimize itself.

As a profit-making organization in a fundamentally nonprofit industry, an important activity for fire department A was demonstrating its legitimacy continually. The efforts to do so had two major goals:

1. To demonstrate that high-quality fire service could be provided at a lower cost than could be provided by a nonprofit fire department.

2. To be a visible part of the community by such actions as participating in parades and placing idle equipment at community activities.

Fire department A's resources were directed to both promoting and demonstrating that the department was efficient. Resources were directed to keep public awareness of fire department A high with the members of the community (the voters). The budget process supported the efficiency focus. Fire department A positioned itself so that efficiency was the focus of the legitimization process.

Fire department B was an integral part of the city government. Its resources were directed at maintaining the status quo in its funding relationship with the city. The manager's goal was to maintain funding through the city council. This approach carried through to its relations with the community and the internal budget process.

General characteristics of the departments' processes discussed were consistent with the argument presented previously. Fire department A's legitimacy came from being efficient; fire department B's legitimacy came from demonstrating to the city council that it was providing service and following the city council's protocols. Fire department A's control systems were oriented to developing efficiency and promoting it; fire department B's control systems provided detailed performance-oriented goals and objectives to the city and did not actively cultivate residents' support.

Concluding Remarks

This study was designed to help develop our understanding of how resources are controlled in organizations with ill-defined technology and output. Departing from research that found differences at the institutional level (e.g., Ansari and Euske, 1987; Boland and Pondy, 1983; Burchell et al., 1980; Covaleski and Dirsmith, 1988), this study was focused on internal operations. Three aspects of the organizations were analyzed: profit orientation of the organization (profit or nonprofit), sources of funding (single or multiple), and proximity of activities to the organization's core transformation process.

The first finding is that the profit-nonprofit distinction, funding source and the ill-defined technology and output (child care) interacted to affect the controls. Different funding sources added a layer of complexity in the control of activities. Use and formality of budget and capacity utilization varied among the child care centers. All used the budget as an internal management tool to some degree. The profit child-care centers had a more internal focus for the budget; the budget was prepared as an internal management tool. The nonprofit child-care centers had a more external focus for the budget; the budgets were prepared to meet legal or organizational requirements. The block-funded child care centers tended to have more formal budget processes than the client-funded centers. Finally, the child care centers that were receiving only subsidized facilities from their sponsoring organization ran at less than full capacity. All other centers, regardless of funding source or profit orientation, operated at maximum capacity.

Second, we found differences in practices and control in peripheral activities carried out by the fire departments. Budgeting and use of public relations differed in the two fire departments. Budgeting in the profit organization was more formal, supporting the organization's external efficiency focus. Budgeting in the nonprofit organization was more informal, geared to maintaining receipt of a "fair share" of the community's budget. Likewise, the public relations function was defined as the key for the profit fire department but not for the nonprofit fire department. These differences contrasted to the similar controls used for core processes (such as manning levels and skill training) of the fire departments.

The third finding is that, when the technology and output were relatively better defined (in fire departments rather than child care centers), the control practices used to monitor activities close to the core transformation process were essentially the same. The fire departments identified fire protection as their primary mission and controlled resources similarly. In child care, where technology and output were less well defined, differences appeared. Quality of care represented fundamentally different concepts among the centers. The differences in defining quality of care can be viewed as weighting performance attributes differently because of different market segments. An important fact is that the expression "quality child care" is ambiguous, apparently leading to diverse controls and use of resources. Notice that the focus is on differences *between* the industries, based on technology and output.

Although the organizations did exhibit differences, they did not look as different internally as they did from outside (e.g., all the organizations used the budget for internal management—only the degree of use varied; both fire departments sought efficiency). These results are generally consistent with previous research (Ansari and Euske, 1987; Boland and Pondy, 1983; Covaleski and Dirsmith, 1983; Macintosh et al., undated). Control systems may have multiple roles, but the differences in the systems may be greater for external than internal matters. DiMaggio and Powell (1983) suggest that the controls are a way for the organization to demonstrate compatibility with the environment. Within limits, however, each organization put some energy into thinking about efficiency.

The study does raise questions about the performance measures used in determining incentive compensation. For instance, how much do subsidies (such as facilities for the child care centers) influence the resources that can be evaluated from an efficiency perspective? If efficiency is used as a basis for evaluating and rewarding managerial behavior, the resources included must be carefully defined. Efficient use of the facilities could be detrimental to the organization's long-run success. The issue here is not the manager's control of resources but rather excluding a controllable resource from the measurement base. More generally, in these organizations, efficiency as a measure of performance should be tempered by other factors.

In this chapter, we describe and illustrate how funding structure and the relative ambiguity of technology relate to control characteristics in a few organizations. The results and analysis are an attempt to provide empirical evidence of the differences in control structures among these organizations. Future research might focus on similar industries, use a representative sample, choose measures that are more amenable to statistical analysis, and produce results that are more generalizable.

NOTES

1. Adopting the position presented by Anthony and Young (1984, p. 35), we use "non-profit" here rather than "not-for-profit."

2. This inductive approach is justified because of the dearth of theory that adequately explains how control systems function in these organizations. In most cases too, theory has not been adequately tested empirically or refined. Hence, one purpose of this study is to test theory empirically and to provide the basis for future deductive, empirical analysis.

3. The original design of the study included two organizations from a third industry— information services. Access and subsequent comparability issues, however, proved that information to be of questionable value.

4. The names of the communities are disguised.

5. A platoon is the crew necessary to staff the fire department for a shift.

REFERENCES

Ackroyd, S., J. A. Hughes, and K. Soothill. "Public Sector Services and Their Management." *Journal of Management Studies*, vol. 26, no. 6 (November 1989), pp. 603–619.

Adams, D. "National Survey of Family Day Care Regulations: Summary of Findings." In *Current Issues in Day Care*, C. H. Thomas, ed. Phoenix: Oryx Press, 1986, pp. 93–98.

Ahlbrandt, R. S., Jr. "Municipal Fire Protection Services: Comparison of Alternative Organizational Forms." *A Sage Professional Paper, Administrative and Policy Studies Series*, Series number: 03-002, vol. 1, 1973.

"America's Child-Care Crisis: The First Tiny Steps Toward Solution." *Business Week* (July 10, 1989), pp. 64–65.

Ansari, S., and K. J. Euske. "Rational, Rationalizing, and Reifying Uses of Accounting Data in Organizations." *Accounting, Organizations and Society*, vol. 12, no. 6 (1987), pp. 549–570.

Anthony, R. N., J. Dearden, and N. Bedford. *Management Control Systems*, 6th ed. Homewood, IL: Richard D. Irwin, 1989.

Anthony, R. N., and D. Young. *Management Control in Nonprofit Organizations*, 3d ed. Homewood, IL: Richard D. Irwin, 1984.

Boland, R. J., and L. R. Pondy. "Accounting in Organizations: A Union of Natural and Rational Perspectives." *Accounting, Organizations and Society*, vol. 8, nos. 2, 3 (1983), pp. 223–234.

Burchell, S., C. Clubb, A. Hopwood, J. Hughes, and J. Nahapiet. "The Roles of Accounting in Organizations and Society." *Accounting, Organizations and Society*, vol. 5, no. 1 (1980), pp. 5–27.

Covaleski, M., and M. Dirsmith. "Budgeting as a Means for Control and Loose Coupling." *Accounting, Organizations and Society*, vol. 8, no. 4 (1983), pp. 323–340.

———. "The Use of Budgetary Symbols in the Political Arena: An Historically Informed Field Study." *Accounting, Organizations and Society*, vol. 13, no. 1 (1988), pp. 1–24.

DiMaggio, P. J., and W. W. Powell. "The Iron Cage Revisited: Institutional Isomorphism and Collective Rationality in Organizational Fields." *American Sociological Review*, vol. 48 (April 1983), pp. 147–160.

Early Childhood Education, GAO/HRD-90-43BR. Washington, DC: United States General Accounting Office, January 1990.

Euske, N. A., and K. J. Euske. "Nonprofit Organizations Employing the Other Side of Rationality." *British Journal of Management*, vol. 2, no. 2 (July 1991), pp. 81–88.

Gilman, D. "Can Private Enterprise Deliver the Goods?" *Dun and Bradstreet Reports Magazine*, vol. 27, no. 1 (January–February 1979), pp. 20–23 +.

Glaser, B. G., and A. L. Strauss. "Theoretical Sampling." In *Sociological Methods*, N. K. Denzin, ed. Chicago: Aldine, 1970, pp. 105–114.

Heskett, J. L. *Managing in the Service Economy*. Boston: Harvard Business School Press, 1986.

Hofstede, G. "Management Control of Public and Not-For-Profit Activities." *Organizations and Society*, vol. 6, no. 3 (1981), pp. 193–211.

Institute for Local Self-Government. *Alternative to Traditional Public Safety Delivery Systems*. Berkeley, CA, September 1977.

Kamerman, S. B. "Child-Care Services: A National Picture." In *Current Issues in Day Care*, C. H. Thomas, ed. Phoenix: Oryx Press, 1986, pp. 4–7.

"Learning from Nonprofits." *Business Week* (March 26, 1990), pp. 66–74.

Levitt, B., and C. Nass. "The Lid on the Garbage Can: Institutional Constraints on Decision Making in the Technical Core of College-Text Publishers." *Administrative Science Quarterly*, vol. 34, no. 2 (1989), pp. 190–207.

Macintosh, N. B., J. C. Moore, and J. J. Williams. "Managerial Roles and Budgeting in Public Sector Organizations." Unpublished manuscript, undated.

Meyer, J. W., and B. Rowan. "Institutionalized Organizations: Formal Structure as Myth and Ceremony." *American Journal of Sociology*, vol. 83 (1977), pp. 340–363.

Meyer, J. W., W. D. Scott, and T. E. Deal. "Institutional and Technical Sources of Organization Structure: Explaining the Structure of Educational Organizations." In *Organizational Environments*, J. Meyer and W. R. Scott, eds. New York: Russell Sage, 1983, pp. 45–67.

Patten, P. "How to Choose the Best Day-Care Program for Your Child." In *Current Issues in Day Care*, C. H. Thomas, ed. Phoenix: Oryx Press, 1986, pp. 62–63.

Scott, W. D. "The Adolescence of Institutional Theory." *Administrative Science Quarterly*, vol. 32, no. 4 (December 1987), pp. 493–511.

Thompson, J. D. *Organizations in Action*. New York: McGraw-Hill, 1967.

Tolbert, P. S., and L. G. Zucker. "Institutional Sources of Change in the Formal Structure of Organizations: The Diffusion of Civil Service Reform, 1880–1935." *Administrative Science Quarterly*, vol. 28, no. 1 (March 1983), pp. 22–39.

APPENDIX A

Interview Protocol

What are the organization's present goals?

How have your organization's goals changed over time?

What are the organization's strategies for achieving its goals?

Explain how the implementation of strategies is monitored.

Does the organization have standard operating procedures (SOPs)? What steps do you take to implement them?

Explain how the organization determines how many people or how much equipment it requires to provide its services.

Starting from the final approval of the budget, describe how you developed the last budget. Are there written budget instructions?

How often is the budget reviewed?

What kind of budget updates are there? How often are they provided?

What is the organization's primary source of revenue? What are the other sources? Get percentages for each.

What have been the most successful techniques to improve income or funding?

Who are the organization's major clients or markets?

How does the organization identify the needs of potential clients?

Describe how the organization establishes the price(s) of its services.

How does the organization measure customer or client satisfaction?

How is the customer-satisfaction information used by the organization?

Does your organization have a formal, internal organizational performance-assessment program? Quality-control program?

What actions have you taken (also ask if organization has taken action) based on the results of the last assessment?

How do you ensure that quality of service is maintained?

Do you think your quality control [performance-assessment program] is unique in any way?

When you hired the last person for your staff, what were the factors that you thought most important for the decision?

Think about the last employee evaluation you conducted. Starting with the final step, describe the process.

How do you ensure that a candidate meets the requirements for advancement?

What importance do professional certification and formal education hold in forming an opinion about a current or prospective member of your staff? [Mention legal requirements.]

Does the organization have written position descriptions?

Does the organization encourage employees to pursue further education or training?

Does the organization provide sponsorship for employees' education?

How many individuals participate in the organization's educational program?

How are new employees introduced to the organization?

What image does your organization attempt to present to the public?

How does the organization attempt to get this image across?

What department within the organization has responsibility for this effort? Is it a separately budgeted activity? [Does the organization have a separate budget for this activity?]

How many resources, dollars and otherwise, does the organization put into its advertising efforts? PR efforts?

What amounts or types of expenditure require approval by the board of directors [or next higher level]?

How often do you talk to the board [next higher level] about issues? Do board members [next higher level] come to your operation to discuss issues?

APPENDIX B

Individuals Interviewed

Child Care Centers

Center	Persons interviewed (by position)
A	Owner
	Director
B	Director or owner
	Assistant director

C   Director

D   Director
           Part-time teacher

E   Director
           Assistant director

F   Director
           Assistant director

G   Director
           Assistant director

H   Director
           Assistant director

Fire Departments

Fire department A   Corporate vice president
                     Fire chief
                     Station chief

Fire department B   Fire chief
                     Assistant fire chief
                     Station chief

APPENDIX C

Archival Data Reviewed

Child Care Centers

Child Care Center A

State Child Day Care General Licensing Requirements
Center A: General-Information Brochure
Center A: Control Card
Center A: Application for Employment
Center A: Accident Report Form
Center A: Daily Sign-in/Sign-out Record Sheet
Center A: Preschool Enrollment Package
Center A: State Immunization Record
Center A: Preschool Brochure

Center A: Job Description: Director, Assistant Director, Aide
Center A: Guidelines for Discipline of Staff, Children
Center A: State Child-Abuse Index Check

Child Care Center B

State Child Day Care General Licensing Requirements
Pamphlet: "What Is Montessori?" (Information Brochure)
Pamphlet: "A Parent's Guide to Understanding Sexual Abuse"
   (Information Brochure)
"Montessori Operations Handbook"
Center B: Parent's Handbook
Center B: Administrative Handbook
Center B: Financial Records; containing:
         Payment records
         Checking-account records
         Financial statements (with accountant's cover letter)
         Payroll records
         Tax information
Center B: Enrollment Application
Center B: Statement of Parental Rights
Center B: Statement of Personal Rights
State Forms: Health History, Emergency Contact; Immunization
   Record; Physician's Report

Child Care Center C

State Child Day Care General Licensing Requirements
Center C: General Information Brochure
Center C: Contract of Employment
Center C: Application for Enrollment
Center C: Sample Budget
Center C: State Facility Review Sheet, Day Care Centers
Center C: Formal Job Description for the Director or Teacher,
   drafted by the Child Care Committee
Center C: Informal Job Description for the Teacher, drafted by the
   Director

Child Care Center D

State Child Day Care General Licensing Requirements
Manual of Administration of Christian Pre-Schools
Center D: Parent's Handbook

Center D: Employment Application Form
Center D: "Suggested Questions" (to be asked during employment
    interviews)
Center D: Teacher Evaluation Form
Center D: Enrollment Application Form
Center D: Family "Background Information" Form (for newly
    enrolled children)
Center D: Statement of Personal Rights
Center D: Emergency Care Information Form
Center D: Tuition Scale
Center D: 1988–1989 Budget
Church Board Minutes from Former Center D Pre-School Board
1987–1988 "Goals and Objectives" for one of Center D's teachers
State Forms: Health History; Emergency Contact; Immunization
    Record; Physician's Report

Child Care Center E

Child Care Conference Agenda
Center E: Bylaws
Center E: Staff Manual
Center E: Staff Meeting Agenda
Center E: Sample Employee Evaluation
Center E: Initial Employee Conference Form
Center E: Financial Records (dated 31 May 1989), including:
            1989 budget
            Balance sheet
            Budget versus actual-income statement
Center E: Board of Directors' Meeting Agenda
Center E: Introductory Brochure
Center E: Parent's Handbook
Center E: New-Employee Welcome Letter
Center E: Tuition-Rate Schedule
Center E: Tuition-Information Package
Community Publication on Child Care Options for Employers and
    Employees
Newspaper Article on Center E
Article from Center E's Corporate Sponsor

Child Care Center F

NAEYC Day Care Center Certification Checklist
Center F: Parent's Handbook

Center F: New-Employee Checklist
Center F: Employee Work Performance Evaluation
Center F: Financial Records, including:
      Income statement
      Budget summary
Center F: Child-Caregiver Position Description
Center F: Employee Handbook
Host Agency Employee Handbook
Government Employee Supplemental Evaluation Form
Host Agency Instruction "Operation of Child Development Center"
Host Agency Organization Chart

Child Care Center G

State Child-Care Quality-Review Instrument
Center G: Employee Roster
State–Teacher's-Union Contract
School-District Personnel Evaluation Procedures
School-District Personnel Evaluation Review Form
Supervisor's Evaluation of Site Director, dated 15 April 1989
Site Director's Goals and Objectives for 1989
School-District Budget Information
Center G: Parent's Newsletter

Child Care Center H

Center H: Policy Handbook for Parents
Center H: Organization Chart
Center H: Personnel Handbook
Center H: Employee-Evaluation Form
Center H: Alternative-Payment Program Handbook

Fire Departments

Fire Department A

Corporation A: Strategic Plan 1, November 1988
Corporation A: Supervisor's Guide to Policies
Operational Plan 1989–1990, City of Glencoe Fire Prevention/
    Fire Operations
Corporation A: Expanded President's I.D.E.A. Program, January
    1989

Corporation A: Pay Structure
Corporation A: Achievement-Evaluation Program Manual
Corporation A: White Paper on Fire Department A, March 1989
Organization Charts for Corporation A (including Fire Department A)
Corporation A's Service Awards Program

Fire Department B

City of Joplin Affirmative-Action Plan, 1988
City of Joplin, Program of Services, 1987–1988
Personnel Manual, City of Joplin, 1 February 1988
Fire Department B: Statistics
Fire Department B: 1988–1989 Accomplishments
Fire Department B: Work Force list
Fire Department B's Management Practices, 17 April 1989
City of Joplin, Employee Performance Program (5)
Fire Department B's Operations Manual

CHAPTER **10**

Total-Factor Productivity Measurement, Pertinent or Passé?

Kiran Verma

Introduction

$\mathbf{P}$ERFORMANCE measurement is an essential part of management control in that it validates whether the results anticipated from planned action are realized. Because what gets measured gets attention, the kind of performance an organization chooses to measure will motivate actions that improve the measure. Traditionally, bottom-line measures such as profit, revenue, and cost have been used to evaluate managers' performance. But in the face of competitive reality, new strategies with new action plans and new performance systems are needed. The traditional measures of profit are no longer considered adequate for motivating desired behaviors such as enhanced productivity and greater focus on customers. Therefore, in recent years, senior executives have been rethinking how to measure their managers' performance. This new thinking has put pressure on organizations to redesign their systems for measuring performance to focus on measures for entities other than financial profit and cost. These new categories include measures for productivity, quality, and customer satisfaction (see Berliner and Brimson, 1988, p. 62).

Within organizations, systems for measuring financial performance are the best developed and entrenched systems because ac-

279

countants have been refining them ever since the double-entry system was invented in the fifteenth century. Overhauling and redesigning these systems therefore requires conviction, careful preparation, and perseverance (see Eccles, 1991).

This paper is focused on issues dealing with the design of performance measurement systems for evaluating and motivating improvements in productivity.

Background of Productivity Measurement Systems

The slowdown in productivity growth of the U.S. economy has attracted much attention among managers and researchers. Analysts from many disciplines have published studies of the causes for the slowdown. Much of the research, particularly that done by economists and political scientists, has focused on comprehensive measures of national and industrial productivity and has failed to yield many insights or prescriptions for the productivity slowdown in general (see Nelson, 1981).

In practice, interest in productivity measurement originated in 1972 as a response to public-utility commissions' requirement that requests for rate changes by regulated firms include productivity measures. Later, even firms in nonregulated industries began to realize that to stay competitive they had to increase and monitor productivity continually. But it was quickly evident that most firms did not know how to define or measure productivity. As a response to growing anxiety about the slowdown in productivity, the American Productivity Center (APC) was founded in 1977. The center's main objective was to develop and promote measurement of productivity at the firm level.

The APC held seminars and conferences to teach companies how to measure and improve productivity. The measure developed by the APC fits in the category of total-factor productivity (TFP) measures because it relates the output of a process to all inputs used to create that output. In contrast, any measure that compares output to just one of the inputs, such as units per hour, is a partial productivity measure. The APC advised firms that although it was acceptable to begin measuring productivity with partial productivity measures, the ultimate goal was to develop a measure of total firm productivity. Such a measure would be focused on the productivity of all factors and would be more thorough because it would incorporate the effects of factor substitution. The measure also had the desirable feature that it could be related to bottom-line results (see Ruch, 1981).

In contrast to the interest in productivity measurement shown by economics researchers and managers, accounting researchers mostly ignored the issue. Kaplan (1983) criticized the lack of research on productivity measurement in accounting literature:

Cost accounting texts do not contain even a minimal discussion of techniques, procedures or properties of productivity measurement. Apparently productivity measurement, perhaps the most basic measure of manufacturing performance over time, has not yet been considered part of the information that will assist managers in their decision making and control activities. (p. 693)

More recently, a few accounting studies have examined TFP measures and compared them to the variance in accounting efficiency reported by traditional cost-accounting systems (see Banker et al., 1989; Barlev and Callen, 1986) and TFP measures have been discussed in a revised textbook on management accounting (see Kaplan and Atkinson, 1989, p. 321). But before accountants get on the bandwagon of productivity measurement, it is worthwhile to ask if productivity measurement has outlived its usefulness. In a recent survey of productivity measures used by U.S. firms, Kraus (1984) reported that the companies surveyed made limited use of productivity measures. Of the companies that measured productivity, fewer than 15% used or planned to use any sort of a TFP measure. This lack of interest in TFP measures was also documented by Armitage and Atkinson (1989).

My main purpose in this paper is to examine why, in spite of careful design and promotion, TFP measures are not widely used in practice. Some of the reasons given by Kraus (1984) and Atkinson and Armitage (1989) are that managers find TFP measures too detailed, too difficult to understand and use, and unnecessary. But these reasons are stated generally and do not help identify improvements that could make TFP measurement systems more useful. These studies also do not distinguish between types of TFP measures and do not examine the appropriateness of TFP measures to the purpose for which they were used. In this study we examine the question of usefulness of TFP measurement systems by exploring in detail the development and subsequent overhaul of one such system at Ethyl Corporation. By interviewing managers and examining company records, I document the features of the old system, its intended purpose, why it became obsolete, and the improvements incorporated in the new system. The analysis sheds light on some of the features that help make productivity measurement systems more useful.

Site Selection

Ethyl Corporation was selected from a sample of firms that had sent managers to the APC's productivity seminars, and had later implemented a TFP measurement system. After contacting several of the firms in the original sample, I found that many of the companies had already abandoned their systems for measuring productivity. These preliminary interviews left the general impression that the productivity measurement programs in these companies had not survived beyond the tenure of their original promoters in the organization. Many of these companies were implementing systems to track other performance measures such as total quality and customer satisfaction. Of the remaining companies with functioning productivity measurement systems, many were in regulated industries. Managers from these companies indicated that the system was used only for reporting productivity measures for rate-increase requests. From the remaining companies in the nonregulated industries, I chose to study Ethyl Corporation for these reasons: (1) because of top management buy-in, the original system had been carefully developed and implemented, (2) management wanted the system to provide useful information, (3) improvements in the system were done systematically rather than ad hoc, and (4) overhaul of Ethyl's productivity measurement system provided an opportunity to evaluate features that might have made the original system more successful.

Company Background

Ethyl Corporation was founded in 1921 when Charles F. Kettering discovered that an automobile engine's performance improved when tetraethyl lead was added to gasoline. Kettering was quick to realize the potential of this discovery, which was great because the automobile was fast becoming an important part of the American life-style and consumers were looking for ways to improve its performance. After years of steady growth, in 1962 Ethyl was bought by a company one-tenth its size, the Albemarle Paper Manufacturing Company of Richmond, Virginia. Albemarle adopted Ethyl's name and the combined company grew to a multibillion-dollar organization with some 5,500 employees. Ethyl now operates mainly in the chemical and insurance industries. Net sales and insurance revenues in 1989 were $2.43 billion.

The TFP Program at Ethyl

Ethyl had always believed in managing its costs. In 1970, it implemented a formal cost-improvement program (CIP) to control manufacturing costs. The program had been very successful for ten years in saving Ethyl millions of dollars, but management was puzzled because those savings were not always reflected in the company's profit picture. When Ethyl added up the savings from CIP, the cost-reduction dollars did not match improvements in the bottom line. It had no system for tracking the flow of cost improvements to the various beneficiaries such as labor, suppliers, or customers. Ethyl needed a way to go beyond cost control, start improving productivity on all fronts, and make a connection between improvements in productivity and the bottom line.

Ethyl began to study the possibility of a broader productivity program in 1981. From this study, it decided that the APC model for measuring productivity was suitable for analyzing improvements in productivity. Ethyl's management especially liked this model because it related changes in productivity to changes in the financial bottom line.

The Ethyl Productivity Analysis System

Ethyl's total productivity-measurement system was called the Ethyl Productivity Analysis System (EPAS); its key elements were profitability, productivity, and price recovery. Profitability was defined as the change in gross margin over time. Productivity was the improvement in utilizing resources that resulted from changes in the relation between the quantity of output produced and the quantity of input used to produce that output. Price recovery was the relation between purchase price and sales price over time. Price recovery could be thought of as an index of an organization's ability or desire to pass on purchase-price changes to its sales prices. According to the

APC model, when profitability, productivity, and price recovery are measured in ratio form, they have this relation,

$$\text{Profitability} = \text{Productivity} * \text{Price recovery}$$

In essence, this relation divides period-to-period changes in the profit margin into a component as a result of price actions and a component as a result of relative volumes.

The EPAS measures were a modified version of the APC measures. The EPAS measures defined profitability, productivity, and price recovery in dollars instead of ratios (see Miller, 1984, for a detailed description). This representation made it easier to relate these measures to financial results, which have traditionally been reported in dollars. Using this formulation, the relationship above is given by,

$$\text{Profitability} = \text{Productivity} + \text{Price recovery}$$

To do TFP measurement at all levels of the organization required that prices and quantities of all inputs be recorded. Like most accounting systems, Ethyl's information system did not routinely collect such data. In particular, data on quantity were not available. This problem was solved by a modified APC system that estimated productivity measures from changes in prices and sales and cost dollars. (See Exhibit 10-1 for a simple example.) To estimate price-recovery measures, deflators for cost and revenue elements had to be calculated and costs had to be divided into appropriate categories to which these deflators could be applied. This process was felt to be difficult and time-consuming. With this limitation in mind, reporting was required only at the division level, and the divisions created and analyzed EPAS charts as part of their Annual Operating Plan (AOP) only once a year. (See Exhibit 10-2 for a sample chart.)

The profitability-productivity chart breaks down changes in profit margins into three components: (1) profitability, (2) the contribution of productivity to profit (calculated by the technique illustrated in Exhibit 10-1), and (3) price recovery, which is the difference between the first two. The EPAS further separated changes in profitability, productivity, and price recovery to associate them with each of the input factors (labor, materials, capital, and energy). An additional chart illustrating trends in inflation factors was also required.

. Ethyl used the system as an aid in planning and coordinating the

Exhibit 10-1 Sample to Illustrate Calculations of the Changes in Profitability, Productivity, and Price Recovery Using the EPAS Technique
P&L Data for ABC Corporation (in millions of dollars)

	1986	1987
Net sales	302.4	342.4
Cost of goods sold	240.8	264.8
Gross profit	61.6	77.6
Gross profit margin	20.4%	22.7%

Price increases, 1986–1987

Change in sales price	7.8%
Change in costs	3.3%

Change in profitability = Actual profit − Projected profit
$$= \text{Sales}_{87} * (\text{Margin}_{87} - \text{Margin}_{86})$$
$$= 342.4 * (0.227 - 0.204)$$
$$= 7.88 \text{ million}$$

Productivity's contribution in 1987
$$= [\text{Deflated sales}] * [\text{Deflated margin}_{87} - \text{Margin}_{86}]$$
$$= \left[\frac{342.400}{1.078}\right] * [0.193 - 0.204]$$
$$= -3.49 \text{ million}$$

Price recovery's contribution in 1987
$$= 7.88 - 3.49 = 4.39 \text{ million}$$

Therefore, 3.49 million of the gains in profitability never reached the bottom line because it was used to offset losses caused by productivity declines.

---

annual budget and to compare results over time. The EPAS productivity and price-recovery measures were used to forecast a "target profit" (see Exhibit 10-3 for a sample). To use the EPAS system as a motivator for improvement, in addition to a graphic analysis of trends in profitability, productivity, and price recovery, Ethyl required division managers to provide a narrative description of their productivity improvement efforts.

In applying the technique, management compared present results with the previous year's results, deflating the numbers by using

Exhibit 10-2 Profitability and Productivity Charts for Division X

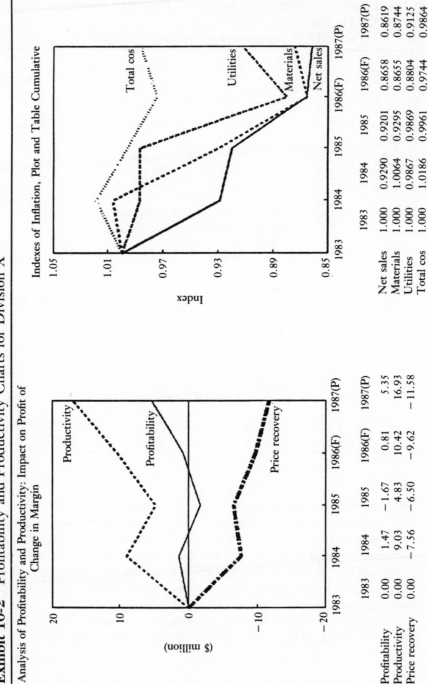

Analysis of Profitability and Productivity: Impact on Profit of
Change in Margin

	1983	1984	1985	1986(F)	1987(P)
Profitability	0.00	1.47	−1.67	0.81	5.35
Productivity	0.00	9.03	4.83	10.42	16.93
Price recovery	0.00	−7.56	−6.50	−9.62	−11.58

Indexes of Inflation, Plot and Table Cumulative

	1983	1984	1985	1986(F)	1987(P)
Net sales	1.000	0.9290	0.9201	0.8658	0.8619
Materials	1.000	1.0064	0.9295	0.8655	0.8744
Utilities	1.000	0.9867	0.9869	0.8804	0.9125
Total cos	1.000	1.0186	0.9961	0.9744	0.9864

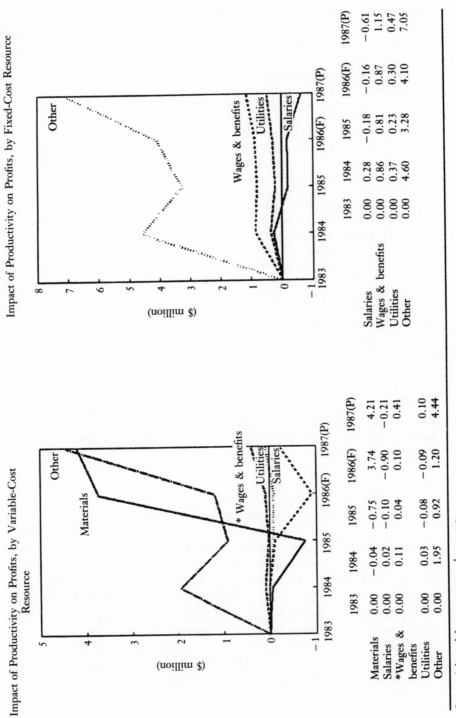

Impact of Productivity on Profits, by Fixed-Cost Resource

	1983	1984	1985	1986(F)	1987(P)
Salaries	0.00	0.28	-0.18	-0.16	-0.61
Wages & benefits	0.00	0.86	0.81	0.87	1.15
Utilities	0.00	0.37	0.23	0.30	0.47
Other	0.00	4.60	3.28	4.10	7.05

Impact of Productivity on Profits, by Variable-Cost Resource

	1983	1984	1985	1986(F)	1987(P)
Materials	0.00	-0.04	-0.75	3.74	4.21
Salaries	0.00	0.02	-0.10	-0.90	-0.21
*Wages & benefits	0.00	0.11	0.04	0.10	0.41
Utilities	0.00	0.03	-0.08	-0.09	0.10
Other	0.00	1.95	0.92	1.20	4.44

Source: Adapted from company documents.

Exhibit 10-3   Computing Target Profit

		Profitability Target
		% or $ million
Annual change in sales volume		8.6%
Annual change in total cost price		2.0%
I.	Net revenue—current-year forecast	124.9
Changes—Plan year/Current forecast:		
	From change in volume	10.8
	From price change in costs	2.7
	Net sales revenue target—plan year	138.4
II.	Gross profit—current-year forecast	46.3
Changes—Plan year/Current-year forecast:		
	From change in sales volume	4.0
	From price change in costs	1.0
	From CIP assumption in plan	1.2
	From impact of volume on fixed cost	2.4
	Gross profit target—Plan year	54.9
	Gross margin target—Plan year	39.7%
III.	Gross profit as proposed in plan	54.5
	Gain (or shortfall) from target in $ million	(0.4)
IV.	Gross margin as proposed in plan	40.3%
	Gain (or shortfall) from target	0.6%

Ethyl's actual cost and price changes. Ethyl established a computerized model to calculate productivity and profitability indexes. This model was small enough to be run on a personal computer, which made it easier to use at the divisional level.

Implementing the Total Productivity-Improvement Program

Ethyl's Total Productivity-Improvement Program was dubbed TPIP. Most simply described, TPIP was to address all resources and involve all employees. Ethyl's management was challenged to make TPIP a way of life. The firm established a network of key people in its operating divisions and staff departments who were "productivity coordinators." (See Exhibit 10-4 for an organization chart.) The coordinators were responsible for encouraging acceptance of TPIP in their areas. Thus, TPIP was designed to be decentralized, with overall planning by the corporate staff.

Exhibit 10-4   Organizational Infrastructure for Productivity
Management

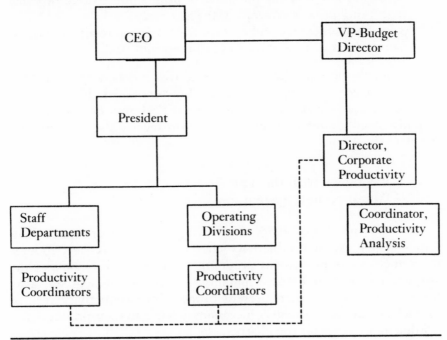

Source: Adapted from Belcher, 1987, p. 196.

Uses of EPAS Measures

In 1986, Ethyl's budget director explained why EPAS measures were considered useful.

1. TFP measures determine the net result of many partial-productivity gains. This net measure points out if gains in partial productivity have been sufficient to offset declines in partial productivity that may also have occurred.

2. Changes in the total-factor approach provide for analyzing the resource components of total productivity. Management therefore can evaluate the results of its overall effort to improve resource utilization.

3. TFP measures provide insight into the net result of pricing actions taken to control costs of resources and expand revenues.

4. Perhaps the most informative feature of this unique approach is that management can learn to understand the relationships between these two key measures of profitability—total productivity and price recovery. Managers can clearly see whether gains from efficiency and cost control are being retained in company profits or passed on to customers and vendors.

Although top management conceded that it was not easy at first to get managers to work with the total-factor model, in time they came around and accepted it. In 1985, Ethyl was one of several Virginia-based manufacturing companies to receive the U.S. Senate Productivity Award.

Problems with the TFP
Measurement System

By the end of 1986, the TPIP progress report stated that despite wider use of productivity charts and narrative descriptions of productivity improvement programs, managers were not making adequate use of their EPAS capabilities. Top management was also disturbed that rather than present profitability-productivity results themselves, division managers increasingly left it to their productivity coordinators to explain the charts.

Explanations in the AOP seldom had any relation to trends in productivity. Given the trends in the charts (see Exhibit 10-2 for a representative division's charts), the productivity line had become a secondary issue; more attention was given to the price-recovery line. This apparent change in Ethyl's strategic direction worried some division managers because they did not believe they could control price recovery.

Many anomalies in the measures were difficult to explain. Because the divisions had very divergent product lines, anomalies were created when at the division level several product lines were lumped together to compute an aggregate performance measure. Applying this measure, it was difficult to pinpoint the source of a problem. Similarly, changes in the product mix gave rise to anomalies that were not explained by the system. Because of these and other problems, EPAS charts lost credibility and became reports generated once a year and never used again. It became clear to top management that the productivity measurement system was ineffective because managers did not use it to make decisions. Because Ethyl believed in scientific research methods, its management decided to study the problem rather than abandon the system for something else.

The Study

The study's objective was to design either a new system or enhancements to the current system for measuring productivity. Such a system was to serve both as a management tool for line managers and a reporting tool to meet the corporate management staff's needs. The study encompassed all Ethyl businesses except insurance. Its major aims were to:

1. Interview line managers (plant managers, marketing managers, sales managers, division managers, division financial managers, and group vice presidents) about the role productivity played in their area of responsibility.

2. Interview corporate staff and corporate officers to determine their need for productivity reporting.

3. Survey the techniques other companies used for productivity measurement.

4. Compare the ability of the present system with the alternatives other companies used to meet the requirements identified in the interviews.

The study team interviewed fifty line managers on their views about the importance of productivity measurement. These interviews revealed that most managers believed productivity measurement was important, but that measurement methods were not clearly understood. Moreover, although these measures took a lot of time and effort to produce, they did not relate to the way in which the businesses were run and therefore were not useful for business analysis. The managers also were not pleased that the corporate staff had implemented the system from the top down, with no input from them. Finally, the managers indicated that they preferred the label "Total Quality" instead of "Productivity."

The study team then interviewed members of the corporate staff to identify their needs for reporting on productivity. These interviews revealed that the present system was not satisfying them, either. Corporate staff strongly felt that to maintain the corporate focus on productivity, reporting of productivity trends should be continued. They recommended that data be reported quarterly rather than annually; that data continue to be reported at the division level, but also at the strategic business unit (SBU) or product-line levels; and finally, that data be backed up with enough detail to allow for analyzing significant changes and anomalies.

Interviews with managers of ten other companies indicated that these companies had faced similar problems, and nearly all had decided to replace the TFP measures with simpler partial measures.

From results of its study on productivity measurement at Ethyl, in February 1989 the study team recommended these steps:

1. Discontinue use of the EPAS system for analyzing productivity and pricing trends.

2. Implement a system for reporting partial-productivity measures in conjunction with quarterly review. The specific measures to be used may be unique for each division and will be developed by the divisions, assisted by members of the Budget Group.

3. Price-recovery trends will also be reported quarterly. The specific measurement technique may also be tailored to a division.

4. The same productivity and price-recovery data reported in the quarterly reviews will be used in the AOP.

5. A Profitability Target will remain in the AOP, but its development will not necessarily require using the EPAS system.

The study team felt that these changes, retaining the spirit and intent of the old measurement system, would give divisions the flexibility to report any measures that most meaningfully indicated performance.

In response to the study team's recommendations, Ethyl's chemicals group formed a steering committee to oversee development of a new measurement system. This was an opportune time for the chemicals group to do so because it had been implementing a new data-base system designed to improve its ability to analyze costs and revenues. Because productivity measurement was so important, the data base included quantity as well as price information. The new data base allowed for directly computing productivity using quantities instead of backing into productivity with price indexes. It also allowed the measures to be computed at a more disaggregated level, as for a product or product line.

Keeping in mind the capabilities of the new data base, the chemicals group developed a new system called the Performance Measurement System.

Performance Measurement System

The objective of the Performance Measurement System was to determine how these factors influenced profits: productivity, inflation, production volume, other manufacturing costs, product distribution, selling price, and sales volume.

Exhibit 10-5 describes the formulas for these measures. The system was designed to provide on-line reports and graphs for any trend indicating changes in any of these performance measures for a strategic business unit (SBU). The SBU could be a product, a group of products, or a division. The data would allow measuring and assigning responsibility to a producing or nonproducing responsibility center. The measures could be generated over monthly, quarterly, or yearly periods. The system was capable of measuring actuals, forecasts, or budgeted amounts.

At first, the steering committee decided to start measuring the partial productivity of the most significant and easiest-to-measure input, raw materials. Exhibit 10-6 gives examples of the new productivity charts and the component business-unit charts. Eventually the system was designed to allow analysis of all significant factors of production. The system would also have been able to aggregate all the partial measures into a total measure. The steering committee is identifying additional performance factors for measuring quality and other key attributes of success.

Analysis of the New System

Ethyl management hopes the new system will prove more useful than the old one. The old system had avoided many of the usual pitfalls common to failed efforts to improve productivity (see Belcher, 1987, pp. 14–16). For example, the productivity program at Ethyl had strong support from top management and was based on the model that was thought to be most appropriate for the organization at that time. Efforts were made to institute a structure for the organization conducive to helping the productivity program, and considerable time and effort had been spent trying to educate and involve personnel at different levels in the organization. The company also evaluated

Exhibit 10-5   Formulas for the Measures Reported
by the Performance Measurement System

1. Productivity Impact

This tool is designed to measure any resource for which units are tracked, including material, salary-wage-benefits, contract labor, and so on. The productivity formula computes an index of productivity directly from information on quantities.

$$\text{Productivity impact gain/(loss)} = \begin{array}{c} \text{Change in} \\ \text{units used/cwt} \\ \text{(parameter)} \end{array} * \begin{array}{c} \text{Current} \\ \text{period} \\ \text{volume} \end{array} * \begin{array}{c} \text{Prior} \\ \text{period} \\ \text{price} \end{array}$$

2. Inflation Impact

Inflation will be measured for all resources, specifically at the product level.

$$\text{Inflation impact gain/(loss)} = \begin{array}{c} \text{Change in price} \\ \text{per unit} \\ \text{consumed} \end{array} * \begin{array}{c} \text{Units consumed} \\ \text{in} \\ \text{current period} \end{array}$$

3. Production Volume Impact

Fixed-cost factors will be applied to each resource at the product level. The system will calculate the effect of changes in unit cost of production caused by changes in unit cost of production because of changes in the volume of production.

$$\begin{array}{c} \text{Production volume} \\ \text{impact} \end{array} = \begin{array}{c} \text{Change in fixed cost} \\ \text{per unit of sales volume} \end{array} * \begin{array}{c} \text{Current-period} \\ \text{volume} \end{array}$$

4. Impact of Other Manufacturing Costs =

Change in other manufacturing costs per unit of sales
* Current-period volume

5. Impact of Product Distribution Costs =

Change in distribution cost per unit of sales volume
* Current-period volume

Impacts 1 to 5 measure the change in cost of sales.

The remaining impacts, 6 and 7, measure the change in sales revenue.

6. Selling-Price Impact = Change in selling price * Current-period volume

7. Sales-volume impact = Change in sales volume * Gross profit margin from
prior period

Exhibit 10-6 Productivity Charts from the New Information System

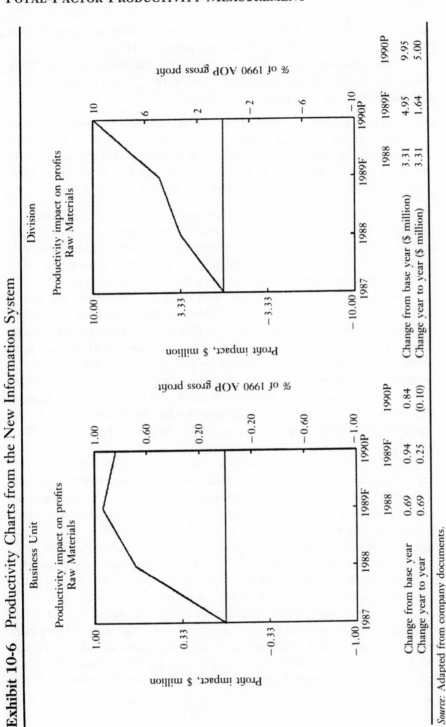

Source: Adapted from company documents.

the results regularly reported by the system of measurement. But despite these efforts, the productivity program failed.

First, line managers did not accept the measures because they found them difficult to understand and apply. The present director of productivity and quality at Ethyl said,

It was perhaps unfortunate for us that we had this model that could compute productivity from accounting data. At that time it allowed us to quickly start reporting productivity measures without having to put in a new data base with quantity data. But in the long run it forced us to deal with measures that were complicated to compute and difficult to understand.

The new system could use information about quantities to compute productivity measures directly. The new measures of productivity and price recovery thus were more intuitive and easier to understand. The experience at Ethyl also emphasizes the need to have the right technology for implementing the right information system.

Second, the old system had been mandated from the top down and did not use the specific knowledge of the managers who were expected to use it. This approach resulted in a measurement system that did not address the needs of the line managers and did not promote buy-in because they did not feel ownership in the system. A number of companies (Beatrice Foods, Continental Group, General Foods, and Kaiser Aluminum and Chemicals) have found it essential that all employees from top to bottom be involved in such programs from the beginning and continuously (see Buehler and Shetty, 1981, p. 237).

Third, the old system was not strategically misleading in pointing out negative price-recovery trends. Because productivity was considered to be related primarily to manufacturing, the marketing and sales function was not part of the measurement and reporting system. Therefore, the line managers responsible for the AOP charts did not feel they should be asked to explain the price-recovery performance. Under the new system, marketing and sales managers were directly involved in designing the system and were expected to be among the principal users of the price-recovery information.

At Ethyl, the systems tracking productivity, quality, and other measures of performance are complementary rather than replacements for each other. Like many other companies, Ethyl has discovered that quality improvements and total-quality measurement are effective ways of improving productivity. As a result, although Ethyl has dropped the banner of TPIP, the management strongly feels it is important for the firm to enhance quality and satisfy customers, and continually to become more efficient. Therefore, whether gains in efficiency are achieved by efforts to improve quality or by CIP, these efforts, to be meaningful, should translate into real gains and relate to the bottom line.

Finally, neither the old nor the new system for measuring productivity at Ethyl is tied to compensation. This neglect is caused not by oversight but by design. Although other compensation systems are available for motivation, Ethyl management feels that the primary use for its productivity measurement system is planning and information. The very fact that line management is asked to create and report productivity measures focuses attention and motivates behavior. But overemphasizing these measures by tying them to compensation has the potential for biasing information, which precludes accurate planning.

The observation above is similar to that made by Merchant (1990) who found that to motivate behavior, organizations did not always feel they needed to tie performance to explicit monetary rewards. Often, organizations have a number of performance measures, of which only a subset may be used in evaluating and rewarding managers. Other performance measures, such as productivity, are meant to direct managers' attention to specific key success factors and to provide information that is useful for achieving goals such as profit targets.

To summarize, Ethyl's old TFP measurement system was found to be deficient not because the concept of TFP measurement is flawed or because understanding TFP measures is inherently too difficult. Instead, the deficiency was that current information technology necessitated a TFP measure that was too aggregative and nonintuitive. At Ethyl Corporation, therefore, productivity measurement is still pertinent; only the method for calculating it is passé.

New Directions and Implications for Research

Although it is difficult to generalize from one organization's experiences, the study does suggest possible directions for future research and practice.

Role for Total Measures of Performance

Total measures of performance including TFP are more appropriate at macro or higher levels of organizations, where they help in the strategic analysis of the organization. But even at these levels, these performance measures are useful for decision making only if they incorporate enough detail to pinpoint problems and suggest solutions. The observed lack of TFP measures to control day-to-day operations on the factory floor is consistent with this hypothesis because such measures are too aggregative for decision making at an organization's micro levels. There, simple partial measures are more relevant. Therefore, the appropriateness of a performance measurement system depends on the intended use of the reported performance measures as well as the level in the organization at which the measures are to be used.

Importance of Labels

Productivity programs in general have had poor acceptance from line managers because productivity traditionally has had an unfortunate association with layoffs and overworked employees. Therefore, many companies have wisely chosen more acceptable labels such as "Total Quality" and "Quality of Manufacturing" for the program that was originally described as productivity. Although many companies claim that they are now promoting quality instead of productivity, closer scrutiny may reveal many similarities in the two.

Relationship Between Types of Performance Measures

At present, many companies have implemented several parallel systems to apply different performance measures. Rather than being mutually exclusive, the measures of financial performance, productivity, quality, customer satisfaction, and so on, are related. In the familiar formula for productivity, if output is defined as the value of the final output to the customer, and inputs as all resources needed to provide that output, the measure includes notions of financial value, quality, and customer satisfaction. Further research is needed to identify the relationships among these different performance measures. Rather than implementing several parallel performance measurement systems, it would be useful for organizations to adopt comprehensive systems that capture the underlying relationships and incorporate the effects of trade-offs between the different measures.

Theory versus Practice

Despite relevance and theoretical rigor, users do not accept performance measures if they appear too complicated and nonintuitive. But researchers evaluating alternative measures have completely ignored the criterion of user acceptability. Instead of focusing on theoretical rigor as the only desirable criterion, it would be fruitful to develop more user-friendly measures. Along with the degree of acceptance, another valid criterion for establishing the merit of such measures would be the desirability of outcomes from decisions based on using these measures. Once again, in-depth case studies would provide the more appropriate mode for studying this question.

REFERENCES

Armitage, H. M., and A. A. Atkinson. "The Choice of Productivity Measures in Organizations." In *Measures of Manufacturing Excellence*, Robert S. Kaplan, ed. Boston: Harvard Business School Press, 1990, pp. 91–126.

Banker, R. D., S. M. Datar, and R. S. Kaplan. "Productivity Measurement and Management Accounting." *Journal of Accounting, Auditing and Finance*, vol. 4 (Fall 1989), pp. 528–554.

Barlev, B., and J. L. Callen. "Total Factor Productivity and Cost Variances: Survey and Analysis." *Journal of Accounting Literature*, vol. 5 (1986), pp. 35–56.

Belcher, John G., Jr. *Productivity Plus.* Houston, TX: Gulf Publishing, 1987.

Berliner, C., and J. A. Brimson. *Cost Management for Today's Advanced Manufacturing.* Boston: Harvard Business School Press, 1988.

Buehler, V. M., and Y. K. Shetty. *Productivity Improvement.* New York: AMACOM, 1981.

Eccles, R. G. "The Performance Measurement Manifesto." *Harvard Business Review* (January–February 1991), pp. 131–137.

Kaplan, R. S. "Measuring Manufacturing Performance: A New Challenge for Managerial Accounting Research." *Accounting Review* (October 1983), pp. 686–705.

Kaplan, R. S., and A. A. Atkinson. *Advanced Management Accounting.* Englewood Cliffs, NJ: Prentice-Hall, 1989.

Kraus, J. *How U.S. Firms Measure Productivity.* New York: National Association of Accountants, 1984.

Merchant, K. A., and A. Riccaboni. "The Evolution of Performance-Based Management Incentives at the Fiat Group." This article is Chapter 3 of this volume.

Miller, D. M. "Profitability = Productivity + Price Recovery." *Harvard Business Review* (May–June 1984), pp. 145–153.

Nelson, R. R. "Research on Productivity Growth and Productivity Differences: Dead Ends and New Departures." *Journal of Economic Literature* (September 1981), pp. 1029–1064.

Ruch, A. W. "Your Key to Planning for Profits." Productivity Brief 6. Houston, TX: American Productivity Center, October 1981.

About the Contributors

GEORGE P. BAKER is an assistant professor of business administration at the Harvard Business School. He has published works on management incentives, leveraged buyouts, and the relationship between a firm's ownership structure and its management. His recent work has focused on the problem of managerial performance measurement, and on the effect of the ownership structure on management incentives and control systems. He teaches a second-year M.B.A. course entitled, "Coordination, Control, and the Management of Organizations." Prior to joining the faculty at Harvard, he worked both as a consultant with Temple, Barker and Sloane, and as a marketing manager with Teradyne Inc. He is an associate editor of the *Journal of Financial Economics*. Dr. Baker holds a Ph.D. in business economics from Harvard University and an M.B.A. from the Harvard Business School.

REGINA F. BENTO is an assistant professor of management at the Robert G. Merrick School of Business, University of Baltimore. Dr. Bento started her career as a psychiatrist, with an M.D. degree from the Federal University of Rio de Janeiro, studying the relationship between work and mental health. Interested in learning more about the nature of work and organizations, she went on to pursue graduate studies in administration, first in Brazil (M.S. in management, Federal University of Rio de Janeiro) and then in the United States (Ph.D. in Management, MIT). Prior to joining the University of Baltimore, Dr. Bento was on the faculty of the University of California, Riverside. Her publications include an award-winning book on managerial decision making, several journal articles, and business cases. Dr. Bento's current research focuses on organizational culture and change, looking at the processes that surround innovations in information technology, production methods, and performance evaluation and compensation.

WILLIAM J. BRUNS, JR. is professor of business administration at the Harvard Business School, where he has taught in the M.B.A. program and educational programs for senior executives. He earned degrees at the University of Redlands (B.A.), Harvard University (M.B.A.), and the University of California, Berkeley (Ph.D.). Before accepting his current appointment, he taught at Yale University and the University of Washington. He is the author of several books, including *The Information Mosaic* with S. M. McKinnon; *Case Problems in Management Accounting* with M. E. Barrett; *A Primer on Replacement Cost Accounting* with R. F. Vancil; and *Introduction to Accounting: Economic Measurement for Decisions*, as well as numerous articles that have appeared in professional journals. He and Robert S. Kaplan co-edited *Accounting and Management: Field Study Perspectives*.

KENNETH J. EUSKE is an associate professor of accounting at the Naval Postgraduate School and was a visiting associate professor of business administration at the Darden Graduate School of Business Administration at the University of Virginia when the research reported in this volume was undertaken. He is the editor of *Behavioral Research in Accounting* and the author of *Management Control: Planning,*

301

Control, Measurement and Evaluation. His articles have appeared in both scholarly and practitioner journals. His most recent work focuses on the differences in the control systems of profit and nonprofit service organizations. He holds an M.B.A. from the Amos Tuck School of Business Administration at Dartmouth and a Ph.D. from Arizona State University.

LOURDES DALTRO FERREIRA is an assistant professor in the School of Accounting at the University of Southern California. Her teaching and research interests are in managerial and cost accounting, and management control systems. She has published in executive compensation, performance measurement, and cost control in highly automated settings. She co-authored several case studies used in M.E.A. and executive education programs. She is currently conducting empirical research on the impact of environmental factors on budgeting decision styles, and transfer pricing for shared corporate resources. She received her D.B.A. from Harvard University in 1989. Before joining the faculty of USC, she was tax analyst at the controller's office of the city of Rio de Janeiro. She obtained her undergraduate degree from the Brazilian School of Public Administration of the Getulio Vargas Foundation, and an M.S. in management from the Federal University of Rio de Janeiro.

EDWARD E. LAWLER III is professor of research at the University of Southern California School of Business Administration. In 1979, he founded and became the director of the university's Center for Effective Organizations, a research unit that works with companies to study organizational change. He is the author and co-author of more than 150 articles and fifteen books. Lawler is a member of many professional organizations and is on the editorial board of several periodicals, including *Human Resource Management, New Management, Personnel,* and *Compensation and Benefits Review.*

EDWARD P. LAZEAR is a senior fellow and coordinator of the domestic studies program at the Hoover Institution, and is the Isidore Brown and Gladys J. Brown Professor of Urban and Labor Economics at the University of Chicago. The founding editor of the *Journal of Labor Economics,* Lazear is also a research associate of the National Bureau of Economic Research, and a fellow of the Econometric Society. He has published more than sixty articles and three books on labor markets; microeconomic theory; issues involving worker compensation and its effects on productivity; pensions and retirement; governmental policies on discrimination; affirmative action and comparable worth; the doctrine of employment at will; distribution of income within the household; and pricing policies.

SHARON M. McKINNON is an associate professor of business administration at Northeastern University. A graduate of the University of North Carolina, she earned an M.P.A. in 1977 and a Ph.D. in 1981 from Georgia State University in Atlanta. Professor McKinnon joined the faculty of Northeastern University in 1980, was awarded tenure in 1986, and served as chairman of the accounting department in 1989–1990 and since 1991. Her teaching interests range from intermediate accounting, advanced accounting, and information systems in the undergraduate and graduate accounting degree programs to financial and managerial core courses in the M.B.A. program. She has also taught in the executive M.B.A. program and in various university and corporate executive workshops and residency programs. Professor McKinnon is co-author (with William J. Bruns, Jr.) of *The Information Mosaic* and (with Thomas Edmonds) of *Financial Accounting: An Elements Approach* and *Accounting Principles* and author of *The Seventh Directive: Consolidated Accounts in the EEC.* She has published articles in the *Financial Analysts Journal*, *Management Accounting*, the *Journal of Business, Finance, & Accounting*, and the *International Journal of Accounting Education & Research*, among others.

KENNETH A. MERCHANT recently joined the University of Southern California as a professor of accounting, after teaching at the Harvard Business School for twelve years. He has degrees from Union College (New York), Columbia University, and the University of California, Berkeley and is a certified public accountant (Texas). He worked for Texas Instruments and Ernst & Whinney prior to joining the Harvard faculty in 1978. He is co-author (with Clive Emmanual and David Otley) of *Accounting for Management Control* and author of *Control in Business Organizations, Rewarding Results: Motivating Profit Center Managers*, and a number of articles in journals such as *The Accounting Review, Accounting, Organizations and Society*, and *Sloan Management Review*. Professor Merchant's research interests are in management control.

ALLAN M. MOHRMAN, JR. is the associate director of research and a research scientist in the Center for Effective Organizations (CEO) at the Graduate School of Business Administration at the University of Southern California. Dr. Mohrman's present interests are: the design of effective organizational systems for human resource management, information technologies in organizations, and the management of teamwork. Of particular interest are the ways in which these elements relate to one another and to the larger organizational context. He has published widely in all these areas. He is the lead author of two books, *Designing Performance Appraisal Systems*, and *Large-Scale Organizational Change*, and he is a co-editor of *Doing Research That Is Useful for Theory and Practice*. Prior to his present position, Dr. Mohrman was a faculty member in the College of Administrative Sciences at the Ohio State University. He earned his Ph.D. from the Graduate School of Management at Northwestern University. His undergraduate degree is in physics from Stanford University. He also has extensive research and consulting experience in both public and private sector organizations.

SUSAN A. MOHRMAN is a senior research scientist in the Center for Effective Organizations (CEO) at the University of Southern California. She received her Ph.D. from Northwestern University and has served on the faculty of the business schools of Ohio State University and the University of Southern California. Her research focuses on innovations in human resource management, organizational change, and organizational design processes. She consulted to a variety of organizations that are introducing employee involvement programs and labor/management cooperative projects. Her publications deal with employee participation, quality of work life, self-designing processes in organizations, high-technology management, and the production of research that is useful to organizations. Dr. Mohrman is active in the Organizational Development Division of the Academy of Management and serves on the review and editorial board of several management journals.

KEVIN J. MURPHY is associate professor of business administration at the Harvard Business School. Professor Murphy received his B.A. from UCLA, and his M.A. and Ph.D. degrees in economics from the University of Chicago. During the 1987–

1988 academic year, he was a Marvin Bower Fellow at the Harvard Business School. Professor Murphy is a nationally known expert on executive compensation, and results from his research have appeared extensively in the popular, business, and professional press.

DAVID OTLEY is the Peat Marwick McLintock Professor of Accounting and head of the Department of Accounting and Finance at Lancaster University in England. His main research interest is in management control systems, with particular emphasis on the operation of budgetary control systems. He has also contributed to the literature on the contingency theory of management accounting. He is co-author (with Clive Emmanual and Kenneth A. Merchant) of *Accounting for Management Control* and also (with Lee Parker and Ken Ferris) of *Accounting for the Human Factor*. An editorial board member of numerous journals, including *Accounting, Organizations and Society*, he has recently been appointed general editor of the new *British Journal of Management*, the official journal of the British Academy of Management.

ANGELO RICCABONI is research fellow in the Department of Accounting at the University of Siena. He received his laureate degree from the School of Economics and Banking in Siena and his Ph.D. in business administration from the University of Pisa. He was formerly a lecturer at the School of Accounting, Banking, and at the University of Wales, Bangor, U.K. and a visiting research assistant at the graduate business schools at New York, Harvard, and Columbia universities. He is author of "La misurazione della performance dei centri di profitto: critica agli strumenti tradizionali e nuovi orientamenti di indagine" ("The Measurement of Profit Center Performance: Analysis of Traditional Tools and New Research Trends"). His present research interests are in management control. He is also conducting a study of accounting practices in Italy, to be published in 1991 as one of the twelve volumes in the "Financial Reporting in Europe" series sponsored by the Institute of Chartered Accountants in England and Wales.

KIRAN VERMA is a visiting assistant professor at the Massachusetts Institute of Technology. Previously she was an assistant professor at the Harvard Business School. She completed her Ph.D. in accounting from Michigan State University. She received her B.Sc. Hons. and M.Sc. Hons. degrees from Punjab University, India. Her recent research, "Effects of Accounting Techniques on the Study of Monopoly Power" is forthcoming in the *International Journal of Industrial Organization*. She is presently researching the measurement of productivity for the purposes of both outside and inside users of financial information. In particular, she is engaged in a field study looking at the evolution of productivity measurement systems within organizations.

KAREN H. WRUCK joined the faculty of the Harvard Business School as an assistant professor in 1987 after she obtained her Ph.D. in finance and accounting from the Simon Graduate School of Business Administration at the University of Rochester. At Harvard Business School, Wruck teaches in the M.B.A. program. Professor Wruck's present research and consulting work deal with managing highly leveraged organizations, including both firms in financial distress and those taken private through leveraged buyouts. She is an associate editor of *The Journal of Financial Economics*.

Index

305